Math WORKSHOP

Grade 4

Credits
Author: Elise Craver
Copy Editor: Carrie Fox

Visit *carsondellosa.com* for correlations to Common Core, state, national, and Canadian provincial standards.

Carson-Dellosa Publishing LLC
PO Box 35665
Greensboro, NC 27425 USA
carsondellosa.com

ISBN 978-1-4838-3973-8
01-345177784

Table of Contents

What Is Math Workshop?

One of the most challenging aspects of teaching mathematics is differentiating instruction to meet the needs of all of the learners in your classroom. As a classroom teacher, you are responsible for teaching the standards that must be met by the end of the year. But, the reality inside the classroom is that one size does not fit all. For some students, the material is too difficult. For others, it is too easy.

With both reading and writing, many teachers have found the workshop model to be an excellent way to teach students at various levels. It allows for whole-group and small-group instruction, and individual practice so teachers can monitor students' progress and vary instruction according to need. The same workshop approach can be used for successful math instruction. This model encourages students to go beyond passive learning and become mathematicians who can think critically.

Like reading and writing workshops, math workshop is a structure, not a curriculum. It can be used with existing curriculums and materials and should be adapted to best fit the needs of the teacher and students. Math workshop will look different from classroom to classroom but usually includes the same building blocks: a warm-up, a whole-class mini-lesson, leveled small-group instruction, and individual practice. For a more in-depth look at the elements of math workshop, refer to pages 4 and 5.

Using a math workshop model allows teachers to:

- meet the needs of learners at all levels
- encourage deeper learning than in traditional lessons
- spiral concepts throughout the year
- work with any curriculum
- group students flexibly so they can move according to their changing needs
- offer repeated opportunities for practice
- keep students consistently engaged in learning

Starting math workshop in your classroom can seem overwhelming if you've never done it before. Use the guides on pages 4 through 14 to help you decide how math workshop will work in your classroom, plan your lessons, and manage the day-to-day details. Then, get started with over 25 preplanned lessons and activities. Use the blank reproducible activities starting on page 183 to create your own practice and review activities to be used throughout the year.

The Elements of Math Workshop

The major parts of math workshop are a warm-up, a mini-lesson, rotations (which include guided math groups, independent practice, and conferencing), and closure. You do not have to follow this format exactly. Instead, mix, match, and tweak things to make math workshop work for your classroom. See page 6 for more information on how math workshop can be changed to better fit your needs. Once you understand the basics, you can use the information below to plan your own math workshop lessons. Refer to pages 9 and 10 for more information on planning math workshop lessons.

1 Warm-Up
about 5 minutes

The warm-up is used to get students thinking mathematically and prepare them for the mini-lesson. It can be the same every day, or changed to relate to the lesson focus. You may choose to discuss only a portion of the assignment, such as a few sections of the calendar bulletin board or a single review problem.

Options*:

- number talks or number study
- problem of the day
- calendar time
- quick games (for example, Buzz or Around the World)
- discussion of an incorrectly solved problem
- number of the day (use the template on page 183)
- fact fluency practice
- daily review problems

2 Mini-Lesson
10–15 minutes

The mini-lesson is a teacher-led, whole-group activity. This is when new vocabulary and foundational information should be introduced and modeled. Teachers should model math thinking as they work through example problems. Often, students work with a practice problem to clear up any misconceptions.

Options*:

- present a textbook lesson
- show an introduction video
- solve a problem and think aloud
- demonstrate a new strategy
- direct a hands-on activity
- create an anchor chart
- share a math read-aloud
- review the previous day's lesson

*Please note that the options provided are a starting point and there are many more options you can explore for each section.

3 Rotations
10–20 minutes each

Students rotate through guided math with the teacher, independent practice, and workstations. This is also the time when teachers may choose to skip small group instruction in favor of one-on-one conferencing with students.

Guided Math

During this time, you work with small (eight or fewer students), flexible, leveled groups of students to extend and enhance the mini-lesson. Students use manipulatives to better understand the reasoning, procedures, strategies, etc., of the topic. Focus on using math talk and math tools to make sure students really understand the topic. Begin with the lowest group so they do not work on independent practice until after small-group instruction. Like the mini-lesson, these lessons can follow the warm-up/explanation/guided practice/independent practice/assessment model, although they don't have to.

Independent Stations

This segment is also known as centers, rotations, workstations, etc. Activities can be individual, partner, or small group and often include both practice of the current skill or topic and review of past skills. Activities should be introduced ahead of time so students can work independently and should be at a level that won't produce frustration. Students can follow a strict rotation or may be given daily choices as long as they complete certain set activities each week.

Options*:

- math games and activities
- fact fluency practice
- Solve the Room activities
- technology centers (including online games and district-mandated math programs)
- practice sheets (*Note*: The practice sheets included in the lessons are all different, so students can progress through them as they gain understanding of the skill.)
- journaling and/or interactive notebooks

Conferencing

Instead of leading guided math groups, you may choose to periodically observe students during independent stations or pull students for one-on-one conferencing. This allows for formative assessment and more targeted instruction for students who need more help with a skill. This is also an ideal time to do state- or district-mandated quarterly testing.

4 Closure/Reflection
3–5 minutes

The closure is a short, targeted way to wrap up the learning students did during math workshop. It is the perfect time to review the math objective or essential question and answer any questions students may still have.

Options*:

- exit tickets
- allow a few students to explain an "ah-ha!" moment they had
- think/pair/share problem-solving
- math talk prompts
- quick journaling
- students can share what they learned in their own words
- Q and A time

*Please note that the options provided are a starting point and there are many more options you can explore for each section.

What Does Math Workshop Look Like?

Due to the nature of the workshop model, math workshop will look different in different classrooms. You can change it however you need so that it works best for your classroom. See below for ideas and examples of how you can reshape math workshop for your needs.

Timing and Structure

- You can conduct math workshop daily, a few times a week, or monthly.
- Or, you can use one or two days to teach longer whole-class lessons and use the remaining days for rotations.
- Meet with each leveled group daily, or only once or twice a week, depending on how long your math block is.
- Have students visit every station daily or visit each station once each week.

Content

- Use your textbook, a prescribed curriculum, or make your own lessons.
- You can have students use math notebooks for recording work and/or journaling.
- Use the same handful of simple games so you don't have to reinvent the wheel (for example, sorting activities, puzzles, concentration, etc.).
- The lessons provided in this book are interchangeable. If you don't like one or more of the suggestions, replace it with your own.

Assessment

- Build in formal assessment as a longer closure, as a station to visit, or take a day off to administer a test.
- You may choose to have students record the results from each activity or use a checklist during rotations.
- See page 13 for more information on accountability during math workshop.

Grouping

- Groups do not have to be the same size.
- You can have more than one group at the same level to ensure small groups.
- To group students, you can use formative assessment, pretests, or group them on the fly after observations made during the previous day or the mini-lesson.
- You can choose to move students between leveled groups as needed (which could even mean daily) or after more formal assessments.

Choice

- You can require students to visit rotations in a certain order and/or on specific days.
- Or, you can allow students to choose which centers to complete each day.
- You may choose to make students responsible for completing all of the rotations by the end of week, or you can make some rotations mandatory each day (such as independent practice, fact fluency, and technology centers).
- Students can complete rotations at their desks so you can keep an eye on them, or you can allow them to work in various spots around the room.

Managing Math Workshop

Math workshop can be daunting to newcomers because of all of the elements that need preparation and upkeep. However, the tips and suggestions below for managing the various parts of math workshop will help you get started on the right foot and maintain it throughout the year.

Starting and Maintaining Math Workshop

- Set student expectations before beginning. See page 11 for more information.
- Don't underestimate the power of positive reinforcement.
- Stop and practice the routines and procedures as needed throughout the year if students aren't following expectations.
- Start slow! Begin with only one game or activity during rotations.
- Practice any new games or activities with the whole group first.
- Keep it simple. To begin with, use familiar activities such as concentration, war, or dominoes.
- As you introduce new activities through the year, use the same formats so you don't have to teach a new set of rules each time.
- If possible, use assistants or parent volunteers to monitor students during the first few weeks.
- During weeks with field trips, assemblies, etc., try to move math workshop to a different time. Or, use the entire week to review old concepts and meet with groups that need more help with old concepts instead of introducing a new topic.

Organizing Materials

- Keep all of the necessary supplies in the area where you meet for guided math. That way, students don't waste time looking for materials such as pencils, paper, and manipulatives.
- Use bins or baskets to organize activities, games, and small group supplies for guided math, so everything needed to complete the activity is in one easy-to-grab place.
- Make all math manipulatives visible and accessible so students can use whatever tools they need whenever they need to.
- Make several copies of each activity so multiple pairs or groups of students can work on the same one.
- Designate a student or students each week to be the Materials Master. Their job is to make sure all materials are cleaned up and organized each day.

Managing Math Workshop, cont.

Classroom Management

Managing Rotations

- Use a bulletin board, pocket chart, or interactive whiteboard for a visual reminder of the rotations order. Refer to the example below.
- Use sticky notes with student names to make reorganizing leveled groups quick and easy.
- Use visual cues and directions on games so students can work independently.
- When students are absent, you can catch them up during conferencing/one-on-one time or temporarily moving them to a lower group.

Student Behavior

- For early finishers: have review, extension, or older activities available; make a packet with word problems or challenges to complete; or create a chart listing things they can move on to.
- Foster independence with an "ask three before me" policy.
- Have students use a special hand signal so they can ask to use the bathroom without interrupting guided math.
- For students who have trouble working independently, remove them from rotations and have them sit at a desk near the guided math group until they are ready to rejoin rotations. It may be helpful to have those students start back slowly, with only one independent activity reintroduced at a time.

Groups · *Rotation order* · *Students in each group* · *Short description of each rotation*

Math Workshop

	A	B	C	D
1st Rotation	Teacher	Seat Work	Computer	Hands-On
2nd Rotation	Hands-On	Teacher	Seat Work	Computer
3rd Rotation	Computer	Hands-On	Teacher	Seat Work
4th Rotation	Seat Work	Computer	Hands-On	Teacher

Group A	Group B	Group C	Group D
Asia, Carson, Ben, Emma, Jose	Drew, Luke, Felicia, Lamar, Nadia	Kade, Nina, Gavin, Ryan, Pilar	Zoe, Ava, Blair, Derek

Planning and Preparation

As with anything, math workshop will be less stressful and have a better chance of success if you plan in advance. Use your district's scope and sequence, textbook curriculum, or similar to plan roughly when and how long to teach each topic. Then, plan the specifics for only a week or two at a time to allow room for remediation or moving on early, depending on what students need. Use the reproducible below to create a high-level plan for a week. Use page 10 to plan more specifically for the guided math groups for that week.

Math Workshop

Week of ______________

Objective:	Essential Question:

Mini-Lesson		Rotations
Monday		
Tuesday		
Wednesday		
Thursday		
Friday		

Guided Math

Week of ______________

Group 1 Level:	Group 2 Level:
Students:	Students:
Group 3 Level:	**Group 4** Level:
Students:	Students:

	Group 1	Group 2	Group 3	Group 4
Monday				
Tuesday				
Wednesday				
Thursday				
Friday				

Student Expectations

Math workshop will not be perfect from the start. It may be a bit chaotic and students may try to play instead of work. But, by setting student expectations early, and with plenty of practice and modeling, math workshop can run smoothly.

Questions to Consider

How should materials be handled? Will there be dedicated students in charge of the materials? Where will they be stored? When can students access them? How and when should cleanup happen? Should there be a one-minute cleanup warning before switching rotations or is cleaning up part of the transition time? Who is responsible for cleaning up common areas?

How and when can students work with others? What activities should be done alone, with a partner, or as group work? Who and when can students ask for help?

What does staying on task mean in math workshop? What level should the volume be? Where should students be working? How should students be accountable for the work they've done? What should the conversations sound like?

What happens if students make mistakes or struggle? Who can they ask for help? What materials and strategies are available if a problem is too hard? Can they skip difficult problems or save them for conferencing?

When is the teacher available? Can students interrupt guided math groups? How can they signal they need to go to the bathroom? What is an appropriate reason to interrupt the teacher? Who else can help students and answer questions?

Setting Expectations

One of the first things you should do when beginning math workshop is to clearly outline the expectations. While you don't have to do this in tandem with making an anchor chart, the visual reminder can be helpful for retaining the expectations as well as serving as a visual reminder throughout the year.

- It can be helpful to frame the expectations simply: What should math workshop look like? What should it sound like? What is the student responsible for? What is the teacher responsible for? Refer to the Questions to Consider in the section above for more specific things to discuss.
- Use the reproducible provided on page 12 for students to complete and keep in their math notebooks or folders. Or, have students and parents sign it as a behavior contract at the beginning of the year. It may be helpful to preprogram the information before copying for students who need it.
- Review the anchor chart often in the first few weeks. Start reviewing it daily before beginning math workshop, and then gradually review it less often as students become more self-reliant.

Don't forget to **model, model, model!** Be sure to start slow, and practice will make perfect!

Looks Like

Sounds Like

Math Workshop

My Job

My Teacher's Job

Ensuring Accountability

While moving to a math workshop model has many benefits, it removes the traditional assessment and accountability options in the traditional teaching model. However, it's still necessary to prove in some way that students are working hard toward learning goals and making progress throughout the year. See the lists below for suggestions.

Accountability During Rotations

- Have students record their math thinking (for example, number sentences solved during a game) on whiteboards or something else that is highly visible. That way, you can see at a glance if students are working or not.
- Use activities with recording sheets that you can collect.
- Or, use a recording sheet where students record the rotations they visited and details about their work at each rotation.
- If desired, collect students' written work and/or recording sheets for a participation grade. Use the reproducible on page 14 as a weekly rotation recording sheet or create your own with the rotations specific to your math workshop (see example below).
- Initial, stamp, or sticker students' work daily. You can circulate and do this quickly during closure each day.
- Have students use a math journal to record their work during rotations.
- Utilize technology if possible—many programs and apps have built-in reports on the teacher side.

Assessment

- When not meeting with groups, use the guided math time to visit different stations and have students explain their math thinking for a quick formative assessment.
- During closure, use exit tickets. Use them as formative assessments, or keep them in a math notebook or portfolio to show progress.
- Designate one math workshop day a week or month for a more formal assessment that can be used for a grade or kept in portfolios.

Name____________________ Date ________

Math Workshop

Mark off each rotation as you complete it. You must do seat work and technology every day!

Mon	Meet with Teacher	Seat Work	Technology	Fast Practice	Math Game
Tues	Meet with Teacher	Seat Work	Technology	Fast Practice	Math Game
Wed	Meet with Teacher	Seat Work	Technology	Fast Practice	Math Game

Name ______________________________ Week of ________________

Math Rotations

Day	Rotation(s) Visited	Done?	Rate Yourself
Monday			
Tuesday			
Wednesday			
Thursday			
Friday			

1	2	3	4
I didn't do any work. I wasn't on task.	I didn't do my best work and was often off task.	I worked well, but was off task a little.	I worked hard and stayed on task.

Multi-Step Word Problems

Essential Question

What strategies can be used to identify and solve multi-step word problems?

Warm-Up/Review

Write or display a single-step word problem on the board and have students solve it with a partner and share their answers. Challenge students to figure out how to rewrite the problem so it uses a different operation. Discuss students' ideas as a class.

Mini-Lesson

Materials: 10 index cards, programmed with 50, 50, 4, 4, 4, 1, 1, 1, 1, 1, copies of word problem (see below)

1. Display or provide copies of the following problem: *At the animal sanctuary, there are 2 elephants, 3 bears, and 5 lions. Each elephant drinks 50 gallons of water a day. Each bear drinks 4 gallons a day and each lion drinks 1 gallon a day. How many gallons of water does the sanctuary need each day?* (117)
2. Assign 10 students animals to play and give them index cards with their gallon amount on them. Challenge the rest of the class to use the "actors" to work through the problem step by step.
3. As a class, record the steps and equations used on the board, relating each number and step to the original problem. If possible, repeat with several different solutions.
4. Place students into small groups and have them work together to solve the following problem: *The tree farm has 12 rows of 30 trees. They cut down 58 trees to sell for lumber. How many trees do they have left?* (302)
5. Allow groups to share their answers and the unique ways they used to solve the problem.

Math Talk

What are you solving for? How do you know?
Why did you choose to do that first?
Could you solve this another way? How?

Journal Prompt

Is there a correct order in which to solve a multi-step word problem? Why or why not? Give examples.

Materials

copies of word problems (see below)
highlighters

Workstations

Activity sheets (pages 17–19)
Multi-Step Word Problem Task Cards (page 20)
Multi-digit addition and subtraction practice

Guided Math

Remediation: Modeling Word Problems

1. Read the following word problem: "There are 2 rooms that each have 24 chairs. There are 61 people who need to sit. How many more chairs does the next room need so everyone can sit?" (13) Provide a copy of the word problem to each student.
2. Explain, "Before starting, figure out what you are trying to answer. You can often look for the question and rewrite it as a statement." Model identifying and highlighting the question. Then, come up with the inverse statement as a group and record it: "The next room needs ___ chairs."
3. Explain, "There are 2 rooms with chairs." Draw 2 boxes. "Each room has 24 chairs." Write *24* in each room. "There are 61 people who need to sit." Write *61* below the boxes. Guide students through one method to solve the problem (subtracting 24 from 61 twice). Then, point out another method (adding 24 and 24, and subtracting the sum from 61).
4. Continue with visual, concrete examples. Encourage students to identify the question, rephrase it, and then use a model.

On Level: Organizing and Labeling Information

1. Read the following word problem: "There are 18 pencils in each pack. Mrs. Oates bought 4 packs. She wants to give each of her 6 groups the same amount of pencils. How many pencils will each group get?" (12) Provide a copy to each student.
2. Have students use highlighters to identify the question and use it to frame the answer they're looking for. (Each group will get ___ pencils.) Then, have students circle the key information in the problem. Explain that context is important. Have students volunteer what operations they think they should perform and why.
3. Have students solve the problem and share their solutions. Connect the operations they used with phrases from the word problem. Emphasize that there are several ways to solve the problem.
4. Continue practicing with other word problems. Encourage students to justify the operations they choose and the order in which they perform the steps.

Enrichment: Writing Word Problems

1. Write $(5 \times 4) + (12 \times 4) = 68$. Review that parentheses tell you what to do first in a problem.
2. Ask students to imagine a word problem to describe the equation. Say, "Multiplication deals with sets or groups of things. What things come in sets of 4? What word signals addition?" Give the example: "The tire shop ordered 5 full sets of tires one week. Next week, they ordered 12 full sets of tires. How many tires did the shop order in all?" Ask students, "Which part of the story says to write 5×4? 12×4? What words suggest using parentheses? Which part indicates addition?"
3. Have students write their own word problems for the same equation. Share and discuss students' stories. Have students identify the clues in their stories.
4. Continue writing word problems for additional multi-step equations.

Assess and Extend

Solve the problem: *The team scored 16 points in the first half. They scored 23 points in the second half. They won by 11 points. How many points did the other team score?* (28) Explain how you know which operations to use in the absence of common key words.

Name ______________________________ Date ______________

Multi-Step Word Problems

Modeling Word Problems

Read each problem. Complete the statements. Then, draw a model to solve. Use the answer to complete your statement.

1. Jose and Emma are playing jump rope. Emma jumped 16 times. She jumped 11 times on her next turn. Jose jumped 3 times as many times as Emma. How many times did Jose jump in all?

   Rewrite the question as a statement.

   ____

   First, I will ____________________. Then, I will ____________________.

2. Whitney went to the carnival. She rode 8 rides 3 times each. She rode 7 rides 4 times each. How many times did she ride in all?

   Rewrite the question as a statement.

   ____

   First, I will ____________________. Then, I will ____________________.

3. The three Sanchez children have 250 toy cars in all. Joe has 104 cars. Emilio has 72 cars. How many cars does Sandy have?

   Rewrite the question as a statement.

   ____

   First, I will ____________________. Then, I will ____________________.

4. There are 40 balloons in a bag. Mark wants to put 3 balloons at each table. There are 12 tables. How many balloons will Mark have left?

   Rewrite the question as a statement.

   ____

   First, I will ____________________. Then, I will ____________________.

Name ______________________ Date ______________

Multi-Step Word Problems

Organizing and Labeling Information

Read each problem. Identify the question and the key information. Then, solve.

1. Each student received 4 ticket books to sell raffle tickets. Each book had 50 tickets. Elliot turned in 64 unsold tickets. How many tickets did Elliot sell?	**2.** The teacher wants to buy cookies for his students. He wants each of his 22 students to get 4 cookies. If the cookies come in packages of 9, how many packages should he buy?
3. Robin's 3 cats each eat 13 ounces of kibble. Jamie's 2 cats each eat 18 ounces of kibble. Whose cats eat the most kibble? How much more?	**4.** Sue read 32 pages in her novel each day from Monday to Friday. On Saturday and Sunday, she read 68 pages each day. How many pages did she read in all?
5. Pilar is training for a marathon. She runs a total of 100 miles each week. Every Saturday and Sunday, she runs 20 miles. On the other 5 days, she runs the same amount. How far does Pilar run each Wednesday?	**6.** On Saturday, the pet store sold 28 fish tank kits. On Sunday, they sold half as many kits. How many kits did they sell that weekend?

Name ______________________ Date ____________

Multi-Step Word Problems

▲ Writing Word Problems

Write a word problem to describe each equation.

1. $(4 \times 5) + 2 = 22$

2. $(12 \times 4) - (2 \times 6) = 36$

3. $210 + (100 - 18) = 292$

4. $1{,}000 - (250 \div 5) = 950$

5. $(7 \times 8) + (7 \times 6) = 98$

Multi-Step Word Problem Task Cards

The bookstore had 50 copies of the new best seller. They sold 28 copies on the first day. They sold 16 copies the next day. How many copies do they have left? **A**	The stunt racing team knows 15 different tricks. Each trick takes 5 minutes to perform. Can they perform all of their tricks in less than an hour? **B**
The toy store had 8 tricycles on display. They had 15 bicycles on display. How many wheels were there in all? **C**	The track is 2,500 feet long. During a four-person relay race, Marcus ran 675 feet, Daniel ran 512 feet, and Beth ran 595 feet. How far does Samira have to run to complete the lap? **D**
Mrs. Avery wanted to buy 4 pencils for each of the 24 students in her class. She saw a sale at the dollar store where she could buy 10 pencils for $1. How much did Mrs. Avery spend on pencils for her class? How many pencils did she have left over? **E**	At the apple orchard, Jayla, Ian, and Seth each picked a dozen apples. Their dad picked double the apples Jayla did. How many apples did the family pick in all? **F**
Olivia is on a competitive gymnastics team. The gym charges $25 for a one-hour training session and $8 an hour to work out in the gym. Olivia trains for 5 hours a week. She works out for another 7 hours a week. How much does Olivia's family pay the gym each week? **G**	John is making bookmarks for his 9 cousins and 5 good friends. He needs 6 inches of paper for each bookmark. He already has 35 inches of paper. How many more inches of paper does he need to make all of the bookmarks? **H**

To prep: Copy on card stock and laminate for durability. Cut apart and place cards in a center. If desired, write the answer on the back of each card to make them self-checking.

Factors

Essential Question

How do factors relate to whole numbers?

Warm-Up/Review

Play Around the World with multiplication and/or division fact flash cards.

Mini-Lesson

Materials: 1–30 game board (hundred chart 1–30)

1. Display a game board showing the numbers 1 to 30. Set up a score chart for two teams: teacher and students.
2. Start by choosing a large prime number, such as 23 or 29. Mark it off of the game board, and record it under the teacher side of the score chart. Mark off the *1* on the game board and record a *1* on the students' side of the score chart. (*Note:* Do not explain the gameplay to the class. They should pay attention to actions and consequences in order to figure out the rules and gain an understanding of factors.)
3. Allow students to choose a number. Mark it off of the game board and record it under the student side of the score chart. Mark off all of the factors of that number on the game board, recording each one under the teacher side of the score chart. If a team chooses a number that has no factors left on the game board, they lose their turn. Continue playing until no more numbers can be marked off, then total the scores. The highest score wins.
4. Have students describe the rules of the game, and how they figured them out. Introduce the term *factor* and relate it to the game the class just played. Ask students why some numbers were better choices than others. If desired, also introduce the terms *prime* and *composite*. (If desired, make a copy of this game to use as a workstation.)
5. Place students in small groups and challenge them to find the factors for each number 31–50. Share and discuss as a group.

Math Talk

How are factors related to multiplication?

Can a number have more than one set of factors?

Do factors always come in pairs? Why or why not?

What is special about the factor *1*?

Journal Prompt

How can understanding factors help you solve other math problems, such as long division, fractions, or measurement problems?

Materials

color tiles
laminated multiplication charts
dry-erase markers
copies of hundred charts

Workstations

Activity sheets (pages 23–25)
Spinning Factors (page 26)
The Factor Game (see mini-lesson on page 21)

Guided Math

Remediation: Using Arrays to Find Factors

1. Give each student 12 color tiles. Have them use all of the tiles to make an array of any size and record the factors. Continue until students have found all of the possible arrays for 12. (1 × 12, 2 × 6, 3 × 4)
2. Have students mark out the duplicates because they are different orientations of the same factors and the same product. Then, have students list the remaining factors in order from least to greatest. Explain, "These are the only numbers that can be multiplied to get the product 12." Point out that the factors come in pairs.
3. Repeat steps 1 and 2 with 16 tiles. Explain, "When a number has the same factor twice (4 × 4), we only record it once. So, the factors of 16 are 1, 2, 4, 8, and 16."
4. Repeat with several more sets of tiles, including at least one prime number (such as 7 or 5). Explain that not all numbers have multiple factors, but that all numbers have the factors of 1 and themselves.

On Level: Relating Multiplication to Factors

1. Give each student a multiplication chart. Say a number, such as 24, and have them circle each instance of the number on the chart. Then, have students draw a line from the circle to the numbers at the head of the columns and rows and record those numbers.
2. Explain, "The numbers that you drew lines to are the factors." Ask students how to treat factors that occur twice (for example, 2 × 6 and 6 × 2). Tell students, "Because of the Commutative property, the order you multiply factors in doesn't matter, so we only include the factors from each pair once."
3. Erase the charts and repeat with several more numbers, including square numbers and prime numbers. Have students describe any patterns they see.

Enrichment: Factor Charts

1. Say a number, such as 30, and challenge students to find all of its factors. (1, 2, 3, 5, 6, 10, 15, 30) Have students share their findings and describe the strategies they used to find all of the factors.
2. Introduce using factor T-charts. Take the factors of 30 that students found and place them in the chart, with each factor in the pair on either side of the line. Order the left-hand factors from least to greatest, beginning with 1. Explain how it keeps the factors organized so you can see if any are missing at a glance.
3. For students who placed factors in a row from least to greatest, introduce the "rainbow" method. Have students draw lines to match factor pairs, so it resembles an arched rainbow. Explain that this easily highlights any missing factors.
4. Have students find the factors of 5, 7, and 11. Explain that these are prime numbers because their only factors are 1 and themselves. Numbers with more than two factors are called composite. Give students a hundred chart, and have them color the prime numbers red and the composite numbers blue.

Assess and Extend

What factors do 12 and 30 have in common? (1, 2, 3, 6) How do you know?

Name ______________________ Date ______________

Factors

Using Arrays to Find Factors

Draw all of the possible arrays for each number. Then, list the factors.

1. 20

Factors: ______________________

2. 18

Factors: ______________________

3. 9

Factors: ______________________

4. 25

Factors: ______________________

5. 24

Factors: ______________________

6. 7

Factors: ______________________

Name ______________________ Date ____________

Factors

Relating Multiplication to Factors

Write the missing factors.

1. 35 = ☐ × 5

2. 72 = 9 × ☐

3. 18 = 3 × ☐

4. 49 = ☐ × 7

5. 20 = 4 × ☐

6. 63 = ☐ × 9

Circle the numbers that are factors of the given number. Not all factors will be included.

7. 36

5 36 7 6 3 2 18 1

8. 40

10 2 6 8 12 5 4 3

9. 25

5 1 3 10 6 4 25 9

10. 42

4 7 2 8 9 10 12 6

List the factors of each number.

11. 28 ______________________

12. 60 ______________________

13. 22 ______________________

14. 16 ______________________

15. 27 ______________________

Name ______________________________ Date ______________

Factors

▲ Factor Charts

Create a factor chart or factor rainbow for each number.

1. 9	**2.** 16
3. 42	**4.** 24
5. 36	**6.** 49
7. 75	**8.** 48

Spinning Factors

Materials: sharpened pencil, paper clip

To play: Use the sharpened pencil and a paper clip to spin each spinner. Use each number to create a two-digit number. Record the number on the chart. List the factors of the number. Then, write *P* or *C* to tell whether the number is prime or composite.

Tens Place

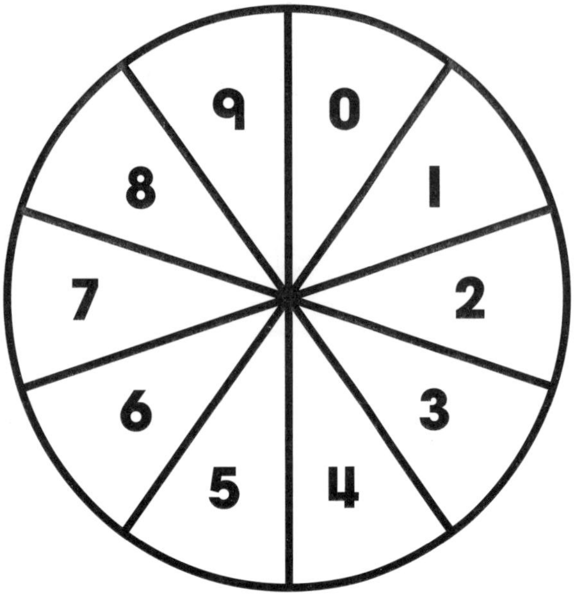

Ones Place

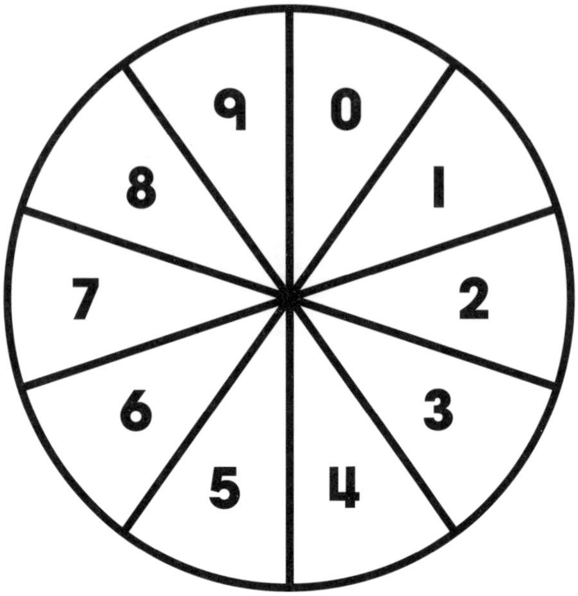

Number	Factors	Prime (P) or Composite (C)?

Multiples

Essential Question

How are factors and multiples related?

Warm-Up/Review

Play Boing. Choose a digit, such as 3, and how to count (by ones, twos, fives, etc.). Students start counting one-by-one. If a student's number includes the chosen number, they say, "boing!" instead. If a student forgets to say "boing," they sit down. Repeat until only one student is left standing.

Mini-Lesson

1. Start skip counting by twos. Say several numbers in the sequence, then point at a student to continue. Start again with a number other than two, say several numbers, then point to a different student to continue. Ask students how they knew which numbers to say next. Repeat with fives and tens.
2. Explain that the numbers they are saying are multiples of the very first number in each sequence other than 0. Each number in the sequence is 2 (or 5, 10, etc.) more than the previous number. Skip counting is repeated addition, and repeated addition is multiplication.
3. As a class, skip count by 2. Start with 0, and hold up a finger each time you say a new number. Stop periodically, and point out how the multiple is the same as the number multiplied by the fingers you have up (2 × 5 fingers = 10). Repeat with the fives and tens before moving on to threes, fours, etc.
4. Divide the class into small groups. Assign each group a number from 2 to 9. Challenge the group to find the first 20 multiples for their number and identify any patterns they notice. Have groups share their multiples and patterns with the class.

Math Talk

Is ____ a multiple of ____? How do you know?

Describe in your own words how multiples are related to multiplication.

What do you notice about the multiples of 2 and 4? 3 and 6? 2 and 5?

Journal Prompt

Is a number a multiple of itself? (For example, is 5 a multiple of 5?) Why or why not?

Materials

multiplication charts
sticky notes
laminated 120 charts
different colors of dry-erase markers

Workstations

Activity sheets (pages 29–31)
Multiples Take Flight (page 32)

Guided Math

◯ Remediation: Finding Patterns in Multiples

1. Give each student a multiplication chart and two sticky notes. Have students use them to cover the chart so only the ×5 row is visible. Explain, "You can easily see the multiples of a number on the multiplication chart because multiples are the products of a number and other whole numbers." Point out the multiples of 5 and emphasize the related multiplication sentences.
2. Have students look at the multiples of 5 and identify any patterns or other things unique to that set of multiples. For example, *all of the multiples end in 0 or 5* or *the tens place repeats twice each time*. Ask, "Could 58 be a multiple of 5? Why or why not? Is 200 a multiple of 5? How do you know? Can you think of another three-digit multiple of 5?"
3. Repeat with other multiples. Have students record their thinking and any patterns for each multiple to refer to later.

☐ On Level: Identifying Multiples

1. Remind students, "A multiple is the product of a number and any other whole number." Have students give examples and rephrase the definition in their own words.
2. Display the number *24*. Ask, "Is 24 a multiple of 2? How do you know? Is it a multiple of any other numbers? Which ones?" Have students justify their answers with the related multiplication sentences.
3. Display the numbers *12, 22, 18, 37, 40,* and *36*. Say, "These are all multiples of 2, except for one. Which number is not a multiple of 2? (37) How do you know? (It is an odd number.)" Repeat with several more sets of multiples.
4. Finally, display a set of multiples and challenge students to figure out which number they are a multiple of. Encourage students to justify their answers.

△ Enrichment: Relationships Between Multiples

1. Give each student a 120 chart and several dry-erase markers. Have students use one color to circle the multiples of 2. Then, have students use a different color to draw an *X* on the multiples of 4. Pause after each multiple to discuss any patterns students notice. Continue marking the multiples of 8, changing colors and using different marks (circles, boxes, slashes, triangles, etc.) for each set of multiples. Discuss any overall patterns students notice, as well as the relationship between 2, 4, and 8, and their multiples.
2. Repeat step 1 with the multiples of 2, 3, 6, and 9.
3. Finally, mark each multiple of the numbers 2 to 10 on the chart. Point out the numbers that have no marks at all. Say, "The blank numbers are prime numbers, which are related to factors. How are factors, multiples, and prime numbers related?"

Assess and Extend

Find the first 10 multiples of 12. Describe how you found the multiples of a larger number.

Name ______________________________ Date ______________

Multiples

Finding Patterns in Multiples

Circle the multiples of each number. Not all multiples will be included for each number.

1. 3

4 2 6
3 9 10
12 15 16
18 21 24
27

2. 4

2 4 8
6 12 14
16 20 22
24 28 32
36 40

3. 6

3 6 9
12 18 24
22 30 36
32 42 48
46 54

4. 7

7 10 14
21 28 32
35 42 48
49 52 56
63 69

5. 8

2 4 8
16 20 24
32 36 40
48 56 64
72

6. 9

3 9 19
27 30 36
39 45 54
63 65 72
81

7. Choose one problem above and justify your answer.

____

____

____

Name ______________________ Date ____________

Multiples

Identifying Multiples

Begin with a shaded square. Draw a path to connect the first nine multiples of each number. You can move in all four directions and diagonally. Use a different color for each shaded square.

43	32	39	6	4	2	6	9
36	27	20	8	12	11	21	13
21	18	24	16	10	27	18	9
10	12	28	30	31	42	36	39
6	32	22	26	36	48	81	45
9	36	16	29	42	72	54	40
17	15	40	49	35	63	35	33
12	32	18	48	56	28	30	25
9	21	24	40	72	64	21	20
5	6	16	27	22	14	15	5
3	2	14	8	15	7	12	10

Choose one of the paths and explain how you found the multiples.

____

____

____

Name ______________________ Date ______________

Multiples

▲ Relationships Between Multiples

Give at least one example for each challenge. If there is no possible example, write *none*.

1. a multiple of 6 between 70 and 80

____

2. a multiple of both 2 and 4 between 50 and 60

____

3. a multiple of 3 between 50 and 70 that is not also a multiple of 6

____

4. an odd multiple of 8 greater than 80

____

5. an even multiple of 5 between 50 and 100

____

6. a multiple of 9 that is not also a multiple of 3

____

7. a multiple of 3 that rounds from the tens place to 100

____

8. Choose a problem where you answered *none*. Justify your answer.

____

____

____

____

Multiples Take Flight

Materials: 2 dice, 1 counter per player

To play: Place counters on the Start space. Players take turns. Player 1 rolls the dice and moves to any space in the first row that is a multiple of the rolled number. For example, if a 2 is rolled, the player can move to the *10, 18, 20,* or *12* spaces. Once on the board, players can only move to adjacent spaces. The first player to reach Finish wins.

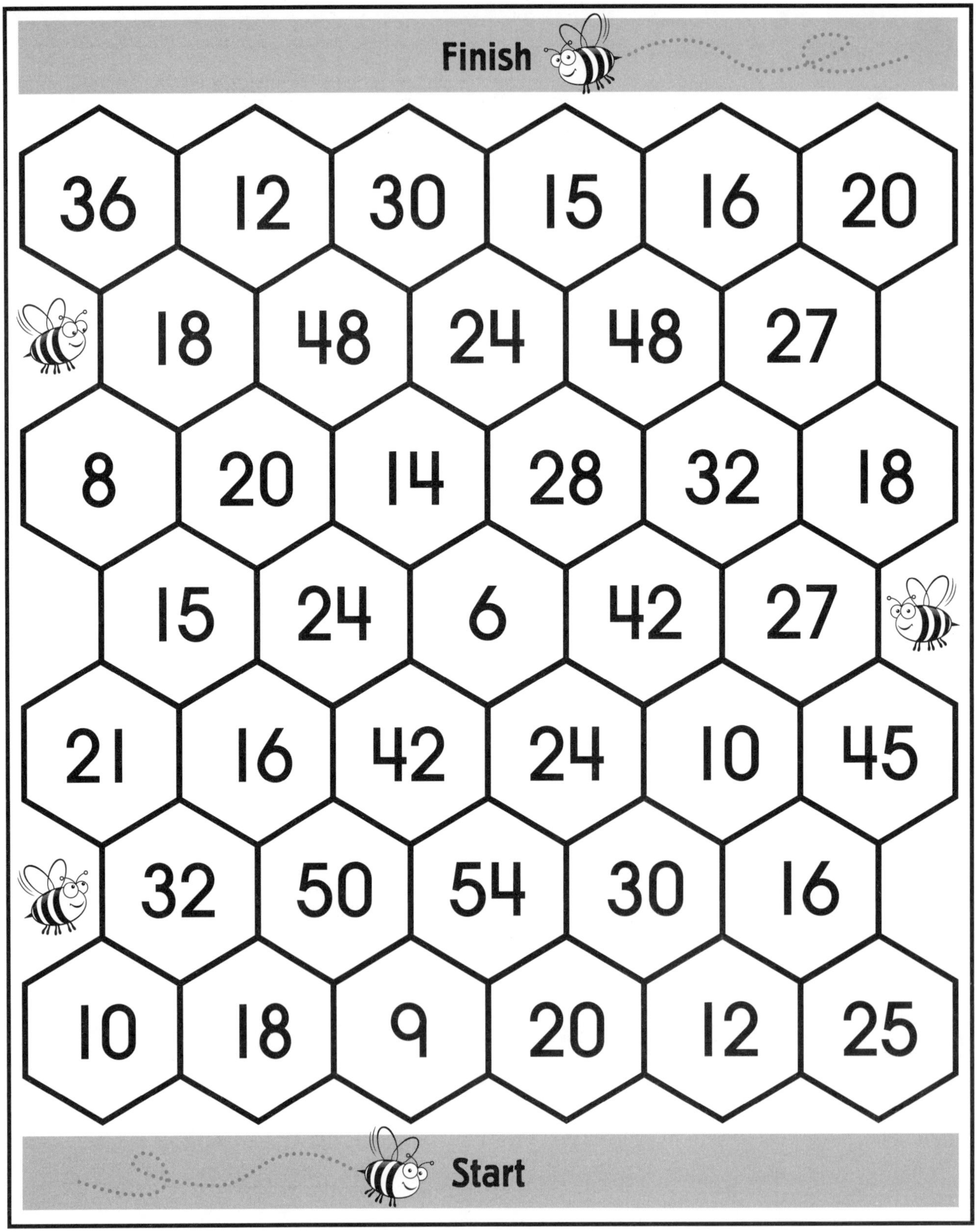

Number and Shape Patterns

Essential Question

How are number or shape patterns related to equations?

Warm-Up/Review

Point out a pattern in the room, such as checkered floor tiles, a pattern on a student's shirt, or a pattern on the classroom calendar. Invite students to share and describe other patterns they notice.

Mini-Lesson

Materials: 120 chart

1. Display the 120 chart. Ask students to identify any patterns they see in the chart, such as *the numbers in each column begin with the same number, the even and odd numbers form alternating columns,* or *all of the numbers on the right side end in 0.*
2. Explain that patterns repeat and can be predicted because they follow a rule. Write the rule *even number + even number* on the board. As a class, record all of the addition sentences with addends less than 10 that fit the rule (0 + 2, 2 + 2, 2 + 4, etc.). Find the sums, and circle them on the 120 chart (all even numbers 0–20). Discuss any patterns students see. Ask, "Is there a conclusion you can make that will always happen when adding even numbers?" Have students test their theory with several larger numbers.
3. Draw five connected squares in a plus sign shape. Add a new square to the end of each "arm" for a total of four new squares. Repeat once more. Have students work with a partner to figure out what will happen next. Challenge students to figure out how many squares will be in the pattern at step 10. (41) Allow students to share their answers and explain how they found them.

Math Talk

What happens next? How do you know?
Is there a way you can test that theory?
Can you explain the pattern in a different way?
What is the base unit? What is the rule?

Journal Prompt

How can finding number patterns help you solve problems?

Materials

color tiles
hundred charts
dot grid paper
multiplication charts

Workstations

Activity sheets (pages 35–37)
Pattern Workshop (page 38)
Manipulatives and laminated 120, addition, and multiplication charts for creating and defining their own patterns

Guided Math

Remediation: Understanding Repeating Patterns

1. Display a pattern with color tiles: yellow, yellow, green, red. Repeat it three times. Explain, "A pattern is something that follows a rule. You always get the same outcome from the rule."
2. Ask, "What pattern do you see? What part repeats?" Identify the core, or unit (yellow, yellow, green, red) and explain, "It is the part that repeats. What color comes next? What is the fifteenth color in the pattern? How do you know?"
3. Give students a hundred chart. Explain that there are patterns in numbers too. Have students color in 3. Display +4. Say, "If I start at 3 and add 4, I get 7." Color in 7. "Then I add 4 again and get 11." Color in 11. Continue with the next several numbers in the pattern. Have students find and color all of the terms in the pattern up to 100. Discuss any patterns they see.
4. On the same chart, have students color in 1 with a different color. Then, have them use the same pattern (+4) and color in all of the terms up to 100. Compare the two patterns and note any new patterns or any shortcuts students were able to use, since those also indicate patterns.

On Level: Relating Shape and Number Patterns

1. Draw a dot. Beside that, draw a triangle with 2 dots per side. Then, draw a triangle with 3 dots per side. Ask, "What shape should I draw next?" (a triangle with 4 dots per side) Draw the triangle.
2. Give students dot grid paper. Have them record the pattern and add the next two shapes. Ask, "How could you describe this pattern? What is changing? What stays the same?"
3. Next, have students count the number of dots in the border of each triangle and record it below the triangle. Explain, "Often, shape patterns are related to number patterns. What do you notice about the numbers?" Give students time to look for more number patterns, such as the lengths of the sides, the number of dots inside each triangle, etc.
4. Challenge students to draw a shape pattern of their own and identify any related number patterns. Allow students to share their work.

Enrichment: Patterns in Square Numbers

1. Give students color tiles and have them make a square up to 10 x 10. Have them record the side lengths of their squares and find the area. Share each square and its area. Find each area on the multiplication chart and color it in. Work together to make any squares that have not been made (including 1 × 1), find their areas, and mark them on the chart.
2. Explain, "These numbers are called square numbers because they form a perfect square. A square number is formed by multiplying a number by itself."
3. Have students start with a single square (1 x 1). Then, using a different color, have them add tiles to create a 2 by 2 square. Record the two colors as an addition sentence (1 + 3 = 4). Note that the sum is also the square number. Use a third color to add on and change it to a 3 by 3 square and add on to the original addition sentence (1 + 3 + 5 = 9). Continue adding tiles to make larger squares and adding to the addition sentence. Discuss any patterns students notice.

Assess and Extend

Look at a multiplication chart and identify a pattern. Give the first 10 numbers in the pattern and explain the pattern using words or an equation.

Name ______________________________ Date ______________

Number and Shape Patterns

Understanding Repeating Patterns

Use a crayon to show each pattern on the section of hundred chart. Then, use the chart to answer the questions.

1. Start at 32.
Rule: +6

31	32	33	34	35	36	37	38	39	40
41	42	43	44	45	46	47	48	49	50
51	52	53	54	55	56	57	58	59	60

2. Describe what you notice about the pattern.

____

____

3. What are the next three numbers in the pattern? ________, ________, ________

4. Start at 99.
Rule: –3

71	72	73	74	75	76	77	78	79	80
81	82	83	84	85	86	87	88	89	90
91	92	93	94	95	96	97	98	99	100

5. Describe what you notice about the pattern.

____

____

6. What are the next three numbers in the pattern? ________, ________, ________

7. Start at 95.
Rule: +4

91	92	93	94	95	96	97	98	99	100
101	102	103	104	105	106	107	108	109	110
111	112	113	114	115	116	117	118	119	120

8. Describe what you notice about the pattern.

____

____

9. What are the next three numbers in the pattern? ________, ________, ________

Name ______________________ Date ____________

Number and Shape Patterns

Relating Shape and Number Patterns

Complete each pattern. Then, use it to answer the questions.

1.

2. Write the related number pattern under each term.

3. Describe the pattern. What is the rule?

____

____

4. What are the next three numbers in the pattern? _____, _____, _____

5.

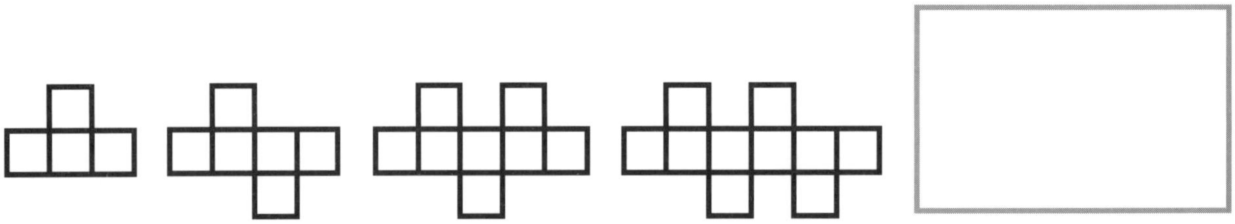

6. Write the related number pattern under each term.

7. Describe the pattern. What is the rule?

____

____

8. What is the tenth shape in the pattern?

How do you know? ______________________________

____

Name ______________________ Date ____________

Number and Shape Patterns

▲ Patterns in Square Numbers

Follow the instructions to complete each section. Then, look for patterns.

1. Write the first 10 square numbers.

2. Find the difference between adjacent numbers. For example, *4 – 1 = 3*.

Step 1

Step 2

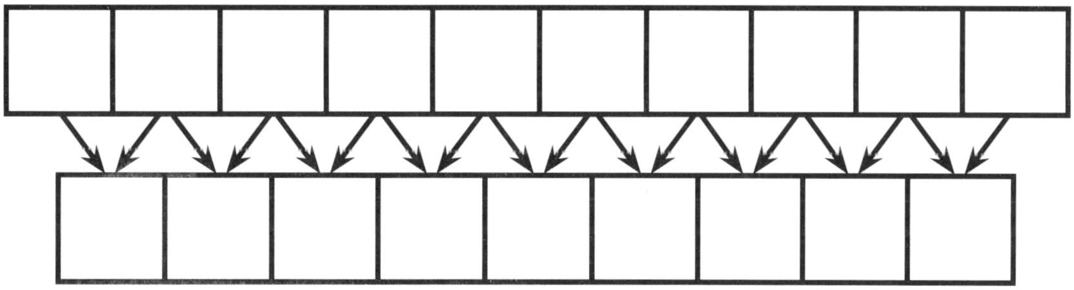

3. What pattern do you notice?

____

____

4. Use two different colors to continue the pattern below. Use the pattern to complete each addition sentence.

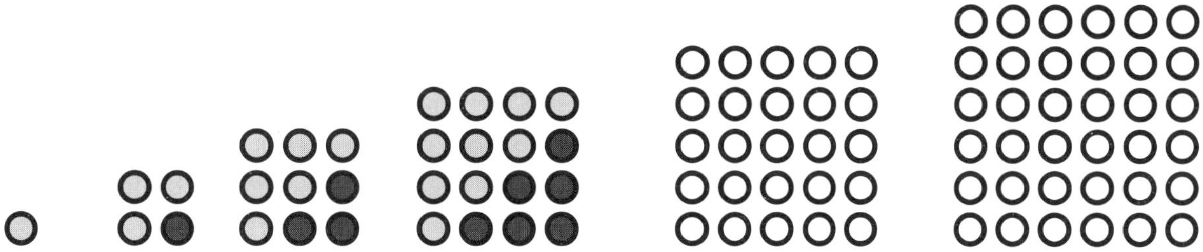

1	4	9	16	25	36
1	1 + 3	3 + 6	16 = ____ + ____	25 = ____ + ____	36 = ____ + ____

5. What pattern or patterns do you notice?

____

____

____

Pattern Workshop

Materials: sharpened pencil, paper clip, pattern blocks

To play: Use a sharpened pencil and a paper clip to spin each spinner and create the basis for your pattern. Use the left spinner for the starting shape. Then, spin the remaining spinners to find out which shapes to add, and how many of each to add each time. Use the pattern to complete the activities and answer the questions. Use the pencil and paper clip to spin the bottom-right spinner and complete the final question before answering.

Starting Shape **Add**

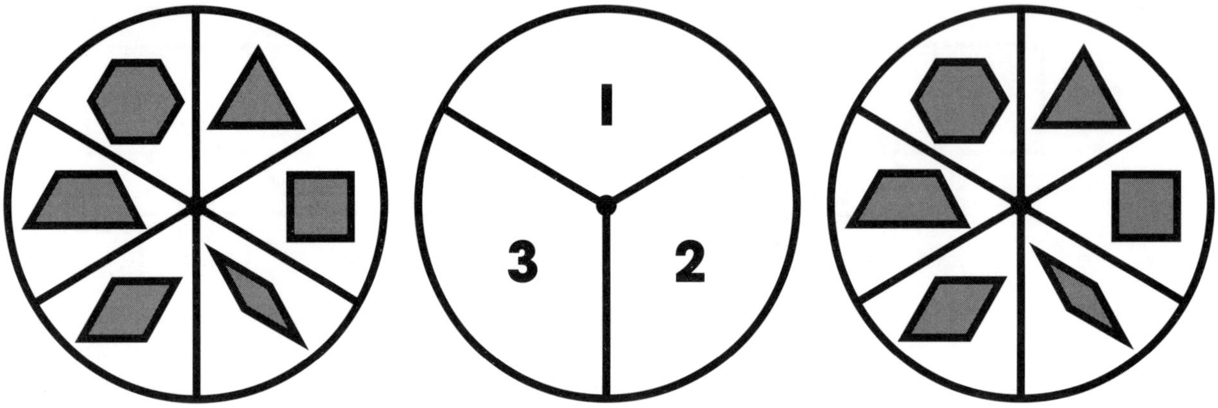

Build the pattern. Record at least the first three terms below.

Describe the pattern.

____

____

____

____

____

____

What is the ______ term in the pattern?

Draw it on the back of the paper.

Place Value Relationships

Essential Question

How are the digits in a number related to each other?

Warm-Up/Review

Give students index cards. Have them write a multiple of 10, 100, or 1,000 on the card. Then, have three students with numbers of different place values stand in front of the class. Have the class say the three-digit number they represent. Repeat several times, switching out a number each time.

Mini-Lesson

Materials: place value chart to millions

1. Display a place value chart. Say, "Dan finds 3 magic beans. He puts them in a cup before bed." Write *3* on the place value chart in the ones place. "In the morning, there are 30 beans in the cup." Write *30* below the 3 on the place value chart in the tens and ones places. "The next morning, the beans have spilled all over the table. Dan counts 300 beans this time!" Add 300 to the chart.
2. Ask students how many beans they think Dan will find the next morning. Have students justify their answers. Continue the story, explaining that the next days there are 3,000, 30,000, etc., beans. Add each new number to the chart. Discuss whether students' predictions were correct and why or why not. Guide students to figure out by how much the beans increase each night (×10) and relate that to the changes on the place value chart.
3. Erase the chart. Explain, "Zoe finds a sack with $2,000,000. She hides it under her bed." Write *$2,000,000* on the board. Say, "The next morning, she counts the money and there is only $200,000 left." Write it on the chart. Continue the story, dividing the money by 10 each night. Have students record the amounts on the chart and describe what is happening (÷10 each night). Relate the changes to the place value chart.
4. Draw two arrows above the place value chart, from ones to millions and from millions to ones. As a class, decide on a rule for moving each direction, and record it above the appropriate arrow (×10, ÷10).

Math Talk

How much larger is this digit than that one? How do you know?

Can you explain how this is related to expanded form?

What is the purpose of 0?

Journal Prompt

Explain how place value can help you compare and order numbers.

Materials

laminated place value mats
base ten blocks
dry-erase markers
0–9 number tiles

Workstations

Activity sheets (pages 41–43)
Guess My Number (page 44)
Multiplying by 10s and 100s fact practice
Drawing number tiles and creating the smallest/largest numbers

Guided Math

◯ Remediation: Relating Place Value to Expanded Form

1. Give each student a place value mat, base ten blocks, and a dry-erase marker. Display the number *1,239*. Direct students to write it correctly on the place value mat.
2. Say, "Three is greater than 2. But, is 3 greater than 2 in this number?" Have students use base ten blocks to model the number on the place value mat, below the digits. "So, the digits 2 and 3 actually represent 200 and 30." Point out the related base ten blocks.
3. Ask, "What does each digit represent?" Have students record each value below the base ten blocks on the mat (1,000, 200, etc.) Explain, "Writing numbers in expanded form shows the actual value of each digit."
4. Repeat steps 1 through 3 with several more numbers, including some with repeated digits and some with zeros. Students should write each number in expanded form.

□ On Level: Multiplying and Dividing by 10

1. Give each student a place value mat and a dry-erase marker. Display the number *6,020*. Have students record it on the mat.
2. Ask, "What happens to the number when we multiply it by 10? Does it get larger or smaller? (larger) How can we show this on the place value mat?"
3. Draw an arrow from each digit to the next higher place value on the mat. Write *× 10* on each arrow. Explain, "When you multiply by 10, each place value increases by 10. Zero times 10 is 0." Write a 0 in the tens place. "Twenty times 10 is 200." Write a 2 in the hundreds place. Continue with each place value to find that 6,020 × 10 is 60,200.
4. Repeat steps 1 through 3 with several more numbers. Encourage students to use place value terminology to explain how the number changes and why. Then, practice dividing by 10 using the process in reverse.

△ Enrichment: Manipulating Place Value

1. Give each student a place value mat and a set of number tiles. Display the number *42,260* and have students create it on their place value mat. Ask students to identify the value of each place.
2. Ask, "How could we change the number so it is greater than 43,000?" (Change the thousands or ten thousands place.) Encourage students to explain their thinking and relate it to place value. Then, investigate: "How could we change the number so it rounds to 42,100? How could we change it so it is 3,000 greater?" etc.
3. Explain, "Multiplying by 10 changes a digit to the next place value. So, it would move each digit left one place value. We have to add a 0 in the ones place as a placeholder. What happens when we divide this number by 10? The digits move right one space and we remove the placeholder."
4. Have students build the number 20,000. Have them multiply and divide by 10, 100, 1,000, etc., and move the number accordingly. Encourage students to explain what is happening in terms of place value each time. Then, multiply and divide by 40, 400, 50, etc.

Assess and Extend

Describe the difference between each 4 in the number 4,444,444.

Name ______________________ Date ______________

Place Value Relationships

Relating Place Value to Expanded Form

Draw base ten blocks to represent each number. Then, write the number in expanded form.

Standard Form	Represent in Base Ten	Expanded Form
1. 4,294		
2. 9,365		
3. 10,372		
4. 92,005		
5. 274,321		

Name ________________________ Date ____________

Place Value Relationships

Multiplying and Dividing by 10

hundred thousands	ten thousands	thousands	hundreds	tens	ones

Use place value to multiply or divide. Use the chart to help you.

1. 6,000 × 10 = ____________

2. 60,000 ÷ 10 = ____________

3. 70,000 × 10 = ____________

4. 4,000 ÷ 100 = ____________

5. 800 × 100 = ____________

6. 700,000 ÷ 100 = ____________

7. 2,000 × 100 = ____________

8. 500 ÷ 10 = ____________

9. 210 × 10 = ____________

10. 390,000 ÷ 10 = ____________

11. 4,622 × 10 = ____________

12. 57,000 ÷ 100 = ____________

13. 836 × 1,000 = ____________

14. 5,240 ÷ 10 = ____________

15. 37 × 10,000 = ____________

16. 142,000 ÷ 1,000 = ____________

17. 4 × 100,000 = ____________

18. 36,000 ÷ 1,000 = ____________

19. 100,000 × 10 = ____________

20. 900,000 ÷ 10,000 = ____________

Name ______________________ Date ____________

Place Value Relationships

▲ Manipulating Place Value

Use place value to multiply or divide.

1. 5 × 60 = ____________
2. 18,000 ÷ 90 = ____________
3. 4 × 9,000 = ____________
4. 500 ÷ 5 = ____________
5. 200,000 × 3 = ____________
6. 4,900 ÷ 70 = ____________
7. 50 × 400 = ____________
8. 30,000 ÷ 300 = ____________
9. 30,000 × 20 = ____________
10. 900 ÷ 90 = ____________
11. 3 × 800 = ____________
12. 21,000 ÷ 3 = ____________
13. 9 × 2,000 = ____________
14. 450 ÷ 90 = ____________
15. 600 × 900 = ____________
16. 600 ÷ 30 = ____________
17. 500 × 300 = ____________
18. 24,000 ÷ 3 = ____________
19. 40 × 7,000 = ____________
20. 800,000 ÷ 400 = ____________
21. 20 × 15,000 = ____________
22. 3,600 ÷ 90 = ____________

Choose two problems above and explain how you solved them.

23. ____

____

24. ____

____

Guess My Number

Materials: dry-erase markers, paper clips

To play: Players take turns. Player 1 thinks of a 4-digit number, writes it in the space at the bottom of the page, and folds the flap over to cover the number. Place a paper clip on the flap to keep the number hidden. Then, Player 1 completes the first statement by giving the two thousands that the secret number is between. Player 2 asks a place value question, such as *Is it greater than 500? Is it an even number?* or *Is there a 6 in the tens place?* and records it in the space provided. Player 1 answers the question and Player 2 records a guess. Player 1 marks if it is higher or lower. Repeat until all sections are complete or until the number is guessed. Reveal the number to check if Player 2's final guess is correct.

Round 1	**Round 2**
The number is between _____ and _____.	The number is between _____ and _____.
Question: __________	Question: __________
Guess: [ ] ☐ higher ☐ lower	Guess: [ ] ☐ higher ☐ lower
Question: __________	Question: __________
Guess: [ ] ☐ higher ☐ lower	Guess: [ ] ☐ higher ☐ lower
Question: __________	Question: __________
Guess: [ ] ☐ higher ☐ lower	Guess: [ ] ☐ higher ☐ lower
Question: __________	Question: __________
Guess: [ ] ☐ higher ☐ lower	Guess: [ ] ☐ higher ☐ lower
Question: __________	Question: __________
Guess: [ ] ☐ higher ☐ lower	Guess: [ ] ☐ higher ☐ lower
Question: __________	Question: __________
Guess: [ ] ☐ higher ☐ lower	Guess: [ ] ☐ higher ☐ lower
Question: __________	Question: __________
Guess: [ ] ☐ higher ☐ lower	Guess: [ ] ☐ higher ☐ lower
Question: __________	Question: __________
Secret Number	Secret Number

To prep: Copy on card stock and laminate for durability. Cut out the game board on the solid line. Cut on the two, short horizontal lines to create two flaps at the bottom. Or, make copies to place in the center. Cut off these directions before copying.

Comparing and Ordering Numbers

Essential Question

What strategies can be used to compare numbers?

Warm-Up/Review

Play a quick place value game with the class. Draw a rectangle for each team and divide each one into six sections (for ones through hundred thousands). Take turns rolling two dice and placing digits to see who can create the largest number (rolling a 10, 11, or 12 equals 0).

Mini-Lesson

Materials: list of the 10 highest mountains in the world (in feet; see below), copies of the list that can be cut apart

1. Display a list of the five highest mountains and their heights (in random order). Ask, "Which mountain is the highest? How do you know?" Discuss how Denali is definitely the highest because it is the only one with a 2 in the ten thousands place. Move it to the top of the list.
2. Work as a class to figure out how to order the remaining four mountains. Model looking at the highest place values first. If any of the mountains can be easily identified as the second highest, move it to the next place in the list. If not, model comparing two heights by comparing the digits in each place and ordering the remaining mountains.
3. Give copies of the list to pairs of students. Partners should cut apart the lists and work together to order the 10 mountains by height, from greatest to least. Review the correct order as a class (see below for correct order).

Highest Mountains in the World (ft.)

Mount Everest	29,029	K2	28,251
Kangshenjunga	28,169	Lhotse	27,940
Makalu	27,825	Cho Oyu	26,906
Dhaulagiri I	26,795	Manaslu	26,759
Nanga Parbat	26,660	Annapurna I	26,545

Note: Mountains are given in height order, so mix them up before giving the list to students.

Math Talk

Which number is larger/smaller? How do you know?
Which place value helped you compare these numbers?
Explain in your own words how you ordered this set.

Journal Prompt

When would knowing how to compare and order numbers be useful in real life? Give several examples.

Materials

laminated place value mats
dry-erase markers

Workstations

Activity sheets (pages 47–49)
Comparison Clash (page 50)
Guess My Number (page 44)

Guided Math

Remediation: Reinforcing Place Value

1. Display the numbers *1,883* and *2,056.* Ask, "What does each digit stand for in these numbers?" Have students record each number correctly on their place value mat, one above the other.
2. Looking at the place value mats, ask, "Which number has more thousands? Hundreds? Tens? Ones? Which place value tells which number is greater?" Emphasize that students should start comparing with the largest place values.
3. Say, "1,883 is less than 2,056. What is another way we can compare them?" (2,056 is greater than 1,883.)
4. Use the same process to compare additional pairs of 4-digit numbers. Remind students to always start with the largest place value. Let students who are ready move on to 5- and 6-digit numbers.

On Level: Comparing Numbers

1. Review place value and reinforce that it increases from right to left. Display the numbers *1,883* and *2,056.* Ask, "What digits are in each place value of each number? Which place value do we compare first? Which number is greater?" Place the numbers on a place value mat to confirm and compare the numbers using the greater than and less than symbols.
2. Follow the same process with 7,021 and 7,453. Ask, "What is the largest place value in these numbers? Can you use that place value to compare them? How should you compare these numbers?" Model moving to the hundreds place and then comparing.
3. Add the number 7,394 to the set. Ask, "How can we order these numbers from least to greatest?" Model using the comparison from step 2. Then, compare the third number to each of the first two numbers. Explain, "This number is greater than 7,021, but less than 7,453, so it belongs between them." Record the comparison using less than symbols.
4. Use the same process to compare additional pairs and sets of 4-digit numbers. Let students who are ready move on to 5- and 6-digit numbers.

Enrichment: Comparing Numbers in Different Forms

1. Display *600,000 + 4,000 + 800 + 2 and 640,820.* Ask, "How would you compare two numbers in different forms?" Explain that one method is to rewrite one of the numbers so they are in the same format. Model rewriting the number that is in expanded form in standard form.
2. Say, "These numbers have the same digits. We can use a place value chart to clearly see the value of each digit." Write both numbers on the place value mat. Model looking to the highest place value first. Then, explain, "Because there are no ten thousands here, and this number has 4 ten thousands, it is greater." Record the comparison using the correct symbol.
3. Repeat with several more pairs of numbers in different forms, including word form and short word form (i.e., 4 hundreds).
4. Add in additional numbers and walk students through the same steps to compare and order larger sets of numbers in different forms.

Assess and Extend

Which number is greater: 32,094 or 32,904? How do you know? Write a number that falls between those two numbers.

Name ______________________ Date ______________

Comparing and Ordering Numbers

● Reinforcing Place Value

Use place value to compare each set of numbers. Color in the place value that helped you compare the numbers.

1. 4,292 ◯ 3,129 | HT | TT | Th | H | T | O |

2. 6,432 ◯ 6,257 | HT | TT | Th | H | T | O |

3. 32,251 ◯ 39,376 | HT | TT | Th | H | T | O |

4. 71,513 ◯ 71,588 | HT | TT | Th | H | T | O |

5. 46,926 ◯ 42,735 | HT | TT | Th | H | T | O |

6. 925,292 ◯ 725,946 | HT | TT | Th | H | T | O |

7. 105,378 ◯ 105,373 | HT | TT | Th | H | T | O |

Write the numbers on the lines to make each statement true.

8. 5,081 6,580 ____________ is greater than ____________.

9. 2,745 2,197 ____________ is less than ____________.

10. 43,024 34,104 ____________ is less than ____________.

11. 7,256 7,500 ____________ is greater than ____________.

12. 13,264 13,604 ____________ is less than ____________.

Name ______________________ Date ______________

Comparing and Ordering Numbers ■ Comparing Numbers

Write each set of numbers in order from least to greatest.

1. 8,589, 8,581, 8,955 ______________________

2. 3,227, 5,325, 2,527 ______________________

3. 17,463, 15,713, 14,734 ______________________

4. 30,412, 43,026, 34,061 ______________________

5. 591,214, 590,758, 509,235 ______________________

6. 76,000, 7,610, 71,600 ______________________

7. 483,243, 487,523, 49,324 ______________________

Write >, <, or = in each box to make the sentence true.

8. 34,292 ◯ 39,129

9. 217,004 ◯ 207,074

10. 10,604 ◯ 1,064

11. 4,538 ◯ 4,835

12. 2,900 ◯ 2,897 ◯ 2,987

13. 568,362 ◯ 658,346 ◯ 685,214

14. 12,473 ◯ 12,421 ◯ 12,387

Name ______________________ Date ______________

Comparing and Ordering Numbers

▲ Comparing Numbers in Different Forms

Use >, <, or = to compare the numbers.

1. 28,941 ◯ 28,914

2. 38,205 ◯ 3,205

3. 130,003 ◯ 130,030

4. 900,267 ◯ 900,267

5. 57,352 ◯ 75,352

6. 741,970 ◯ 741,790

7. 891,745 ◯ 891,145

8. 16,661 ◯ 106,661

9. 40,000 + 2,000 + 700 + 1 ◯ 42,701

10. six hundred eighty thousand four hundred thirty ◯ 60,000 + 800,000 + 400 + 30

11. 507,129 ◯ 20 + 7,000 + 100,000 + 500 + 9

12. 300,000 + 10,000 + 6,000 + 90 ◯ 90 + 6,000 + 100 + 300,000

13. four hundred ninety-seven thousand eight hundred fifty-two ◯ 497,852

14. three hundred thousand forty-five ◯ 345,000

15. 20,000 + 8,000 + 600 + 1 ◯ twenty-eight thousand one

16. nine hundred thirteen thousand three hundred nineteen ◯ nine hundred thirty thousand three hundred nine

Comparison Clash

Materials: several sets of 0–9 number cards, dry-erase markers (if laminated)

To play: Shuffle the number cards and place them facedown. Players take turns. Decide on the number of digits for the round, such as 4-digit numbers or 5-digit numbers. Player 1 draws one fewer card than the chosen number of digits. So, if working with 4-digit numbers, draw 3 cards. Arrange the cards in any order to make the greatest number. Choose a digit from the digit bank (0–9), mark it off, and place it at any point to complete the number. Numbers from the digit bank cannot be reused within a round. Record the final number on the first space. Player 2 draws and arranges cards, chooses a digit from the digit bank, and records the number in the second space. Use symbols to compare the numbers. The player with the greater number gets a point. Record it in the Points area. Continue until all six comparisons are complete. The player with the most points wins.

Round 1

Player 1	Points								
0	1	2	3	4	5	6	7	8	9

Player 2	Points								
0	1	2	3	4	5	6	7	8	9

Round 2

Player 1	Points								
0	1	2	3	4	5	6	7	8	9

Player 2	Points								
0	1	2	3	4	5	6	7	8	9

To prep: Copy on card stock and laminate for durability. Use with dry-erase markers. Place the game board and directions in a center.

Multiplication: Multi-Digit by 1-Digit

Essential Question

How can multiplication facts be used to solve more complex multiplication problems?

Warm-Up/Review

Review multiplication facts by chanting the skip counting as a class. For each factor, hold up one finger and say the product. So, for the 2s, you would hold up one finger and say "2" ($2 \times 1 = 2$); two fingers would be "4," etc. Complete each chant as a class, from $n \times 1$ to $n \times 10$.

Mini-Lesson

Materials: laminated place value mats, dry-erase markers

1. Review multiplying 1-digit numbers by multiples of 10 by solving several problems aloud as a class. Have several students explain how they found the answers.
2. Write *32 × 2* on the board. Explain, "Thirty-two is 3 tens and 2 ones, so we can break this into two problems: 30 × 2 and 2 × 2." Record the problems on the board. Work together to find the product of each problem. Then, explain that because the original factor was split up, it needs to be added together to find the final answer. Model adding the products.
3. Give students place value mats and markers. Rewrite the same problem in a vertical format on a place value mat. Explain, "We can also solve this problem a different way. First, we multiply the ones places. 2 ones times 2 equals 4 ones, which we record in the ones place. Then, we multiply the ones by the tens. 3 tens, or 30, times 2 ones equals 60, or 6 tens, which we record in the tens place."
4. Practice with a few more problems with no regrouping. (41 × 3 (123); 22 × 4 (88))
5. Write *36 × 2* on the place value mat. Emphasize that it is important to think of the digit in the tens place as 30, not 3. Walk students through solving the problem, as in step 3. Show the regrouping, explaining that 6 ones times 2 is 12, so you regroup the ten into the tens column and record the 2. Multiply the tens like before, but add the ten from the previous step. (72)
6. Practice with several more problems, encouraging students to follow along on their place value mats.

Math Talk

Can you explain how place value is related to multiplication?

How is regrouping in multiplication the same as regrouping in addition and subtraction? How is it different?

What is the value of this digit? How do you know?

Journal Prompt

Describe how you would explain to a friend how to multiply 34 × 6.

Materials

laminated place value mats
dry-erase markers
base ten blocks
sticky notes

Workstations

Activity sheets (pages 53–55)
Multiplication Lab (page 56)

Guided Math

Remediation: Modeling Multiplication

1. Give each student a place value mat and marker. Write *41 × 2* on the mats. Then, have each student use base ten blocks to model 41 on the mat below the problem.
2. Explain, "We always begin with the ones place. What is in the ones place? What is 1 times 2?" Have students model the product by doubling the base ten blocks on their mat. Say, "We have 2 ones now, so we record a 2 in the ones place."
3. Say, "Next, we multiply the tens. What is in the tens place? What is 40 times 2?" Have students model the product by doubling the tens rods on their mat. Say, "Now there are 8 tens, or 80, so we record an 8 in the tens place."
4. Repeat with several more problems. When students are ready, introduce regrouping.

On Level: Using the Standard Algorithm

1. Work with students to use the algorithm to solve 73 × 4. (292)
2. Ask, "How would the answer change if the problem was 273 × 4 instead? We can use the same method to multiply larger numbers as well."
3. Have students record the new problem on their place value mats. Walk through each step together. Explain, "In the original problem, 70 times 4 equaled 280, and we could write the 28 in the answer. Now, we need to regroup before we can multiply the hundreds place. We regroup 28 tens into 2 hundreds and 8 tens." Write *2* and *8* in the correct places on the mat. "Now, multiply the 2 hundreds by 4 to get 8 hundreds. Add in the 2 hundreds that we regrouped for a total of 10 hundreds." Record the hundreds in the answer. (1,092)
4. Practice with several more problems with factors of 3 or more digits.

Enrichment: Multiplying Larger Numbers

1. Work with students to use the algorithm to solve 521 × 3. (1,563)
2. Ask, "How would the answer change if the problem was 521 × 30 instead?" (15,630) Students may note that you can "just add a 0," but make sure students understand why adding a zero works.
3. Remind students of breaking apart the problem in the mini-lesson, so that the tens were multiplied separately from the ones. Explain, "When multiplying by factors larger than one digit, it works the same way." Have students record the new problem on their place value mats. Have students cover the tens place (3) with the sticky note. Say, "First we multiply 521 by the ones like normal." Model multiplying 521 by 0, and record all zeros below the equal bar.
4. "Next, we multiply by the tens." Move the sticky note to cover the 0. "One times 3 tens is 30." Write *3* in the tens place. Ask, "Will there ever be a number in the ones place during this step?" Allow students to think through it, and guide them toward understanding that because you are multiplying by tens, not ones, there will never be ones in the second row. Continue multiplying the tens row. Explain, "Now, because we broke the problem into tens and ones, we add the answers together to find the final product."
5. Practice with several more problems, encouraging students who can solve the problems mentally to explain their reasoning.

Assess and Extend

What is the product of 39 × 7? (273) How can knowing 40 × 7 help you check your answer?

Name ______________________ Date ______________

Multiplication: Multi-Digit by 1-Digit

Modeling Multiplication

Rewrite each equation on the place value chart. Then, solve. Show your work.

1. 14 × 2 =

H	T	O

2. 15 × 4 =

H	T	O

3. 12 × 2 =

H	T	O

4. 14 × 3 =

H	T	O

5. 15 × 6 =

H	T	O

6. 21 × 3 =

H	T	O

Solve.

7. $\begin{array}{r} 13 \\ \times\ 4 \\ \hline \end{array}$

8. $\begin{array}{r} 16 \\ \times\ 7 \\ \hline \end{array}$

9. $\begin{array}{r} 28 \\ \times\ 7 \\ \hline \end{array}$

10. $\begin{array}{r} 12 \\ \times\ 5 \\ \hline \end{array}$

Name ______________________ Date ______________

Multiplication: Multi-Digit by 1-Digit

Using the Standard Algorithm

Solve.

1. $\begin{array}{r} 94 \\ \times\ 3 \\ \hline \end{array}$

2. $\begin{array}{r} 24 \\ \times\ 7 \\ \hline \end{array}$

3. $\begin{array}{r} 36 \\ \times\ 9 \\ \hline \end{array}$

4. $\begin{array}{r} 37 \\ \times\ 5 \\ \hline \end{array}$

5. $\begin{array}{r} 59 \\ \times\ 8 \\ \hline \end{array}$

6. $\begin{array}{r} 32 \\ \times\ 2 \\ \hline \end{array}$

7. $\begin{array}{r} 28 \\ \times\ 3 \\ \hline \end{array}$

8. $\begin{array}{r} 72 \\ \times\ 7 \\ \hline \end{array}$

9. $\begin{array}{r} 43 \\ \times\ 5 \\ \hline \end{array}$

10. $\begin{array}{r} 24 \\ \times\ 6 \\ \hline \end{array}$

11. $\begin{array}{r} 34 \\ \times\ 6 \\ \hline \end{array}$

12. $\begin{array}{r} 94 \\ \times\ 3 \\ \hline \end{array}$

13. $\begin{array}{r} 86 \\ \times\ 7 \\ \hline \end{array}$

14. $\begin{array}{r} 58 \\ \times\ 5 \\ \hline \end{array}$

15. $\begin{array}{r} 47 \\ \times\ 8 \\ \hline \end{array}$

16. $\begin{array}{r} 43 \\ \times\ 2 \\ \hline \end{array}$

17. $\begin{array}{r} 31 \\ \times\ 6 \\ \hline \end{array}$

18. $\begin{array}{r} 24 \\ \times\ 8 \\ \hline \end{array}$

19. $\begin{array}{r} 32 \\ \times\ 4 \\ \hline \end{array}$

20. $\begin{array}{r} 21 \\ \times\ 7 \\ \hline \end{array}$

Name ______________________ Date __________

Multiplication: Multi-Digit by 1-Digit

▲ Multiplying Larger Numbers

Solve.

1. 214×3
2. 284×2
3. 510×5
4. 243×4
5. 131×8
6. 123×6
7. 514×4
8. 213×7
9. 412×9
10. 842×3
11. 354×5
12. 126×8
13. 408×6
14. 237×3
15. 543×4
16. 985×2
17. $3{,}123 \times 3$
18. $4{,}243 \times 2$
19. $4{,}321 \times 6$
20. $1{,}228 \times 4$
21. $2{,}752 \times 4$
22. $4{,}523 \times 5$
23. $8{,}463 \times 2$
24. $8{,}427 \times 3$

Multiplication Lab

Materials: several sets of 0–9 number cards, dry-erase marker

To play: Draw three, four, or five number cards. Use all of the digits to create a multiplication problem that fits each challenge below. Draw again to create a new problem. Use the space below to test problems. Record each problem and answer that meets a challenge in the blank problem beside each challenge. (*Note*: Not all challenges may be possible.)

×

A. A problem with a product greater than 500	×	**B.** A problem with a product between 500 and 1,000	×
C. A problem with an even product	×	**D.** A problem with a 0 in the product	×
E. A problem with a 3 in the tens place in the product	×	**F.** A problem with a product that repeats the same digit at least twice	×

To prep: Copy on card stock for durability. Laminate so students can test multiplication problems as needed. Cut off these directions before copying and laminating.

Multiplication: Arrays and Area Models

Essential Question

How are arrays related to multiplication of larger numbers?

Warm-Up/Review

Arrange students in arrays. Have the remaining students give the related multiplication sentence and product for each array. Challenge students to figure out if there is an array that can contain the entire class without actually modeling an array, and explain why or why not.

Mini-Lesson

Materials: large grid to display

1. Write *2 × 4* on the board. Have a volunteer draw and label the related array on the grid and show how to find the answer.
2. Add digits to the problem so it reads *26 × 41*. Ask, "How would we solve this using an array?" Explain that it works the same way, but the side lengths are much longer. Draw and label the related array.
3. Ask, "How could we use this array to find the product?" Students may suggest counting every block. If so, begin counting but don't count the entire array.
4. Explain that while counting would give you the correct answer, it takes a long time and it is easy to lose count, skip numbers, or otherwise make mistakes. Ask, "Is there an easier way to quickly count large chunks of the array?" Allow students to work with partners or small groups to come up with solutions. Let students share their solutions, and guide the class toward understanding that they can find larger chunks, such as 10 by 10 and mark it as 100 without counting. Then, they can add the chunks they find to get the final product. (1,066)
5. Write *72 × 12* on the board and have students work together to find the product using arrays. (864)

Math Talk

Describe the array method in your own words.
How is this array related to the problem?
Is there a faster way to use an array to solve the problem?
How can you relate that to using equations?

Journal Prompt

Is the array method an efficient way to solve for products? Why or why not?

Materials

graph paper
colored pencils, markers, or crayons

Workstations

Activity sheets (pages 59–61)
Multiplying Models (page 62)
Multiplication Lab (page 56)

Guided Math

○ Remediation: Using Arrays

1. Display *37 × 14*. Give each student graph paper. Ask, "How would we show this problem as an array?" Model counting 37 and 14, drawing the borders of the rectangle, and labeling each side. Have students model along with you on their own graph paper.
2. Say, "This is too many blocks to count without making mistakes. I know that 10 times 10 is 100, so first I will color in 10 by 10 arrays. I know this side is 14, so 4 less is 10." Draw a line to separate the 10 from the 4. "Next, I can count 10 in the other direction and start blocking off 10 by 10 arrays. Since I know each of these blocks equals 100, I'll write it on the space." Label the sections *100*.
3. Ask, "What can I do with the remaining blocks? Can I divide them into smaller chunks that I can count easily?" Think aloud as you section off smaller chunks and use multiplication to label each one. Explain, "There are many different ways to divide this into smaller arrays. Now, we add all of the numbers to find the product." (518) Model skip counting when possible.
4. Have students practice with several more problems.

□ On Level: Arrays and Area Models

1. Display *37 × 14*. Have students draw the related rectangle, label it, and model along with you. Think aloud: "I know I can divide this into smaller chunks so it is easier to count. But, I can use place value to quickly figure out how many tens are in each direction. There are 3 tens in 37." Draw lines to mark each ten. "There is 1 ten in 14." Mark off the ten. "Each 10 by 10 array equals 100." Label each section *100*.
2. Then, explain, "I know this section is the 7 ones. I can use the 10 I've already marked off to make a 7 by 10 chunk. Seven times 10 is 70." Mark it and label it *70*. Repeat with the 4 by 10 sections at the bottom. "This final section is 7 ones wide, and 4 ones tall. Seven times 4 is 28." Label the section *28*.
3. Model adding the sections together to find the product (518), using skip counting when possible.
4. Have students practice creating and labeling arrays for additional problems without using graph paper.

△ Enrichment: Using Area Models

1. Display *37 × 14*. Have students draw an array and use it to solve for the product. (518) Ask, "Is there a way to use place value and larger chunks to find the product?"
2. Draw a rectangle and label each side. Say, "I know that there are 3 tens and 7 ones in 37." Draw a line to divide the rectangle into roughly proportional sections. Label the sections *30* and *7*. Repeat with the 14.
3. Explain, "Now, I can multiply the tens and ones to find and label the product of each section. Thirty times 10 is 300. Thirty times 4 is 120. Ten times 7 is 70. Four times 7 is 28. Now, I can add the sections together to find the product." (518)
4. Have students practice using area models to solve several more problems.

Assess and Extend

Use an array or area model to solve 45 × 16. (720) How can you check that your answer is reasonable?

Name ____________________ Date ____________

Multiplication: Arrays and Area Models

Using Arrays

Draw an array to solve each problem. Show your work on the array.

1. 18 × 17 = ____________

2. 19 × 12 = ____________

3. 34 × 16 = ____________

4. 41 × 11 = ____________

Name ______________________________ Date ______________

Multiplication: Arrays and Area Models

Arrays and Area Models

Sketch an array to solve each problem. Show your work.

1. 45 × 13 = ______________

2. 62 × 21 = ______________

3. 56 × 33 = ______________

4. 48 × 43 = ______________

5. 75 × 36 = ______________

6. 91 × 24 = ______________

Name ________________________________ Date ______________

Multiplication: Arrays and Area Models

▲ Using Area Models

Draw an area model to solve each problem.

1. 35 × 14 = ______________

2. 73 × 52 = ______________

3. 84 × 63 = ______________

4. 52 × 41 = ______________

5. 88 × 23 = ______________

6. 59 × 35 = ______________

Multiplying Models

Materials: sharpened pencil, paper clip, base ten blocks, dry-erase markers

To play: Use a sharpened pencil and a paper clip to spin the left spinner. Repeat with the right spinner. Record each factor in the space provided. Then, use the Model It section to make an array or area model to solve the problem. You may draw it or use base ten blocks. If playing with a partner, have the partner use a calculator to check your answer. If you answered incorrectly, try to identify your mistake.

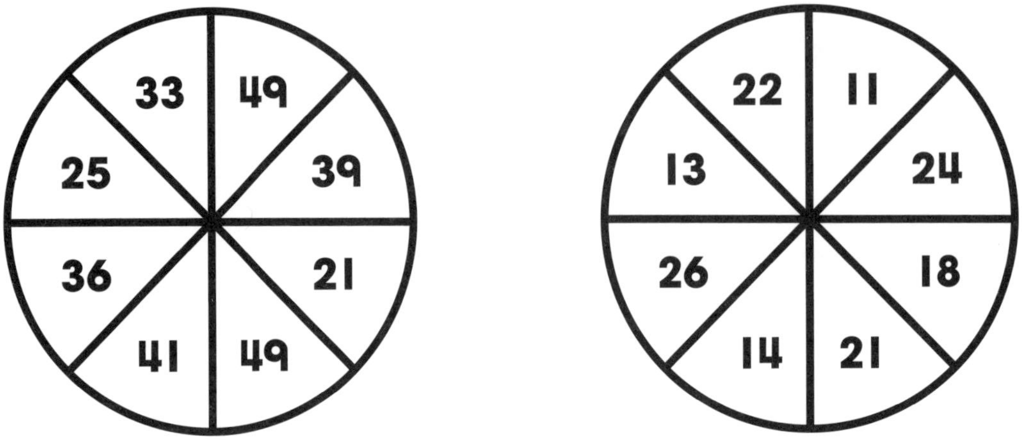

____ × ____ = ____

Model It

To prep: Copy on card stock for durability. Laminate so students can use dry-erase markers to model problems. Cut off these directions before copying and laminating.

Multiplication: Using the Algorithm

Essential Question

How is multiplying 2-digit numbers the same as multiplying larger numbers by a single digit? How is it different?

Warm-Up/Review

Write the numbers *0, 1, 3, 6,* and *7* on sticky notes. Place them on the board to create the number 3,671; set 0 to the side. Explain that 0 is powerful. Challenge students to use it to make the number 10 times bigger; greater than 29,000; less than 3,500; etc.

Mini-Lesson

Materials: sticky note

1. Work with students to use the algorithm to solve 52 × 13.
2. Cover the 1 with a sticky note. Work together to review multiplying 1-digit and multi-digit numbers and solve 52 × 3 using the algorithm.
3. Move the sticky note so it covers the 3. Remind students of the method where they can break apart the problem so the tens are multiplied separately from the ones. Explain, "When multiplying by factors larger than one digit, it works the same way. Remember, we are not multiplying by 1, we're multiplying by 10." Write a *0* on the sticky note. Ask, "What is the same about numbers that are multiplied by 10?" Give several examples, and guide students toward understanding that because you are multiplying by tens, not ones, there will always be a 0 in the ones place in the second row of the product. Record the 0 in the ones place.
4. Model multiplying 52 by 1, recording the answer beside the 0. Emphasize the role of the 0.
5. Then, explain that because the problem was separated into tens and ones to get the two answers, you have to add the answers together to get the final product. (676)
6. Practice with several more problems, encouraging students to explain the method in their own words.

Math Talk

What do you do next? How do you know?
Can you use place value to explain why that happens?
Why is zero so important here?

Journal Prompt

Joey solved 27 × 13 and got 128. Is his answer reasonable? If not, what do you think he did incorrectly? Explain his mistake to him.

Materials

place value mats
base ten blocks

Workstations

Activity sheets (pages 65–67)
Multiplication Ups and Downs (page 68)
Multiplying Models (page 62)

Guided Math

Remediation: Modeling Multiplication

1. Display the problem *21 × 15*. Say, "Let's look at this as two separate problems. We can separate the second factor into tens and ones and create four multiplication problems." Record *20 × 5, 1 × 5, 20 × 10,* and *1 × 10*. Point out where each problem comes from.
2. Have students model 20 with base ten blocks on their place value mat. Say, "Look at the problem 20 times 5. What is 20 times 5?" Have students use base ten blocks to model the product and regroup tens into hundreds. "What is 1 times 5?" Have students model the ones. Record each product beside the problems recorded in step 1.
3. Repeat step 2 with the second set of problems. Emphasize that because each problem includes a factor that is a multiple of 10, every answer will end in at least one 0.
4. Finally, add all of the recorded products together to find the final product. (315)
5. Repeat with several more problems, encouraging students to relate the model to the algorithm and to break the problem into two instead of four problems when ready.

On Level: Checking for Reasonableness

1. Use the algorithm to solve 21 × 15. (315) Have students solve along with you, and correct any misconceptions as they arise.
2. Ask, "How can I check to see if my answer is reasonable?" Explain that they can round one or both of the factors and see how the product of the rounded numbers compares. Have students round 21 to 20. Say, "If I mentally multiply 15 by 2, I get 30. Then, because I'm multiplying by a multiple of 10, I place a 0 in the ones place to get 300. It is close to our original answer, so our answer is reasonable."
3. Model solving a problem incorrectly by leaving out the 0 when multiplying the tens. Have students assess the reasonableness, explain their method, and figure out what you did incorrectly.

Enrichment: Finding Multiplication Mistakes

1. Write *48 × 35 = 384*. (1,680) Tell students you need their help. You know the answer is incorrect. But, you don't know where the mistake is. Have students work the problem and identify the mistake.
2. Discuss students' findings. "When multiplying by the 30, I forgot the 0, so it was like multiplying by 3 instead."
3. Continue with similar problems, including 86 × 23 = 1,868 (1,978; forgot to regroup at all) and 42 × 39 = 1,588 (1,638; addition error).

Assess and Extend

Solve 53 × 17. (901) Explain how regrouping was used to solve the problem.

Name ______________________ Date ____________

Multiplication: Using the Algorithm

Modeling Multiplication

Break apart each problem using place value and record the related problems. Solve and add to find the product. The first problem has been started for you.

1. 58 × 22

8 × 2 = ____

50 × 2 = ____

8 × 20 = ____

50 × 20 = + ____

[ ]

2. 47 × 32

× = ____

× = ____

× = ____

× = + ____

[ ]

3. 96 × 38

× = ____

× = ____

× = ____

× = + ____

[ ]

4. 51 × 13

× = ____

× = ____

× = ____

× = + ____

[ ]

5. 33 × 14

× = ____

× = ____

× = ____

× = + ____

[ ]

6. 38 × 11

× = ____

× = ____

× = ____

× = + ____

[ ]

7. 89 × 17

× = ____

× = ____

× = ____

× = + ____

[ ]

8. 65 × 32

× = ____

× = ____

× = ____

× = + ____

[ ]

9. 67 × 28

× = ____

× = ____

× = ____

× = + ____

[ ]

10. 95 × 39

× = ____

× = ____

× = ____

× = + ____

[ ]

11. 97 × 29

× = ____

× = ____

× = ____

× = + ____

[ ]

12. 88 × 14

× = ____

× = ____

× = ____

× = + ____

[ ]

Name ______________________ Date ____________

Multiplication: Using the Algorithm

☐ Checking for Reasonableness

Multiply. Check to see if it is a reasonable answer. Show your work.

1. 41×32

2. 35×24

3. 34×21

4. 42×16

5. 52×21

6. 36×31

7. 71×25

8. 48×12

9. 44×32

10. 71×18

11. 49×35

12. 35×29

13. 72×58

14. 89×13

15. 98×20

16. 44×29

Name ____________________ Date __________

Multiplication: Using the Algorithm

▲ Finding Multiplication Mistakes

Find the mistake or mistakes in each problem. Circle each mistake. Then, redo each problem to find the correct answer.

1.
$$\begin{array}{r} 25 \\ \times\ 17 \\ \hline 175 \\ +\ \ 25 \\ \hline 200 \end{array}$$

2.
$$\begin{array}{r} 42 \\ \times\ 30 \\ \hline 126 \end{array}$$

3.
$$\begin{array}{r} 36 \\ \times\ 12 \\ \hline 62 \\ +\ 360 \\ \hline 422 \end{array}$$

4.
$$\begin{array}{r} 54 \\ \times\ 27 \\ \hline 358 \\ +\ 1080 \\ \hline 1438 \end{array}$$

5.
$$\begin{array}{r} 49 \\ \times\ 28 \\ \hline 372 \\ +\ 880 \\ \hline 1{,}252 \end{array}$$

6.
$$\begin{array}{r} 86 \\ \times\ 42 \\ \hline 172 \\ +\ 3440 \\ \hline 3{,}522 \end{array}$$

7.
$$\begin{array}{r} 68 \\ \times\ 32 \\ \hline 126 \\ +\ 1824 \\ \hline 1{,}950 \end{array}$$

8.
$$\begin{array}{r} 58 \\ \times\ 63 \\ \hline 174 \\ +\ 348 \\ \hline 522 \end{array}$$

9. Choose one problem and explain how it was solved incorrectly.

____

____

____

____

____

____

____

Multiplication Ups and Downs

Materials: 2 dice, 1 counter per player, calculator

To play: Place the counters on the Start space. Players take turns. Roll the dice and move that number of spaces. Solve the problem. If you answer correctly, stay on the space. If you answer incorrectly, move back to your previous space. Use the calculator to check answers. If you land on a space with a slide, move your counter down the slide and lose your turn. If you land on a ladder, move your counter up the ladder. You do not have to solve that problem to stay on the space. The first player to reach the Finish space wins.

Finish	67 × 24	88 × 62	66 × 34	69 × 48	53 × 24	68 × 59
39 × 28	45 × 27	70 × 47	89 × 24	38 × 22	56 × 45	62 × 46
48 × 28	73 × 58	76 × 49	29 × 89	66 × 38	73 × 28	48 × 37
55 × 63	55 × 33	62 × 44	67 × 49	51 × 40	50 × 42	73 × 63
48 × 38	41 × 18	38 × 22	81 × 72	64 × 47	68 × 32	42 × 18
36 × 12	91 × 43	49 × 28	73 × 46	86 × 42	35 × 28	73 × 56
72 × 43	42 × 30	56 × 13	86 × 75	58 × 63	62 × 44	83 × 27
Start	82 × 51	25 × 17	70 × 60	54 × 27	48 × 38	53 × 38

Division with Remainders

Essential Question

How are remainders useful information?

Warm-Up/Review

Play Around the World with division flash cards, but include a twist. Instead of competing to be the first to say the answer, challenge students to be the first to give the complete related multiplication fact.

Mini-Lesson

1. Tell students that some friends are planning a surprise party. There will be 31 people attending and they want each person to have at least 1 cupcake. Explain that the bakery sells cupcakes in dozens, so they need to figure out how many dozen cupcakes to order.
2. Place students in pairs or small groups and challenge them to use models, manipulatives, or other methods to solve the problem.
3. Allow students to share their answers as well as their methods. Record each new method on the board.
4. Explain, "No matter what method was used, the friends can't buy the exact number of cupcakes they need. What happens if they buy 2 dozen? (There aren't enough cupcakes.) What happens if they buy 3 dozen? (There are extra cupcakes.) So, they have to buy 3 dozen. How many cupcakes will be left over? (5) How do you know?"
5. Explain that the leftover amount is the remainder. Explain that when numbers can't be divided evenly, there is a remainder. Show students that the answer is written with an *r* to show the remainder. For the cupcake problem, the answer is 3r5, or 3 dozen cupcakes with 5 left over.
6. Give students several more simple division problems with remainders to solve using any method they prefer.

Math Talk

What information do you need to know first?

How can you use multiplication facts to divide more quickly?

Explain what the remainder in this probem represents in your own words.

Journal Prompt

Give a definition of *remainder* in your own words. Include examples and nonexamples.

Materials

laminated multiplication charts
dry-erase markers
counters or similar manipulatives

Workstations

Activity sheets (pages 71–73)
Racing Remainders (page 74)
Division facts practice

Guided Math

Remediation: Division Using Tools

1. Remind students how multiplication and division are related. Give a set of three numbers (9, 8, 72) and have students give the multiplication and division facts in the fact family.
2. Give each student a multiplication chart. Display the problem *46 ÷ 5*. Ask, "What is the divisor?" (5) Guide students to find the ×5 row and look at the products to find out where the dividend, 46, falls. Have students circle the two products that the number is between. (45 and 50) Ask, "Five times what is 45? Five times what is 50? So, the quotient must be between 9 and 10, or 9 with some left over." Record *9 and ?*.
3. Ask, "How can we find out how much is left over?" Allow students to share ideas and explain that they can find the product of 5 and 9 and subtract it from the dividend to find a remainder of 1.
4. If some students need a visual, use counters to show the division and the remainder. Practice using the tools to solve several more division problems with remainders.

On Level: Interpreting Remainders

1. Work as a group to find the quotient and remainder for the problem 63 ÷ 8. (7r7) Ask, "What does the remainder mean to you?"
2. Read this problem: "Mr. Garcia has 63 pages left to read in his book. He has to return it to the library in 8 days. How many pages should he read each night so he finishes on time?" Guide students to identify the dividend (63), the divisor (8), and the problem to be solved (how many pages to read each day). Have students solve the problem.
3. Say, "This is the same problem we solved earlier; the quotient is 7 with a remainder of 7. What does that mean for Mr. Garcia?" Allow students to share their ideas. (He should read 8 pages each day for 7 days, and read 7 pages on the last day.)
4. Give students this problem and work together to solve the problem and interpret the remainder: "Pens come in packs of 6. There are 27 students in the class. How many packs should the teacher buy so each student can have a pen?" (5 packs) Emphasize that remainders are not always treated the same.

Enrichment: Remainders as Fractions

1. Pose the following problem: "Julia's family ordered 2 pizzas, with 6 slices each. There are 5 people in Julia's family. How much of the pizza should each person get, so there is no pizza left over?"
2. Have students identify the dividend (6 × 2 = 12 slices), the divisor (5), and the problem to be solved (how many slices each person should get to avoid leftovers). Ask, "How can we use the information to solve the problem?" (12 ÷ 5)
3. Have students solve the division problem on their own. (2r2) Say, "The quotient tells us that each person gets 2 slices, but there are 2 slices left over. We can't have leftovers, so we have to divide those 2 slices between how many people? (5) The way we show this is to show the remainder as a fraction. Use the remainder as the numerator, and the divisor as the denominator. So, each person gets 2 2/5 slices."
4. Repeat with several more similar problems.

Assess and Extend

Divide 48 by 2, 3, 4, 5, 6, 7, and 8. What does the pattern in the remainders tell you?

Name ______________________ Date ______________

Division with Remainders

● Division Using Tools

Divide. Use the multiplication chart or other tools to help you find the quotient.

×	1	2	3	4	5	6	7	8	9	10
1	1	2	3	4	5	6	7	8	9	10
2	2	4	6	8	10	12	14	16	18	20
3	3	6	9	12	15	18	21	24	27	30
4	4	8	12	16	20	24	28	32	36	40
5	5	10	15	20	25	30	35	40	45	50
6	6	12	18	24	30	36	42	48	54	60
7	7	14	21	28	35	42	49	56	63	70
8	8	16	24	32	40	48	56	64	72	80
9	9	18	27	36	45	54	63	72	81	90
10	10	20	30	40	50	60	70	80	90	100

1. $8\overline{)34}$ **2.** $4\overline{)26}$ **3.** $7\overline{)67}$ **4.** $3\overline{)17}$

5. $9\overline{)29}$ **6.** $5\overline{)42}$ **7.** $6\overline{)47}$ **8.** $9\overline{)83}$

9. $6\overline{)39}$ **10.** $4\overline{)19}$ **11.** $5\overline{)24}$ **12.** $8\overline{)79}$

13. $7\overline{)41}$ **14.** $6\overline{)23}$ **15.** $9\overline{)60}$ **16.** $4\overline{)15}$

Name ______________________ Date ____________

Division with Remainders

Interpreting Remainders

Solve each problem. Then, explain how the remainder affected your answer.

1. Becca has a package of 49 bracelets. She wants to share them equally with her 4 best friends. Becca plans to keep any leftover bracelets. How many bracelets will Becca keep?

____

____

2. Mrs. Ryan has 80 erasers. She gave each of the 6 students in her group the same number of erasers. How many erasers did each student get?

____

____

3. Heath is training for a track meet. He needs to run at least 40 miles this week. He wants to run the same amount each day. How much should he run each day to run 40 miles or more this week?

____

____

4. Malia needs 75 balloons for a party. Balloons come in packs of 10. How many packs does Malia need to buy?

____

____

5. There were 27 students playing basketball. The coach divided them into 2 teams. How many students were on each team?

____

____

Name ______________________ Date ______________

Division with Remainders

▲ Remainders as Fractions

Solve. Interpret each remainder as a fraction.

1. Kim was decorating a parade float. She used 93 sheets of tissue paper to make flowers. Tissue paper comes in packs of 6 sheets. How many packs did she use in all?

2. The trail from Patterson Forest to the waterfall is 41 miles long. It took Luke's family 3 days to hike to the waterfall. If they hiked the same distance each day, how many miles did they hike each day?

3. Nathan's book had 29 chapters. He finished the book in 4 days. If he read the same amount daily, how many chapters did he read each day?

4. Ana bought 50 yards of fabric. She wants to make 4 quilts using all of the fabric. How many yards of fabric will each quilt have?

5. The bag of Zip Zaps had 74 pieces of candy in all. Trey divided the Zip Zaps evenly between himself and his 2 best friends. How many pieces of candy did each person get?

6. The fourth-grade teachers ordered pizza for the class celebration. There were 88 slices in all. Each of the 3 classes got the same amount of pizza. How much of the pizza did each class get?

Racing Remainders

Materials: sharpened pencil, paper clip, 1 counter per player

To play: Players take turns. Use the sharpened pencil and paper clip to spin the spinner. Divide the number of the space you are on by the number you spin. The remainder is the number of spaces you can move your counter forward. If there is no remainder, stay on the same space. The first player to reach the Finish space wins.

26	11	51	33	86
74	62	47	70	29
23	82	31	14	71
41	37	18	92	53
39	25	67	95	

Division Strategies

Essential Question

What strategies can I use to divide larger numbers?

Warm-Up/Review

Give students the following problems to solve: A. 82 ÷ 9; B. 46 ÷ 7; C. 22 ÷ 4; D. 69 ÷ 8; and E. 39 ÷ 6. Have students place the problems in order by their remainders, from least to greatest. (A. 9r1; C. 5r2; E. 6r3; B. 6r4; D. 8r5)

Mini-Lesson

Materials: counters

1. Display the problem *154 ÷ 4.* (38r2) Place students in small groups and challenge them to work together to solve the problem using any method they want. Provide counters as needed.
2. Allow groups to share their answers and the strategies they used. Record each different strategy on the board. Identify and correct any misconceptions or mistakes. Explain that there are many valid ways to solve division problems, but some ways are faster and less prone to mistakes than others. Using known multiplication facts, multiples, and "easy" numbers is a reliable strategy.
3. Model using the partial quotient method to solve the problem. Think aloud as you complete each step: "I know that 10 is an easy number. Four times 10 is 40, so I will record the 10 and subtract 40 from the dividend." Continue modeling until the problem is solved. Guide students to see that depending on which easy numbers and multiplication facts are chosen, it could look very different from person to person, but they will all end up with the same answer.
4. Practice another problem together as a group. If desired, have students follow along at their desks.

Math Talk

Is there another way you could do that?
How is that related to place value?
Explain how knowing multiplication facts can help you solve this problem.

Journal Prompt

How can memorizing your multiplication facts help you divide more quickly and easily?

Materials

Blank paper

Workstations

Activity sheets (pages 77–79)
Division Dash (page 80)
Racing Remainders (page 74)

Guided Math

Remediation: Using Bar Diagrams

1. Display the problem *123 ÷ 3*. Have students draw a long rectangular bar. Ask, "What does the whole bar represent?" (the dividend, 123) Have students draw a bracket above the bar and label the rectangle 123. "What is the divisor?" (3) Have students divide the bar into three sections.
2. Explain that students can start dividing with a good guesstimate. Ask, "What is a round number that goes into 123 three times? Let's start with 10." Have students write 10 in each box, then skip count to find out how much has been divided so far and subtract it from the dividend. (30) Continue adding round numbers, placing them in the boxes with plus signs in between each new number. When done, each box will have something similar to *10 + 10 + 10 + 10 + 1*.
3. Guide students to add the numbers in one box to find the quotient. (41)
4. Next, have students use the same method to work through the problem 241 ÷ 4. (60r1) Explain, "Any amount left over that cannot be divided between the boxes is the remainder. It should always be less than the dividend, or else you can divide some more."

On Level: Partial Quotient Division

1. Display the problem *125 ÷ 3* in the traditional format. Have students identify the dividend and divisor. Draw a long line extending straight down from the right-hand end of the horizontal line.
2. Explain, "One way to divide larger numbers is to use what you know about multiplication facts and multiplying by round numbers like tens and hundreds to find parts of the quotient. I know that 3 times 30 is 90, which fits into 125." Record 30 to the right of the vertical line, one level below the dividend. "Three times 30 is 90, so I can subtract that from the dividend to see how much is left to divide into." Write 90 below 125 and subtract. (35)
3. Repeat step 2 with the new dividend. (35) Say, "I know 3 times 11 is 33." Write *11* to the right of the line, then model multiplying 3 and 11 and subtracting 33 from 35. "There are 2 left over, which I can't divide by 3. Two is the remainder. Now, I can add my partial quotients to find the complete quotient." Add 30 and 11 to get 41. Record *41r2* above the problem.
4. Have students practice the method with several more problems.

Enrichment: Using Area Models

1. Explain that area models can also be used to solve division problems. Display the problem *467 ÷ 6*. Draw a rectangle. Identify the divisor and write it to the left of the rectangle.
2. Explain, "With this method, you use what you know about multiplication facts and place value to find parts of the quotient, then add them to find the final answer. First, I look at the largest place values. I know that 6 times 6 is 36, 6 times 7 is 42, and 6 times 8 is 48. So, multiplying 6 by those factors times 10 gives me 360, 420, and 480. The dividend is between 420 and 480, so I can use 6 times 70." Write 70 above the left side of the rectangle. Draw a vertical line to divide the rectangle into two parts. Model multiplying 6 and 70 and write the product (420) inside the rectangle below the 70. Subtract 420 from 467. (47)
3. Repeat step 2 with the new dividend. (47) Say, "I know 6 times 7 is 42, and 6 times 8 is 48, so I have to use 7. Write the seven above the right rectangle. Forty-seven minus 42 is 5. I can't divide 5 by 6, so it is the remainder. Now, I add the partial quotients above the rectangle to find the final quotient." (77r5)
4. Have students practice with several more problems, including 4-digit dividends.

Assess and Extend

Solve 821 ÷ 7. (117r2) How do you know your answer is reasonable?

Name ______________________ Date ______________

Division Strategies

Using Bar Diagrams

Divide. Use a bar diagram to help you find each quotient.

1. $3\overline{)41}$

2. $5\overline{)59}$

3. $2\overline{)71}$

4. $7\overline{)80}$

5. $4\overline{)91}$

6. $4\overline{)89}$

7. $2\overline{)93}$

8. $3\overline{)47}$

9. $8\overline{)982}$

10. $6\overline{)794}$

11. $5\overline{)792}$

12. $7\overline{)951}$

Name ______________________ Date ____________

Division Strategies

Partial Quotient Division

Divide. Use the partial quotient method to help you find each quotient.

1. $2\overline{)119}$ **2.** $4\overline{)227}$ **3.** $5\overline{)444}$

4. $3\overline{)337}$ **5.** $6\overline{)445}$ **6.** $7\overline{)660}$

7. $8\overline{)775}$ **8.** $6\overline{)251}$ **9.** $7\overline{)169}$

10. $4\overline{)335}$ **11.** $3\overline{)520}$ **12.** $9\overline{)680}$

Name ______________________ Date ____________

Division Strategies

▲ Using Area Models

Divide. Use an area model to help you find each quotient.

1. $4\overline{)317}$
2. $6\overline{)351}$
3. $5\overline{)214}$
4. $8\overline{)511}$
5. $7\overline{)200}$
6. $4\overline{)159}$
7. $6\overline{)166}$
8. $3\overline{)290}$
9. $4\overline{)291}$
10. $6\overline{)173}$
11. $7\overline{)552}$
12. $3\overline{)292}$

Division Dash

Materials: 2 dice, 1 counter per player, calculator

To play: Players take turns. Roll the dice. Divide the number on your space by the number rolled or follow the directions on the space. Check your answer with the calculator. If you are correct, move forward the amount rolled. If you are not correct, lose a turn. The first player to reach the Finish space wins.

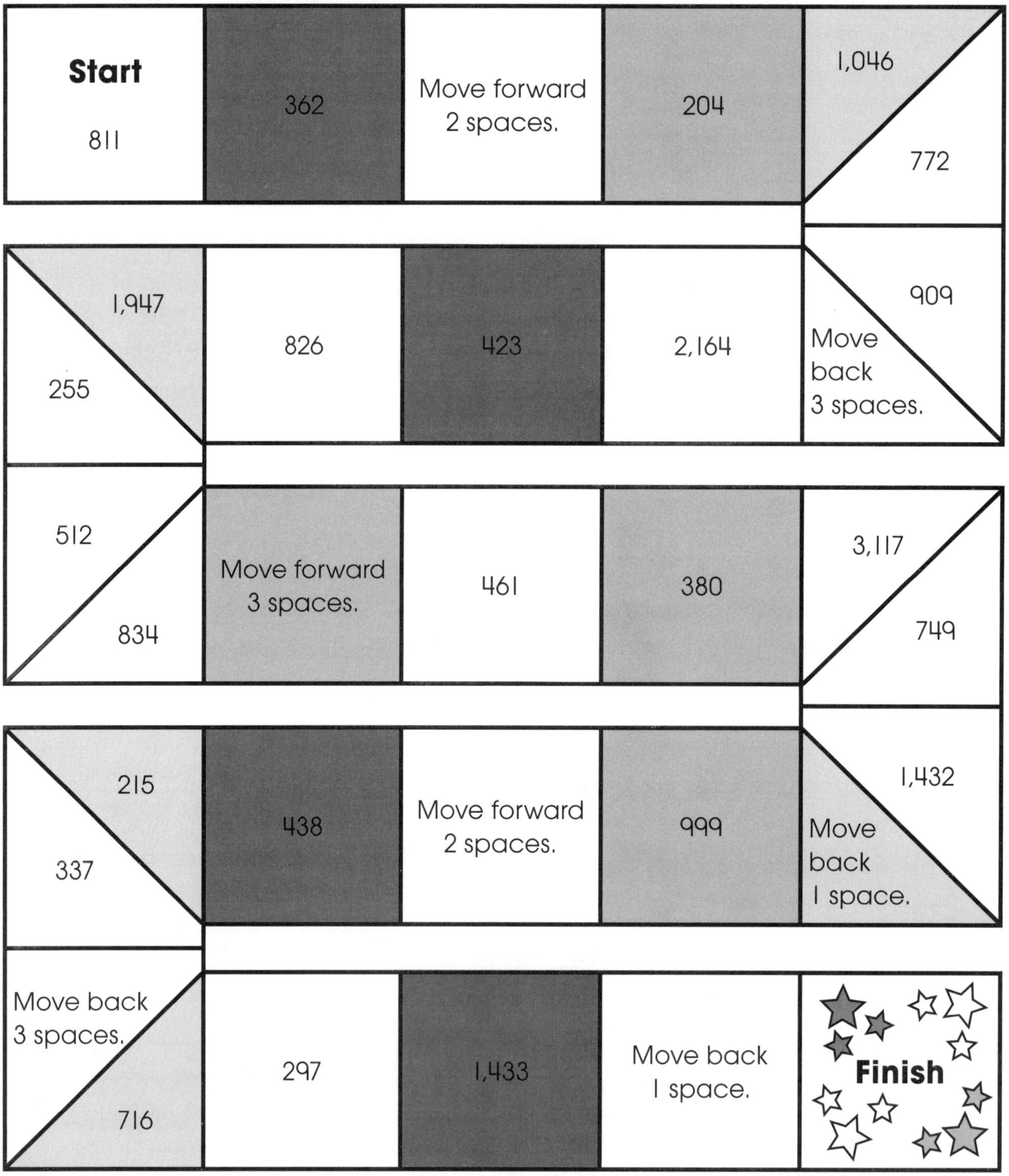

Long Division

Essential Question

How are strategies like the partial quotient method and area models related to the standard algorithm?

Warm-Up/Review

Write *416 ÷ 3* on the board. Have three students solve the problem, each using a different method: a bar diagram, the partial quotient method, and an area model. As a class, discuss how they are similar and different.

Note: Save these problems for the mini-lesson.

Mini-Lesson

Materials: solved problems from the warm-up, sticky notes

1. Explain, "The standard algorithm, also called long division, works a lot like the methods we used in the warm-up. You are looking at place values or chunks of place values and figuring out how many times the divisor can go into that section." Rewrite the warm-up problem in the "house" format (see page 84). As you work through the problem, refer to the other methods in the warm-up to point out similarities.
2. Say, "We always start with the greatest place value. In this case, it is the hundreds. We won't look at the rest until later." Cover the 16 with sticky notes. Ask, "How many times does 3 go into 4? (1) Because this 4 is in the hundreds, don't forget that its value is 400. By writing the 1 above the 4, it is also in the hundreds place and has a value of 100."
3. Explain, "As in the other methods, we have to multiply and subtract to find out how much we have left to divide into." Model the multiplication and subtraction. "We have 1 left. Can we divide 1 by 3? (No) That's a clue that we used the right number in the first step. To keep dividing, we have to bring down the next place value." Remove the sticky note from the 1. Draw a line straight down and record the 1 beside the 1.
4. Repeat steps 2 and 3 to complete the division, emphasizing the place value of each digit as it is used in the dividend and quotient.
5. As a class, work through several more problems. Have students follow along at their desks.

Math Talk

How is this step like the other methods? How is it different?

What is the value of this digit? How do you know?

How can you check that you divided correctly?

Journal Prompt

Xander solved 639 ÷ 7 and got 102. Is he correct? (No, 91r2) How do you know? If he is incorrect, show him how to correctly solve the problem.

Materials

place value mats
base ten blocks

Workstations

Activity sheets (pages 83–85)
Division Tic-Tac-Toe (page 86)
Division Dash (page 80)

Guided Math

Remediation: Hands-On Division

1. Give students a place value mat and base ten blocks. Display the problem *274 ÷ 2*. Have students model 274 on their mats and record the problem.
2. Say, "We always start division with the largest place value. We have 2 hundreds. If we divide that by 2, how many hundreds do we have?" (1) Model the division and help students record the 1 correctly in their problem. "Is there anything left after dividing 2 by 2?" (No) Model and record the multiplication and subtraction.
3. Explain, "Now there is nothing left in the hundreds, so we look at the tens. We have 7 tens. If we divide 7 by 2, we get 3 in each group with 1 left over." Record the quotient and walk students through the multiplication and subtraction. "The 1 here represents the 1 ten we had left over after dividing. Since we've already divided the tens, we include this leftover ten when dividing the ones." Continue modeling to find the quotient. (137)
4. Next, walk students through the problem 343 ÷ 4 (85r3) and explain how to use both the hundreds and tens when the hundreds place isn't divisible by the divisor.

On Level: Checking Quotients

1. Display the problem *752 ÷ 7*. (107r3) Work through the problem with students, pausing to teach to any errors or misconceptions.
2. Explain, "You can use estimation to check your answer. Round 752 to 750. You know that 7 goes into 750 at least 100 times because 7 times 100 is 700. But, 7 times 200 is 1,400, which is too large. So, the answer should be over 100, but not by much because 752 is much closer to 700 than 1,400."
3. Explain that you can use multiplication to reverse the problem and check your answer. Model multiplying the quotient by the divisor. Say, "107 groups of 7 equal 749. Add the remainder of 3, and you get 752, the original dividend."
4. Work through several more problems. Students should use multiplication to check each quotient.

Enrichment: Finding Errors in Division

1. Write *386 ÷ 5 = 70*. Ask students to identify whether the quotient is correct or incorrect without dividing. Guide students to understand that a dividend ending in 6 cannot be divided by 5 without remainders.
2. Then, tell students you need their help to find the mistake. Have students work the problem and identify the mistake.
3. Discuss students' findings (the quotient should be 77r1). "After dividing into 38, I forgot to bring down the 6 and continue dividing."
4. Continue with similar problems, including 946 ÷ 9 = 15r1 (105r1; didn't add 0 as the placeholder in the tens place before dividing the ones) and 528 ÷ 6 = 79r5 (88; divided 52 by 6 incorrectly).

Assess and Extend

Solve 627 ÷ 4. (156r3) Show how to check your answer.

Name ____________________ Date ____________

Long Division

Hands-On Division

Divide. Show the long division.

1. $5\overline{)27}$

2. $2\overline{)17}$

3. $6\overline{)25}$

4. $7\overline{)23}$

5. $4\overline{)79}$

6. $6\overline{)84}$

7. $6\overline{)99}$

8. $8\overline{)91}$

9. $5\overline{)78}$

10. $9\overline{)302}$

11. $6\overline{)135}$

12. $4\overline{)445}$

13. $5\overline{)192}$

14. $9\overline{)506}$

15. $7\overline{)441}$

Name ______________________ Date ______________

Long Division

Checking Quotients

Divide. Check each quotient. Show your work.

1. $5\overline{)527}$

2. $2\overline{)597}$

3. $9\overline{)973}$

4. $6\overline{)653}$

5. $3\overline{)784}$

6. $4\overline{)486}$

7. $2\overline{)301}$

8. $5\overline{)637}$

9. $4\overline{)862}$

10. $7\overline{)5{,}001}$

11. $2\overline{)6{,}841}$

12. $6\overline{)9{,}469}$

Name ______________________ Date ____________

Long Division

▲ Finding Errors in Division

Find the mistake or mistakes in each problem. Circle each mistake. Then, redo each problem to find the correct answer.

1.
```
     18 r1
 4 ) 721
    -4
     32
    -32
      0
```

2.
```
      11 r2
 6 ) 808
    -8
     008
    -  6
       2
```

3.
```
      204 r 4
 5 ) 1,224
    -10
       2
      -0
       24
      -20
        4
```

4.
```
      924 r2
 3 ) 3,446
    -27
      74
     -72
       2
```

5.
```
      718 r 8
 9 ) 800
    -63
     170
    -162
       8
```

6.
```
      110 r5
 7 ) 821
    -77
      5
```

7.
```
      184 r 1
 2 ) 3,649
    -2
     16
    -16
      09
      -8
       1
```

8.
```
      74 r5
 8 ) 617
    -58
      37
     -32
       5
```

9. Choose one problem and explain how it was solved incorrectly.

____

____

Division Tic-Tac-Toe

Materials: sharpened pencil, paper clip, dry-erase markers, calculator

To play: Players take turns. Decide who is *X* and who is *O*. Use the sharpened pencil and paper clip to spin the spinner. Write the number in the space above the board. That will be the divisor for the round. To win a spot, a player must divide the number in that spot by the divisor. Use a calculator to check the whole-number part of the quotient. If the player is correct, she should draw an *X* or *O* in the spot. The first player to get three in a row wins.

Divisor:

924	133	1,504
720	823	612
2,117	451	923

Divisor:

193	340	622
784	2,218	785
354	219	1,553

Divisor:

726	198	305
1,343	861	456
321	842	3,515

Divisor:

2,412	526	313
405	826	741
996	1,123	144

To prep: Copy on card stock for durability. Laminate so students can use dry-erase markers. Cut off these directions before copying.

Equivalent Fractions

Essential Question

What are equivalent fractions and how are they formed?

Warm-Up/Review

Write a simple fraction on the board, such as 3/4. Challenge the class to come up with as many ways to model or describe it as they can. Repeat with more fractions as time allows.

Mini-Lesson

1. Draw a pizza on the board and divide it into 8 slices. Draw 3 more circles of the same size. Divide the circles into fourths, sixths, and halves, respectively.
2. Tell students, "A family ate 4 slices of this pizza. (eighths circle) Two sections of this tire got damaged. (fourths circle) Three slices of this cake are left. (sixths circle) This half of the moon is lit up tonight." (halves circle) Color in 4 out of 8, 2 out of 4, 3 out of 6, and 1 out of 2 parts on each respective circle as you give each description. Be sure to color the same section of each circle.
3. Ask, "How could we use fractions to describe each situation?" Guide students toward identifying 4/8, 2/4, 3/6, and 1/2. Label each circle with the correct fraction.
4. Ask, "How else could you describe these circles? Think of a term that would describe all four situations." Guide students toward *half.*
5. Ask, "Could we write that as a fraction?" (1/2) Explain that all of the fractions on the board are equivalent fractions, or different fractions that name the same part.

Math Talk

How are these numerators related?
How are these denominators related?
Do you notice any patterns? If so, describe them.

Journal Prompt

Can a fraction have more than one equivalent fraction? Why or why not? Give examples.

Materials

fraction bars or paper copies of fraction bars
crayons or colored pencils
laminated blank number lines
dry-erase markers
laminated multiplication charts

Workstations

Activity sheets (pages 89–91)
Equivalent Fractions Bump (page 92)
Fraction modeling practice

Guided Math

Remediation: Modeling Equivalent Fractions

1. Give each student a set of fraction bars, or a copy of fraction bars to cut apart. (Have students shade each bar a different color if the copies are blank.)
2. Have students find the halves, fourths, sixths, and eighths bars and set the rest to the side. Ask them to show one-half using the halves bar. (If using paper bars, students can fold the unused portion behind.) Model lining the left edge up with fourths bars and explain, "One-half matches exactly with two-fourths, so they are equivalent." Repeat with sixths and eighths. Then, challenge students to find any other equivalent fractions on the remaining bars. (5/10, 6/12)
3. Ask, "Why can't the fifths bar show an equivalent fraction?" Line the halves and fifths bars up and show how they don't match up.
4. Have students explore with the fraction bars to find other sets of equivalent fractions. Record the sets as students share their findings.

On Level: Finding Equivalent Fractions

1. Give each student a number line and a dry-erase marker. Have them model the fraction 1/3 on the number line, labeling the tick marks below the line.
2. Ask, "What happens if we divide each section on the number line in half? How would we label the new tick marks?" Guide students to draw new tick marks halfway between the old ones and count them to understand that the number line is now divided into sixths. Have students label the new tick marks above the number line.
3. Explain, "One-third is equivalent to 2/6 because they fall at the same place on the number line. Can you find any other equivalent fractions on this number line? (2/3 and 4/6) Is 3/6 equivalent to a third? Why not?"
4. Repeat steps 1–3 with additional sets of related fractions: fourths and eighths, fifths and tenths, etc.

Enrichment: Using Multiplication to Form Equivalent Fractions

1. Display the fractions *1/2, 2/4, 3/6, 4/8, 5/10,* and *6/12* in a row.
2. Ask, "What do you notice about these fractions?" (they are equivalent, the numerators count up by 1, the denominators double, the denominator is always double the numerator, etc.)
3. Give students a multiplication chart. Have them use a dry-erase marker to circle two complete, adjacent rows, such as ×3 and ×4. Point out how each vertical pair of numbers forms a fraction, and all of the fractions in the row are equivalent. It also works with non-adjacent rows. Simply have students cover the rows in between to focus on the correct rows. Say several fractions, such as 5/6, 1/4, and 3/8, and have students use the chart to find equivalent fractions for each.
4. Explain, "When you multiply the numerator and denominator by the same number, it forms an equivalent fraction. You can also divide the numerator and denominator by the same number to find equivalent fractions." Have students multiply and divide to find equivalent fractions for 1/8. Students should justify their answer by giving the related factor or divisor.

Assess and Extend

Is 2/3 equivalent to 3/4? Why or why not?

Name ______________________ Date ____________

Equivalent Fractions

Modeling Equivalent Fractions

Write the equivalent fractions.

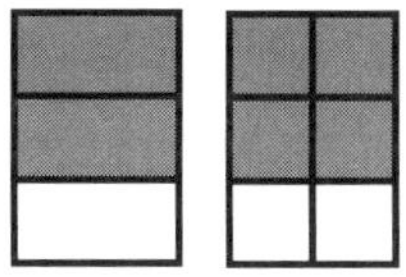

1. _____ = _____

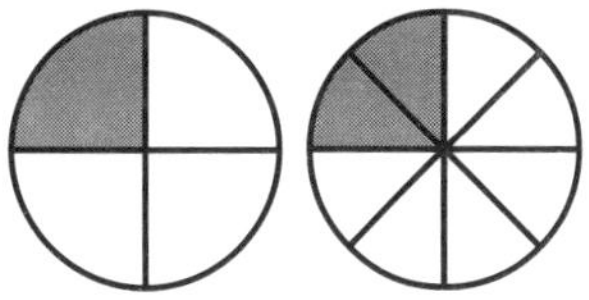

2. _____ = _____

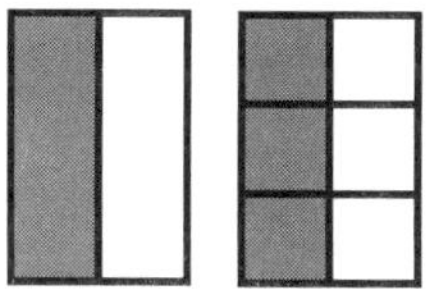

3. _____ = _____

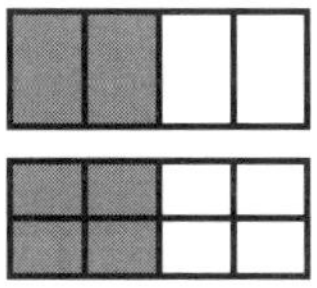

4. _____ = _____

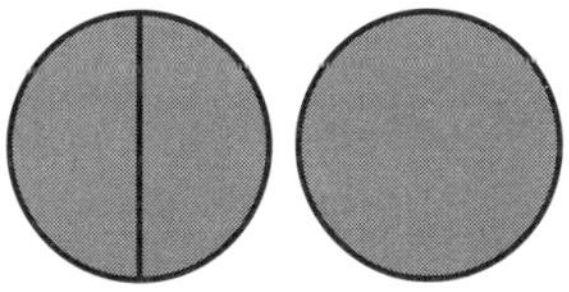

5. _____ = _____

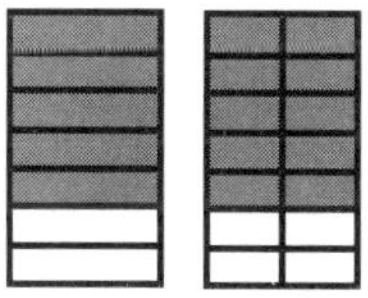

6. _____ = _____

Shade in the equivalent fraction. Then, write the equivalent fractions.

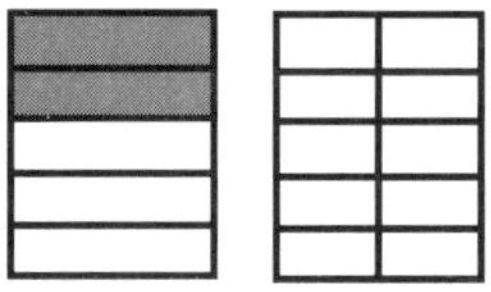

7. _____ = _____

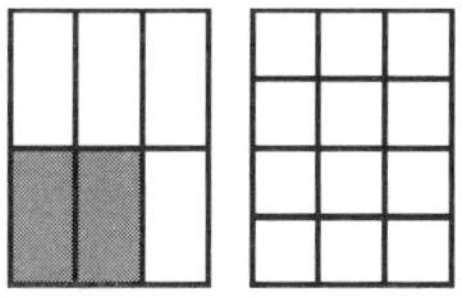

8. _____ = _____

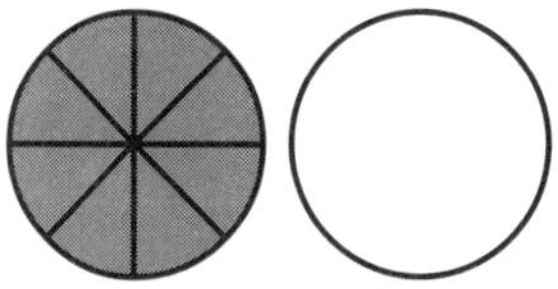

9. _____ = _____

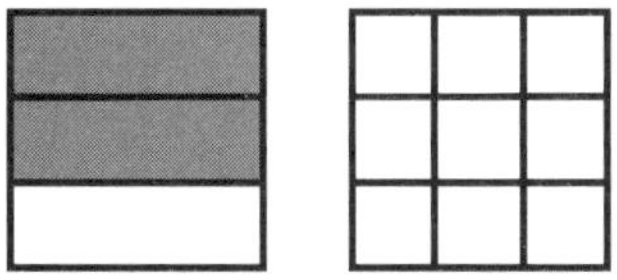

10. _____ = _____

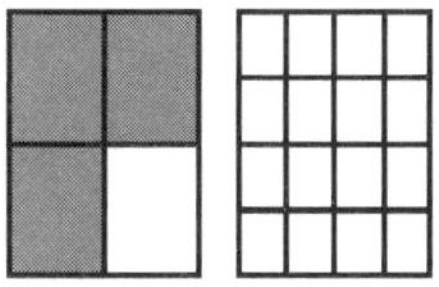

11. _____ = _____

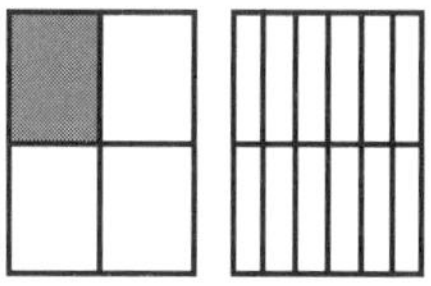

12. _____ = _____

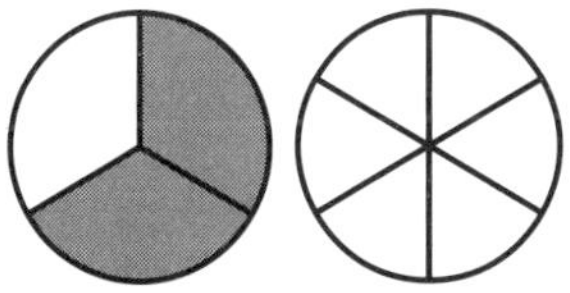

13. _____ = _____

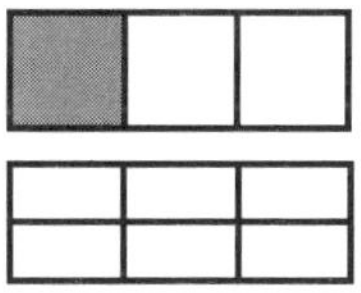

14. _____ = _____

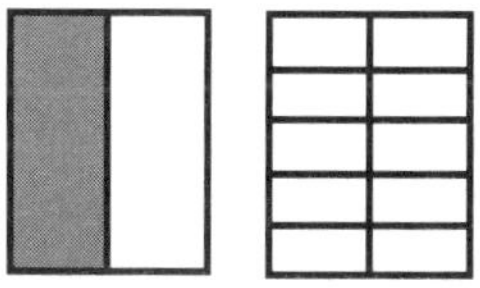

15. _____ = _____

Name ______________________ Date ____________

Equivalent Fractions

Finding Equivalent Fractions

Write the missing numerator or denominator to make each pair equivalent.

1. $\frac{2}{3} = \frac{\quad}{12}$

2. $\frac{8}{9} = \frac{\quad}{18}$

3. $\frac{1}{2} = \frac{5}{\quad}$

4. $\frac{1}{8} = \frac{\quad}{16}$

5. $\frac{4}{9} = \frac{36}{\quad}$

6. $\frac{2}{9} = \frac{\quad}{18}$

7. $\frac{3}{4} = \frac{12}{\quad}$

8. $\frac{1}{2} = \frac{\quad}{12}$

9. $\frac{4}{5} = \frac{\quad}{25}$

10. $\frac{2}{5} = \frac{12}{\quad}$

11. $\frac{7}{8} = \frac{\quad}{16}$

12. $\frac{2}{3} = \frac{\quad}{15}$

13. $\frac{2}{5} = \frac{\quad}{10}$

14. $\frac{3}{8} = \frac{6}{\quad}$

15. $\frac{5}{8} = \frac{\quad}{24}$

16. $\frac{3}{4} = \frac{\quad}{12}$

17. $\frac{3}{5} = \frac{\quad}{15}$

18. $\frac{3}{7} = \frac{\quad}{14}$

19. $\frac{1}{6} = \frac{2}{\quad}$

20. $\frac{4}{5} = \frac{16}{\quad}$

21. $\frac{3}{7} = \frac{\quad}{21}$

22. $\frac{5}{6} = \frac{\quad}{12}$

23. $\frac{1}{6} = \frac{6}{\quad}$

24. $\frac{5}{8} = \frac{10}{\quad}$

Name ______________________ Date ____________

Equivalent Fractions

▲ Using Multiplication to Form Equivalent Fractions

Write the missing numerators to make the fractions in each row equivalent. Below each equivalent fraction, write the factor you multiplied by.

1. $\frac{1}{2} = \frac{\_\_}{36} = \frac{\_\_}{18} = \frac{\_\_}{16} = \frac{\_\_}{42} = \frac{\_\_}{48}$

× ____ × ____ × ____ × ____ × ____

2. $\frac{5}{6} = \frac{\_\_}{48} = \frac{\_\_}{12} = \frac{\_\_}{30} = \frac{\_\_}{18} = \frac{\_\_}{24}$

× ____ × ____ × ____ × ____ × ____

3. $\frac{1}{3} = \frac{\_\_}{9} = \frac{\_\_}{27} = \frac{\_\_}{90} = \frac{\_\_}{6} = \frac{\_\_}{12}$

× ____ × ____ × ____ × ____ × ____

4. $\frac{3}{4} = \frac{\_\_}{24} = \frac{\_\_}{16} = \frac{\_\_}{8} = \frac{\_\_}{20} = \frac{\_\_}{36}$

× ____ × ____ × ____ × ____ × ____

5. $\frac{4}{9} = \frac{\_\_}{18} = \frac{\_\_}{45} = \frac{\_\_}{36} = \frac{\_\_}{54} = \frac{\_\_}{27}$

× ____ × ____ × ____ × ____ × ____

6. $\frac{7}{8} = \frac{\_\_}{16} = \frac{\_\_}{56} = \frac{\_\_}{24} = \frac{\_\_}{48} = \frac{\_\_}{32}$

× ____ × ____ × ____ × ____ × ____

7. $\frac{3}{7} = \frac{\_\_}{21} = \frac{\_\_}{42} = \frac{\_\_}{14} = \frac{\_\_}{35} = \frac{\_\_}{28}$

× ____ × ____ × ____ × ____ × ____

8. $\frac{2}{5} = \frac{\_\_}{50} = \frac{\_\_}{10} = \frac{\_\_}{40} = \frac{\_\_}{15} = \frac{\_\_}{25}$

× ____ × ____ × ____ × ____ × ____

Equivalent Fractions Bump

Materials: 1 die, 10 counters per player

To play: Players take turns. Roll the die. Cover a fraction equivalent to the fraction you rolled with a counter. You can "bump" the other player off of a space if they only have one counter on it. Once you place two counters on a space, it is yours and cannot be bumped. The first player to use all of their counters wins.

1	$\frac{1}{2}$	2	$\frac{1}{3}$	3	$\frac{2}{3}$
4	$\frac{1}{4}$	5	$\frac{3}{4}$	6	$\frac{1}{5}$

$\frac{10}{15}$ $\frac{4}{8}$ $\frac{4}{12}$ $\frac{6}{12}$

$\frac{9}{12}$ $\frac{5}{10}$ $\frac{8}{12}$ $\frac{3}{12}$

$\frac{4}{6}$ $\frac{2}{10}$ $\frac{3}{15}$ $\frac{6}{8}$

$\frac{4}{20}$ $\frac{3}{9}$ $\frac{2}{8}$

$\frac{3}{6}$ $\frac{5}{15}$ $\frac{15}{20}$ $\frac{2}{6}$

$\frac{5}{20}$ $\frac{6}{9}$ $\frac{2}{4}$

Comparing Fractions

Essential Question

Why does the whole matter when comparing fractions?

Warm-Up/Review

Write *3/8* and *7/8* on the board. Ask students to identify the greater fraction and justify their answer with a model. Repeat with 1/2 and 1/3.

Mini-Lesson

1. Tell students, "Two fourth-grade classrooms have the same number of metersticks. Two-sixths of Mrs. Beck's metersticks are new. One-fourth of Mr. Diaz's metersticks are new. Which class has more new metersticks?"
2. Have students identify the important numbers in the problem (2/6, 1/4) and the problem to be solved (which class has more new metersticks). Set up the comparison on the board.
3. Explain, "We need to compare these fractions, but both the numerators and the denominators are different. So, we have a few options. We can draw a model." Set up a number line to compare the fractions. Model with a bar diagram as well to emphasize that models should show the same whole.
4. Say, "Or, we can find equivalent fractions with the same denominator." Walk through creating equivalent fractions for each.
5. Explain, "Another option is to draw a picture. But, we don't know how many metersticks they have. We can choose a test number that divides easily by both denominators, such as 12 or 24." Draw a picture to show each class set and circle the correct portion of each.
6. Have students work in pairs and use any method to solve the following problem: "Jake and Lila both have the same box of crayons. Jake has broken 1/3 of his crayons. Lila has broken 3/8 of her crayons. Who has the fewest broken crayons?" (Jake, 1/3 < 3/8) Allow students to share their answers and methods.

Math Talk

How does the denominator affect the size of the fraction? (For example, with 1/2 and 1/10.)

Describe another way to model this problem.

Journal Prompt

The Jets have 12 players on their team. The Tigers have 21 players on their team. One-third of each team is fourth-graders. Do the Jets and the Tigers have the same number of fourth-grade players? Why or why not?

Materials

laminated number lines
dry-erase markers

Workstations

Activity sheets (pages 95–97)
Compare and Collect (page 98)

Guided Math

Remediation: Understanding Fraction Comparisons

1. Give each student a pair of number lines. Display the fractions *1/2* and *3/4*. Work with students to model each fraction on one of the number lines.
2. Have students compare the number lines. Point out where each fraction lies. Say, "One-half is less than 3/4. Three-fourths is greater than 1/2."
3. Ask, "What happens if I use a longer number line to model 3/4? Can we still compare the fractions?" (No) Guide students to understand that you can only compare fractions from the same whole, which means using number lines that are the same length.
4. Repeat steps 1 and 2 with several more pairs of fractions. Guide students toward marking the fractions on the same number line as they are ready.

On Level: Using Benchmark Fractions

1. Display *1/2* and *3/4*. Explain, "One-half is an easy fraction to work with, because I know the equivalent fractions." Have students provide several fractions equivalent to 1/2. "Because I am comparing it to a fraction with a denominator of 4, I can convert 1/2 to the equivalent fraction with a denominator of 4, or 2/4. Now I can easily compare. One-half is less than 3/4." Record the comparison with the correct symbol.
2. Display *4/5* and *1/3*. Explain, "I can also use the benchmark fraction 1/2 to compare these fractions. I know that 4/5 is greater than 1/2. I know that 1/3 is less than 1/2. So, 4/5 is greater than 1/3." If needed, draw models to prove each statement. Record the comparison with the correct symbol.
3. Repeat with several more pairs of fractions. Encourage students to explain their reasoning using benchmark fractions.

Enrichment: Using Cross-Multiplication to Compare Fractions

1. Set up a comparison problem with 5/6 and 7/8. Explain, "Using benchmark fractions isn't as helpful with this problem. Both fractions are greater than 1/2 and close to 1. So, I need to create equivalent fractions with the same denominators."
2. Work with students to use multiples to find a common denominator (48) and convert the fractions. (5/6 = 40/48 and 7/8 = 42/48) Then, compare.
3. Explain that there is a faster way to do the same thing. Remind students that you can create equivalent fractions by multiplying the numerator and denominator by the same number. You are doing the same thing when you find equivalent fractions with a denominator equal to the product of the denominators (i.e., 6 × 8 = 48).
4. Say, "To convert 5/6 to a fraction with a denominator of 48, we multiply both parts by what?" (8, or 8/8) Show the multiplication. Repeat with 7/8 (multiply by 6, or 6/6). Ask, "What do you notice?" (You multiply each fraction by the denominator of the other fraction.) Explain, "We can do this more quickly by cross-multiplying." Demonstrate multiplying 6 × 7 and 8 × 5, and recording and comparing the products.
5. Have students practice cross-multiplying with several more sets of fractions. Encourage students to explain why each cross-multiplication works.

Assess and Extend

Place 2/6, 4/5, and 1/2 in order from least to greatest. (2/6, 1/2, 4/5) Explain how you compared and ordered the set.

Name ______________________ Date ______________

Comparing Fractions

Understanding Fraction Comparisons

Write a fraction for the shaded area of each figure. Then, write >, <, or = to compare each pair of fractions.

1.

____ ◯ ____

2.

____ ◯ ____

3.

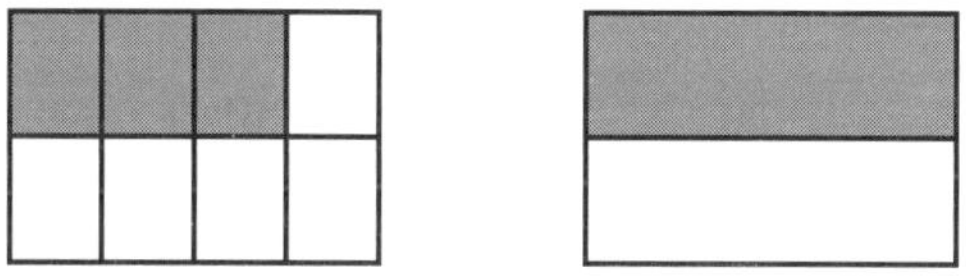

____ ◯ ____

4.

____ ◯ ____

5.

____ ◯ ____

6.

____ ◯ ____

7. Circle the fraction that is less.

$\frac{2}{3}$ $\frac{2}{5}$	$\frac{2}{6}$ $\frac{2}{8}$
$\frac{4}{6}$ $\frac{3}{4}$	$\frac{4}{10}$ $\frac{1}{3}$

8. Circle the fraction that is greater.

$\frac{3}{6}$ $\frac{3}{5}$	$\frac{4}{8}$ $\frac{4}{5}$
$\frac{9}{10}$ $\frac{2}{3}$	$\frac{4}{10}$ $\frac{2}{6}$

Name ______________________ Date ______________

Comparing Fractions

Using Benchmark Fractions

Check each comparison. Write *C* if it is correct. Circle and correct the false comparisons. Justify each correction with a model or benchmark fraction.

1. $\frac{5}{10} > \frac{2}{5}$

2. $\frac{1}{6} > \frac{2}{3}$

3. $\frac{5}{8} > \frac{6}{16}$

4. $\frac{5}{10} < \frac{1}{2}$

5. $\frac{1}{12} > \frac{3}{8}$

6. $\frac{6}{7} > \frac{3}{21}$

7. $\frac{4}{7} = \frac{8}{14}$

8. $\frac{5}{12} > \frac{3}{4}$

9. $\frac{4}{6} < \frac{7}{8}$

10. $\frac{1}{7} > \frac{4}{21}$

11. $\frac{3}{8} > \frac{1}{2}$

12. $\frac{3}{6} < \frac{1}{18}$

13. $\frac{1}{2} < \frac{3}{4}$

14. $\frac{1}{6} < \frac{2}{12}$

15. $\frac{3}{5} > \frac{1}{15}$

16. $\frac{1}{4} > \frac{1}{8}$

17. $\frac{4}{10} > \frac{3}{5}$

18. $\frac{4}{12} < \frac{2}{6}$

Name ______________________ Date ____________

Comparing Fractions

Using Cross-Multiplication to Compare Fractions

Write >, <, or = to compare each pair of fractions. Show your work.

1. $\frac{1}{14}$ ◯ $\frac{6}{7}$

2. $\frac{3}{10}$ ◯ $\frac{4}{5}$

3. $\frac{1}{2}$ ◯ $\frac{3}{4}$

4. $\frac{1}{6}$ ◯ $\frac{2}{3}$

5. $\frac{12}{20}$ ◯ $\frac{6}{10}$

6. $\frac{3}{7}$ ◯ $\frac{2}{4}$

7. $\frac{3}{5}$ ◯ $\frac{1}{2}$

8. $\frac{1}{3}$ ◯ $\frac{4}{9}$

9. $\frac{8}{9}$ ◯ $\frac{3}{5}$

10. $\frac{2}{3}$ ◯ $\frac{7}{9}$

11. $\frac{1}{3}$ ◯ $\frac{2}{5}$

12. $\frac{5}{8}$ ◯ $\frac{15}{24}$

13. $\frac{6}{7}$ ◯ $\frac{1}{3}$

14. $\frac{1}{8}$ ◯ $\frac{3}{4}$

15. $\frac{4}{6}$ ◯ $\frac{3}{8}$

16. $\frac{1}{3}$ ◯ $\frac{5}{7}$

17. $\frac{5}{8}$ ◯ $\frac{2}{3}$

18. $\frac{4}{5}$ ◯ $\frac{1}{4}$

19. $\frac{2}{5}$ ◯ $\frac{3}{4}$

20. $\frac{1}{4}$ ◯ $\frac{3}{9}$

21. $\frac{8}{12}$ ◯ $\frac{3}{5}$

Compare and Collect

Materials: 3 sets of 1–9 number cards

To play: Shuffle the number cards and place them facedown. Choose a board to work on: > or <. Players take turns drawing cards and placing them in any of the four empty spaces on the board. Once the board is full, Player 1 decides if the statement is true. If she is correct and the statement is true, she takes all four cards. If it is not true, she gets a chance to rearrange the numbers to make the statement true and take the cards. If she is still not correct, Player 2 gets a chance to correct the statement. Then, Player 2 begins the next turn. The player with the most cards after all cards have been used wins.

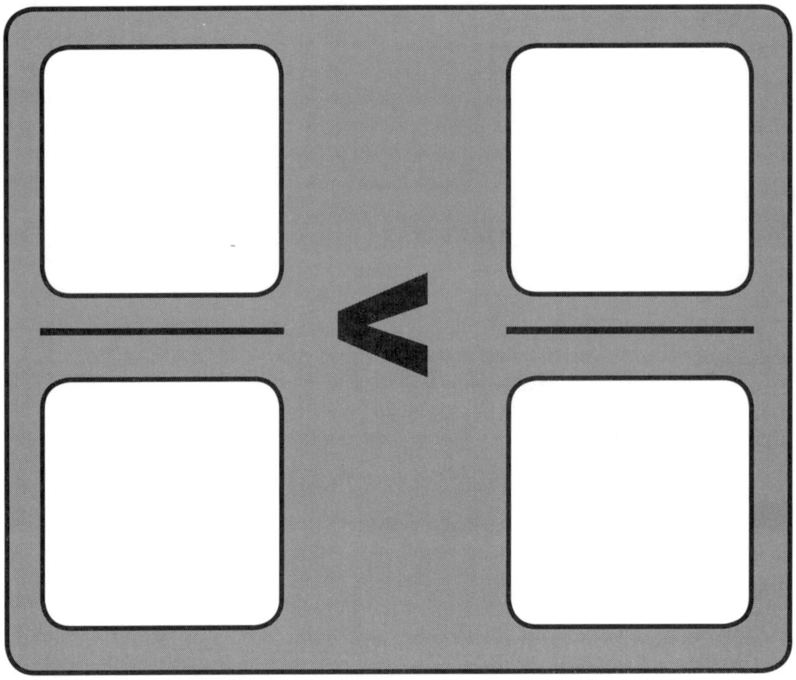

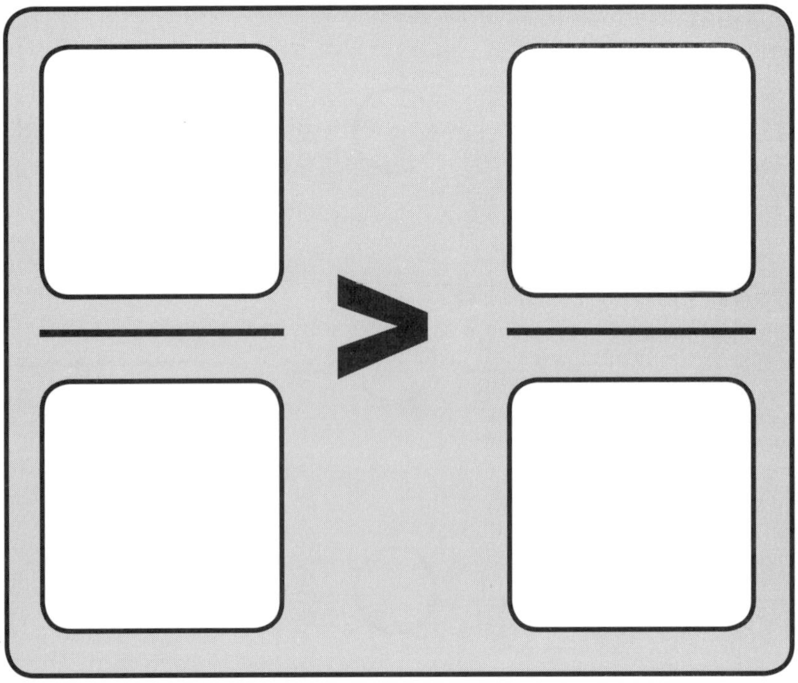

Adding and Subtracting Fractions

Essential Question

What strategies help to add and subtract fractions?

Warm-Up/Review

Give each student two sets of 1–9 number cards or tiles. Assign partners. Display a blank fraction, such as a circle divided into eighths or a number line divided into sixths. Challenge each pair of students to hold the number tiles to show each whole as a fraction (i.e., 8/8).

Mini-Lesson

Materials: two colors of sticky notes

1. Draw a rectangle on the board that is two sticky notes high and four sticky notes wide.
2. Add one sticky note to fill the top-left corner of the rectangle. Have students identify the fraction shown and explain where the numerator and denominator come from. Record the fraction on the note. (1/8) Say, "Now I'm going to add another part." Place a second note on the rectangle. "What fraction does it show now? (2/8) What fraction did the new piece represent? (1/8)" Record 1/8 on the new note. Continue until the entire rectangle is filled and labeled.
3. Explain, "This shows one whole, or 8/8. We added eighths one at a time to get 8/8." Place the sticky notes as addends in an addition sentence showing the decomposition (1/8 + 1/8 + . . . = 8/8). Say, "The denominator stays the same, because it still counts the total number of divided parts of the same whole. The numerators are added together to equal 8." Skip count the numerators by ones to 8.
4. Explore different compositions, such as 3/8 + 5/8, using the two different colors of sticky notes. Then, work with examples that equal less than 1, such as 1/8 + 4/8.
5. Finally, demonstrate subtraction with the same model. Start with 1, and subtract different amounts by removing sticky notes and recording the related number sentences. Finally, subtract from amounts less than 1.

Math Talk

Why does the denominator stay the same?

How is this like adding and subtracting whole numbers? How is it different?

Explain in your own words what it means to decompose a fraction.

Journal Prompt

Does 1/6 + 2/6 = 1/2? Why or why not? Justify your answer.

Materials

copies of blank fraction models (a variety)
scissors

Workstations

Activity sheets (pages 101–103)
Fraction Feud (page 104)

Guided Math

Remediation: Decomposing Fractions

1. Give each student a blank fraction. Have students identify their whole as a fraction and share it with the group. Then, have students use scissors to cut their fraction apart on the lines and reassemble it.
2. Explain, "Fractions can be taken apart and put back together by adding and subtracting parts." Have students separate the pieces to show decomposition into unit fractions. Say, "Each part is worth 1 because it is 1 section of the fraction. You can write this as an addition sentence." Demonstrate writing an addition sentence with unit fractions. Then, have students record the addition sentence for their fraction.
3. Have students explore and record decompositions with numerators other than 1 by creating piles of pieces. Then, work with decompositions with sums other than 1 by removing pieces.
4. Repeat steps 2 and 3 to demonstrate subtraction as well. Have students switch models to gain practice with additional fractions.

On Level: Operations with Fractions

1. Draw a rectangle. Explain that it represents a sub sandwich. Say, "The sandwich shop divided it into 4 equal sections." Draw lines to divide the rectangle into 4 equal sections.
2. Explain, "The first day, a boy ate 1 of the 4 pieces, or 1/4 of the sandwich." Shade 1 section. "The next day, the boy was hungrier and ate 2 pieces, or 2/4 of the sandwich." Shade 2 sections with a different color. Ask, "How much of the sandwich did the boy eat in all?"
3. Write __ + __ = __. Ask, "How many sections is the sandwich divided into?" Write this number as the denominator of all of the fractions. Point out that when adding fractions, the denominator remains the same because the total number of pieces of the sandwich never changes.
4. Then, ask, "How many pieces of the sandwich were eaten each day?" Write those numbers as the numerators of the first two fractions. Model adding the numerators to complete the final fraction.
5. Repeat steps 1 through 4 to model subtraction and find how much of the sandwich is left.

Enrichment: Improper Fractions and Mixed Numbers

1. Write *2/4 + 3/4*. Next to it, draw a rectangle divided into 4 sections.
2. Shade 2 of the 4 sections. Say, "The second part of the equation tells me to add 3 sections, but I only have 2 sections left. What should I do?" Draw a new, identical rectangle that is divided into 4 sections. Explain, "The denominator always stays the same. Now, do I have 3 sections to shade?" Shade the remaining 2 sections of the first rectangle and 1 section of the second rectangle.
3. Ask students to add the fractions and write the sum. (5/4) Explain, "Because the numerator is larger than the denominator, this is called an improper fraction. We can convert an improper fraction into a mixed number, which includes a whole number and fraction." Show how 1 whole rectangle was filled in along with 1 of the 4 pieces of the second. Ask students to write *5/4* as a mixed number. (1 1/4)
4. Continue with other equations, including those that produce improper fractions as well as those with mixed numbers as addends.

Assess and Extend

Sabrina says 4/10 + 6/10 = 1. Is she correct or incorrect? Justify your answer.

Name ______________________ Date ____________

Adding and Subtracting Fractions • Decomposing Fractions

Add or subtract. Show your work by shading each model.

1. $\frac{1}{4} + \frac{1}{4} =$ ___

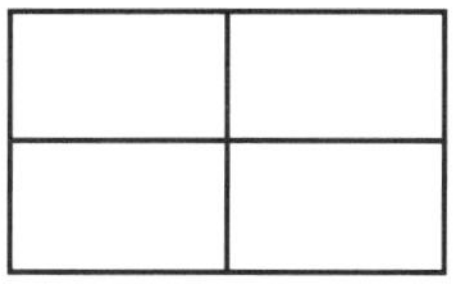

2. $\frac{1}{6} + \frac{3}{6} =$ ___

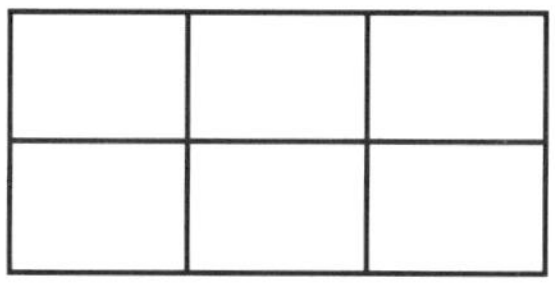

3. $\frac{5}{8} + \frac{2}{8} =$ ___

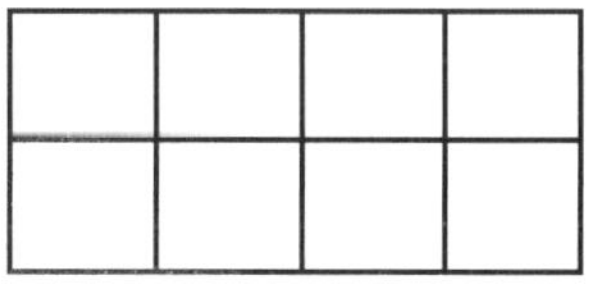

4. $\frac{1}{3} + \frac{1}{3} =$ ___

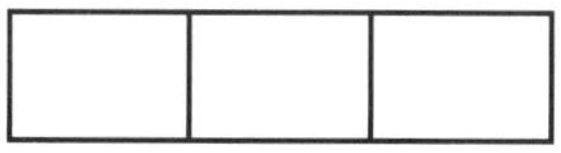

5. $\frac{1}{8} + \frac{4}{8} =$ ___

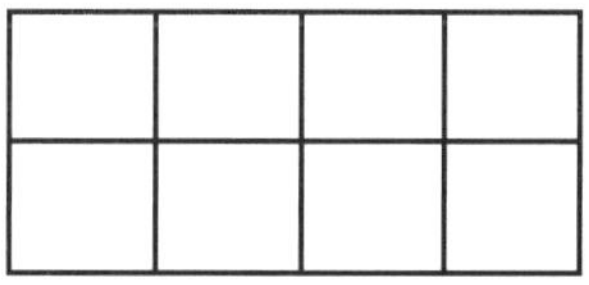

6. $\frac{2}{4} + \frac{1}{4} =$ ___

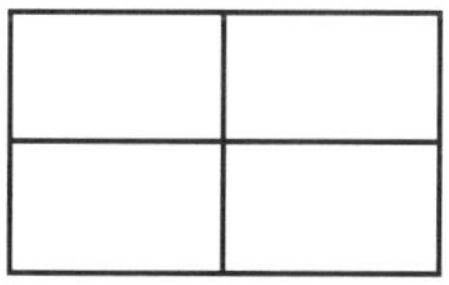

7. $\frac{7}{8} - \frac{4}{8} =$ ___

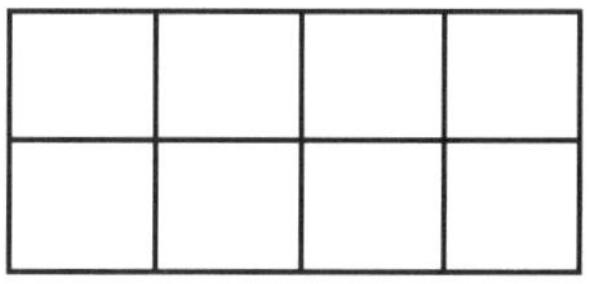

8. $\frac{4}{6} - \frac{2}{6} =$ ___

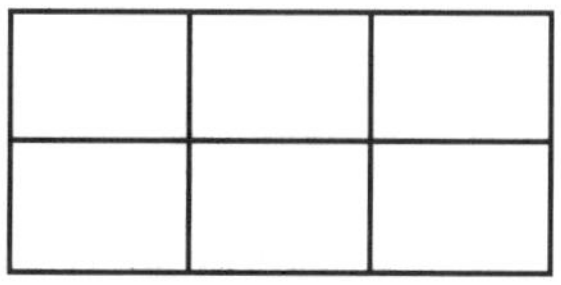

9. $1 - \frac{1}{4} =$ ___

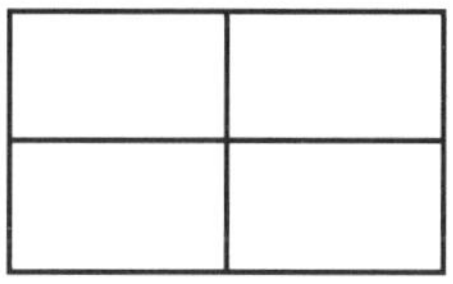

10. $\frac{4}{5} - \frac{2}{5} =$ ___

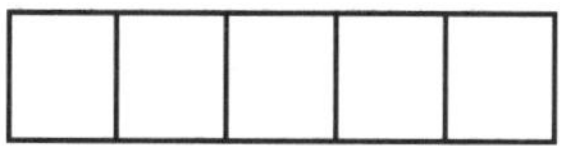

11. $\frac{3}{10} - \frac{2}{10} =$ ___

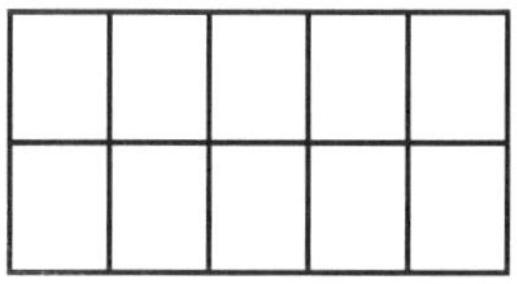

12. $\frac{5}{8} - \frac{2}{8} =$ ___

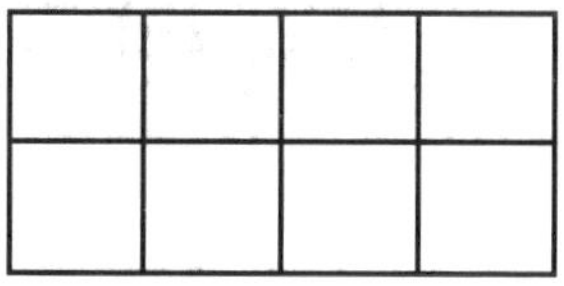

Name ______________________ Date ____________

Adding and Subtracting Fractions

Operations with Fractions

Add or subtract.

1. $\frac{1}{4} + \frac{2}{4} =$

2. $\frac{6}{8} - \frac{4}{8} =$

3. $\frac{1}{5} + \frac{3}{5} =$

4. $\frac{4}{10} + \frac{5}{10} =$

5. $\frac{7}{8} - \frac{5}{8} =$

6. $\frac{9}{10} - \frac{3}{10} =$

7. $\frac{6}{9} + \frac{2}{9} =$

8. $\frac{10}{12} - \frac{6}{12} =$

9. $\frac{15}{20} - \frac{7}{20} =$

10. $\frac{68}{100} + \frac{12}{100} =$

11. $\frac{5}{50} + \frac{15}{50} =$

12. $\frac{12}{15} - \frac{9}{15} =$

13. $\frac{4}{15} + \frac{2}{15}$

14. $\frac{5}{13} - \frac{2}{13}$

15. $\frac{5}{8} - \frac{3}{8}$

16. $\frac{3}{10} + \frac{1}{10}$

Name ______________________ Date ______________

Adding and Subtracting Fractions

▲ Improper Fractions and Mixed Numbers

Add or subtract.

1. $1\frac{1}{5} + 3\frac{3}{5}$

2. $2\frac{4}{10} + 7\frac{4}{10}$

3. $5\frac{4}{14} + 4\frac{5}{14}$

4. $3\frac{3}{10} + 3\frac{2}{10}$

5. $4\frac{2}{12} + 6\frac{9}{12}$

6. $1\frac{6}{8} + 1\frac{5}{8}$

7. $3\frac{6}{9} + 5\frac{5}{9}$

8. $6\frac{4}{12} + \frac{8}{12}$

9. $6\frac{5}{8} - 3\frac{2}{8}$

10. $9\frac{2}{5} - 4\frac{1}{5}$

11. $2\frac{9}{10} - 1\frac{8}{10}$

12. $9\frac{8}{14} - \frac{8}{14}$

13. $8\frac{5}{9} - 2\frac{4}{9}$

14. $5\frac{2}{4} - \frac{3}{4}$

15. $6\frac{8}{18} - 2\frac{3}{18}$

16. $10\frac{20}{27} - 5\frac{18}{27}$

Fraction Feud

Materials: 2 sets of 1–9 number cards, denominator cards, dry-erase markers, sharpened pencil, paper clip

To play: Shuffle the denominator cards and place them facedown. Give each player a set of 1–9 number cards. Keep the cards faceup. Use the sharpened pencil and paper clip to spin the spinner so players know if they are aiming to make the greatest or least fraction. Draw a denominator card and place it in the Denominator space. Then, each player should choose to make either an addition or subtraction sentence by using their number cards in the numerator spaces. Add or subtract to find the sum or difference. The player with the greatest (or least) sum or difference wins the round and colors in a circle. After a tie, players do not color in a circle. Place the used number cards to the side and draw a new denominator for the next round. Once number cards have been used, they cannot be used again until the next game.

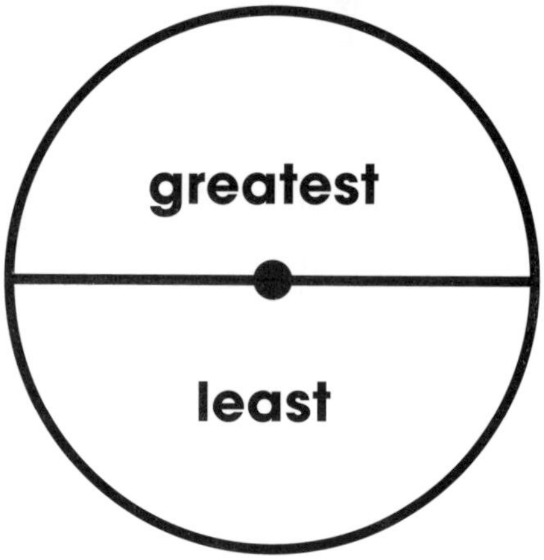

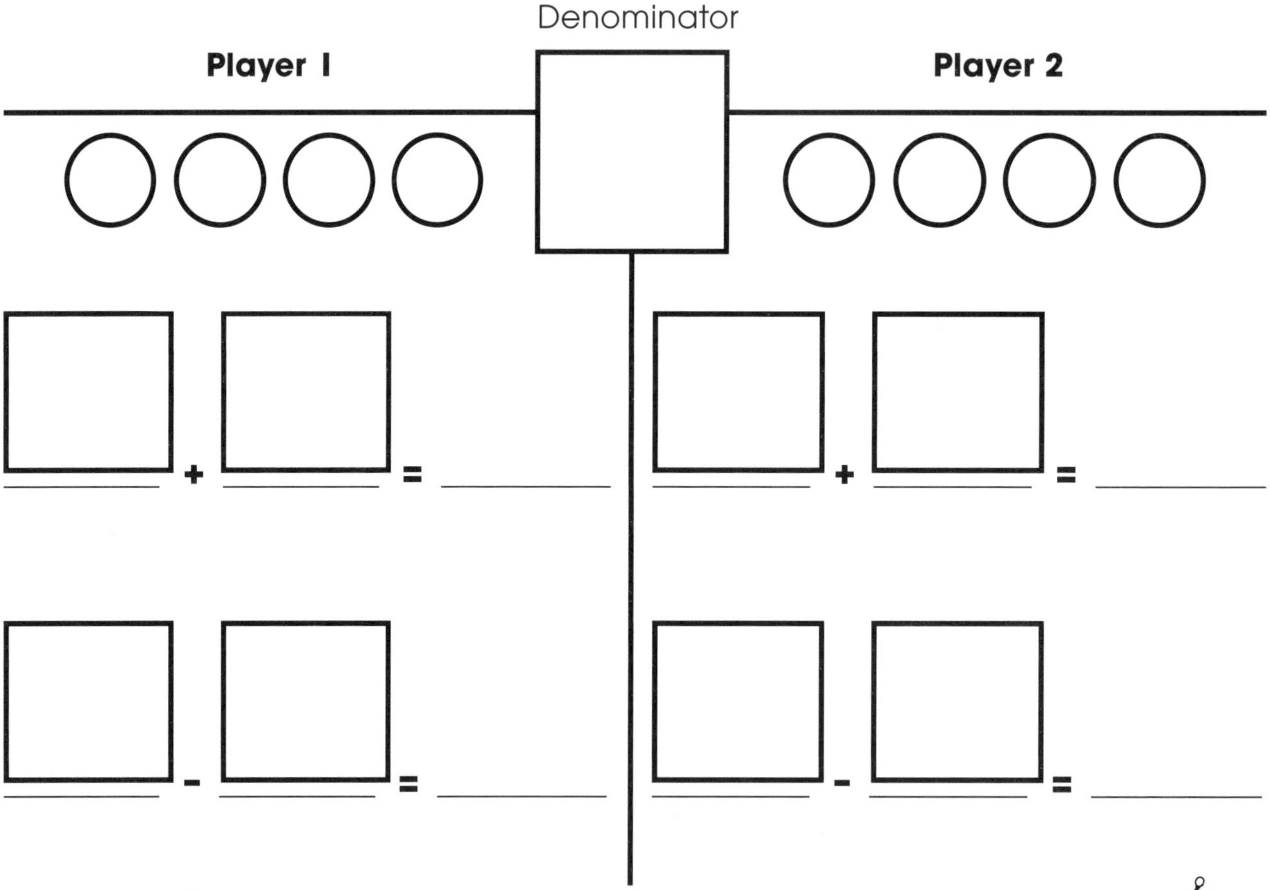

2	3	4	5	6	8	10	12	100

To prep: Copy on card stock for durability. (If desired, use different colors for the number cards and the denominator cards.) Cut apart the denominator cards and discard these directions. Laminate the game board so it can be used with dry-erase markers. Place the game board, number cards, and other materials in a center.

Multiplying Fractions

Essential Question

Can fractions have multiples?

Warm-Up/Review

Have students give their own definition of *multiples*. Then, practice counting by multiples. Give a number, such as 3, then have each student say the next multiple. Repeat with several numbers.

Mini-Lesson

1. Tell students, "A craft uses 1/3 of a bag of beads. Five students have made the craft." Draw five rectangles on the board and divide each rectangle into thirds. Explain that the rectangles represent the bags of beads, one bag per student. Color in 1 section of each rectangle to show 1/3.
2. Ask, "How many bags of beads did they use in all?" Model adding 1/3 five times to get 5/3. Remind students that repeated addition is multiplication. Explain, "I can rewrite this problem as a multiplication problem." Write *1/3 × 5 = 5/3.*
3. Have students observe the multiplication problem and share what they notice. Guide students to notice that as in addition, the denominator stays the same because the multiplication happens to the same whole. Observe that the product of the numerator multiplied by the whole number is the numerator of the final product. If desired, model rewriting the improper fraction as a mixed number.
4. As a class, work through the problem 2/5 × 4. If needed, draw a model to support the multiplication. If time allows, have students independently solve a problem.

Math Talk

What happens to the denominator? Why?
What happens to the numerator? Why?
What patterns do you notice?
How is this related to multiplying whole numbers?

Journal Prompt

Find 5 multiples of 1/4. Write the related multiplication fact for each multiple.

Materials

pattern blocks

Workstations

Activity sheets (pages 107–109)
Multiplication Maze (page 110)
Multiples Take Flight (page 32)

Guided Math

Remediation: Using Models to Multiply Fractions

1. Give each student several yellow hexagons. Review that a green triangle represents 1/6, the blue rhombus represents 1/3, and the red trapezoid represents 1/2. If needed, place multiple copies of each shape on a hexagon to model.
2. Display the problem *1/6 × 4*. Have students model 1/6 by placing a triangle on a hexagon. Then, have them make 3 more copies to show the multiplication.
3. Ask, "How many sixths are there? (4) How would you write that as a fraction? (4/6)" Move all of the triangles to one hexagon to show 4/6.
4. Repeat steps 2 and 3 with the problem 2/3 × 4. When moving the rhombuses to show 4/3, explain that it is an improper fraction because the numerator is greater than the denominator. Use a second hexagon to show how it is 1 1/3.
5. Repeat with several more problems, moving on to drawn models when students are ready.

On Level: Understanding Fractions as Multiples

1. Give each student a set of pattern blocks. Review that a green triangle represents 1/6, the blue rhombus represents 1/3, and the red trapezoid represents 1/2.
2. Have students use the pattern blocks to model 2/6 × 4. Guide students to place 2 triangles on each of 4 hexagons. Ask, "How many multiples of the unit fraction, 1/6, are there? (8) How could you rewrite the problem as a multiple of unit fractions? (8 × 1/6) What do you notice about these problems?" Guide students to see the related multiplication facts. (2 × 4 = 8 × 1)
3. Count the triangles to find the product. (8/6 or 1 2/6) Repeat step 2 with several more problems, such as 1/2 × 5 (2 1/2) and 2/3 × 2 (1 1/3). Encourage students to explain why they can multiply the numerator by the whole number to find each product.

Enrichment: Multiplying Fractions in Word Problems

1. Tell students, "The team drinks 3/8 of a jug of water every quarter during a game. There are 4 quarters in the game. So, how many jugs of water will the players use?"
2. Have students identify the important numbers (3/8, 4) and the problem to be solved (how many jugs will be used). Then, set up the number sentence. Draw a model if needed.
3. Solve the multiplication problem, walking through each step: "First, I record the denominator, since it stays the same. Then, I multiply the numerator and the whole number to find the numerator of the product. Since the product is an improper fraction, I need to rename it as a mixed number. (1 4/8) So, the players will use 1 4/8 (or 1 1/2) jugs of water."
4. Repeat with several more word problems, letting students solve the problems independently.

Assess and Extend

Is the product of 3/4 × 3 greater than or less than 1? (greater than) How do you know? Justify your answer.

Name ______________________ Date ______________

Multiplying Fractions

Using Models to Multiply Fractions

Solve each problem. Rewrite improper fractions as mixed numbers. Draw a model to show your work.

1. $\frac{1}{2} \times 3 =$

2. $\frac{1}{3} \times 5 =$

3. $\frac{1}{4} \times 2 =$

4. $6 \times \frac{2}{3} =$

5. $4 \times \frac{3}{4} =$

6. $3 \times \frac{2}{8} =$

7. $2 \times \frac{4}{5} =$

8. $\frac{1}{8} \times 4 =$

9. $\frac{2}{3} \times 4 =$

10. $\frac{1}{6} \times 6 =$

11. $5 \times \frac{1}{4} =$

12. $\frac{7}{8} \times 2 =$

Name ______________________ Date ______________

Multiplying Fractions

Understanding Fractions as Multiples

Rewrite each problem as the product of a unit fraction. Draw a model below each problem.

1. $5 \times \frac{2}{3} =$

2. $2 \times \frac{4}{5} =$

3. $\frac{2}{7} \times 4 =$

Solve each problem. Write the answer in simplest form.

4. $3 \times \frac{5}{6} =$

5. $4 \times \frac{1}{4} =$

6. $\frac{2}{12} \times 3 =$

7. $\frac{1}{8} \times 6 =$

8. $\frac{5}{7} \times 5 =$

9. $2 \times \frac{2}{3} =$

10. $\frac{2}{16} \times 4 =$

11. $\frac{1}{3} \times 8 =$

12. $4 \times \frac{3}{4} =$

13. $\frac{6}{8} \times 5 =$

14. $5 \times \frac{4}{5} =$

15. $\frac{2}{3} \times 3 =$

Name ______________________ Date ____________

Multiplying Fractions

▲ Multiplying Fractions in Word Problems

Solve each problem. Show your work on a separate sheet of paper.

1. Carlos is making a potato dish for a party. The recipe calls for $\frac{2}{3}$ cup of cheese. He needs to make 4 times the recipe to make enough for everyone. How much cheese does Carlos need?	**2.** The track around the field at Flynn Elementary School is $\frac{1}{4}$ of a mile. Alexis ran around the track 7 times. How far did she run?
3. Ellis uses $\frac{1}{8}$ of a pot of glue each time he works on his model airplanes. He worked on them 5 times last week. How much of a pot of glue did he use last week?	**4.** Casey's mom spent $85 at the grocery store. She spent $\frac{2}{5}$ on fresh produce. How much did Casey's mom spend on produce?
5. Holly is making punch for her sleepover. Each glass holds $\frac{4}{5}$ of a cup of lemonade. She is having 6 friends over. How much punch should Holly make so she and her friends each get one glass?	**6.** Jack is helping his mom make curtains for his room. He needs 4 curtains to cover his windows. Each curtain needs to be $2\frac{1}{8}$ yards tall. How much fabric does Jack need?
7. Ms. Unger is ordering pizza for her after-school club. She estimates that each of the 9 students will eat $\frac{2}{8}$ of a pizza. How many pizzas should she order?	**Challenge:** At Forrest's party, the guests ate $\frac{3}{4}$ of the birthday cake. The next day, Forrest's dad had $\frac{1}{4}$ of the leftover cake. How much of the cake did Forrest's dad eat?

Multiplication Maze

Solve each problem. Follow the path of the matching answer to get to the next problem. Continue until you reach the end. Highlight or draw a line through your final path. *Hint:* Be sure to reduce your answers to lowest form.

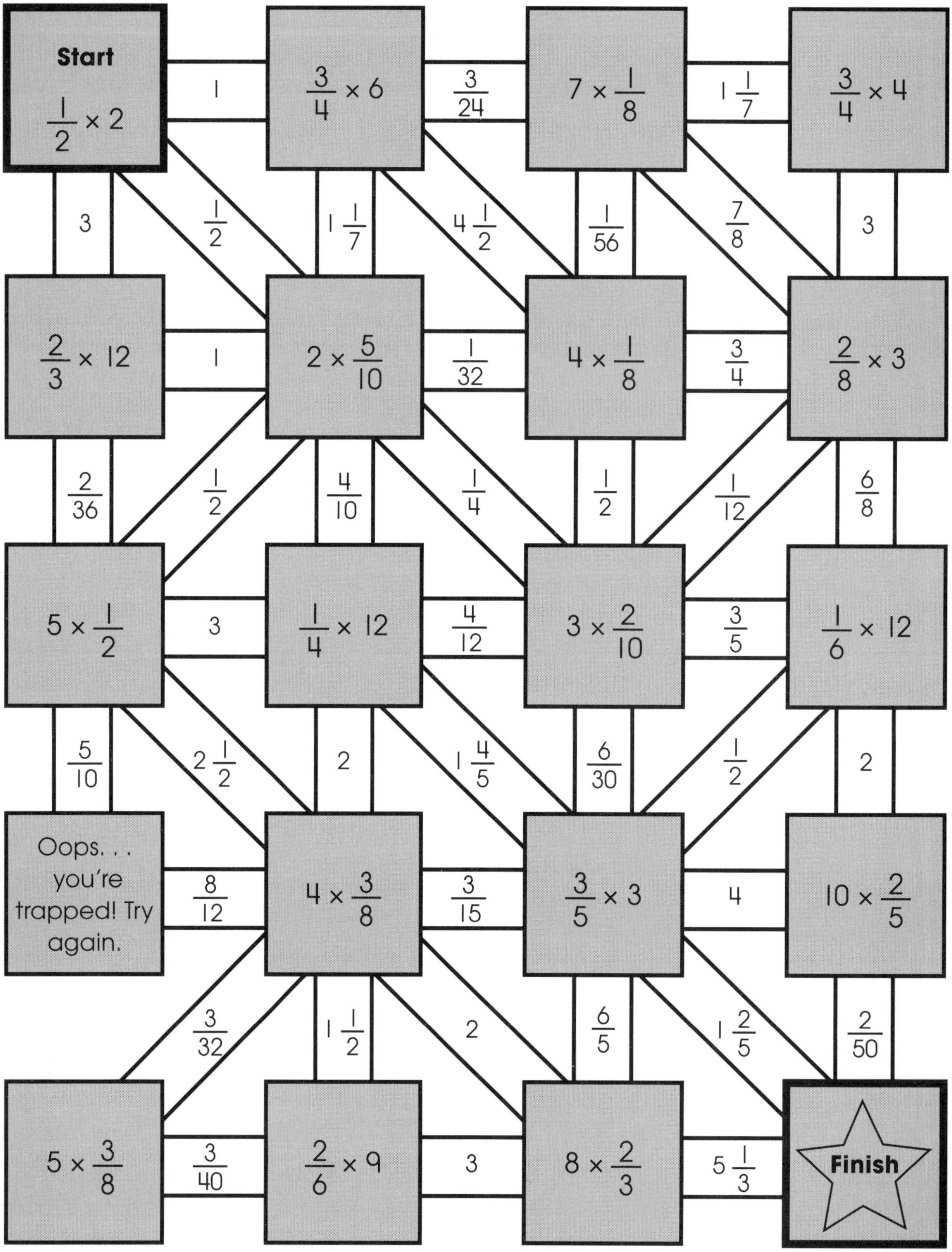

Fractions with Denominators of 10 and 100

Essential Question

How do you add fractions with unlike denominators?

Warm-Up/Review

Preprogram index cards with common equivalent fractions, such as 5/10, 6/8, etc. Give each student an index card. Say common fractions, like 1/2, 2/3, 1/4, etc. Students should stand if their fraction is equivalent. Switch cards and repeat as time allows.

Mini-Lesson

Materials: play dimes and pennies, base ten blocks

1. Tell students you found some dimes on the floor. Hand 3 dimes to a student and have her count them to find the total. Then, tell students you also found some pennies. Hand 6 pennies to another student to count. Ask, "How much money do I have in all? How do you know?" (36¢)
2. Have students solve 3/10 + 6/10. Then, add a 0 to the second denominator so it reads 6/100. Ask, "How does this change the problem? Six out of 100 is very different from 6 out of 10."
3. Discuss how they have already solved this problem using money instead. Explain that the dimes represent 3/10 of a dollar, and the pennies represent 6/100 of a dollar. Ask, "How would you write the total you found, 36¢, as a fraction? (36/100)"
4. Give students base ten blocks and have them model the same problem. Say, "We can change 3/10 to an equivalent fraction with a denominator of 100. The 3 tens rods are the same as 30 ones cubes, or 30/100. Now, we can add 30/100 and 6/100. Thirty plus 6 is 36/100."
5. Explain, "You can add zeros to the end of the numerator and denominator of a fraction with a denominator of 10 to make an equivalent fraction with a denominator of 100." Have students explain why that works. (You are multiplying by 10/10 to create an equivalent fraction.)
6. Have students work with a partner and use base ten blocks if needed to add 7/10 + 12/100 (82/100) and 2/10 + 2/100 (22/100).

Math Talk

How are 10 and 100 related?
Can you add these fractions as they are? Why or why not?
Can tenths and hundredths be from the same whole? Explain.

Explain why 4/10 + 4/100 is not equal to 8/10 or 8/100.

Materials

dime and penny manipulatives
laminated hundredths board
dry-erase markers

Workstations

Activity sheets (pages 113–115)
Money, Money, Money! (page 116)
Equivalent Fractions Bump (page 92)
Fraction Feud (page 104)

Guided Math

Remediation: Using Models

1. Explain, "Sometimes it is easier to understand adding tenths and hundredths by using money. What coin represents 1/10 of a dollar? 1/100?"
2. Have students represent 8/10, 3/100, 26/100, and 20/100 with coins. With 26/100 and 20/100, point out that students can "trade in" some pennies for dimes. State each amount using fractions: "26/100 is 2 tenths and 6 hundredths."
3. Once students are comfortable using money to represent fractions, give them laminated hundredths boards. Explain that each square represents 1/100, or 1 penny. Have students color in the same fractions from step 2 on the hundredths board. Emphasize thinking of each column as a group of 10. Explain, "We know there are 10 squares in this column, so like trading in 10 pennies for a dime, you can 'trade in' 10 hundredths for 1 tenth."
4. Have students use either model to solve 3/10 + 7/100 (37/100) and 1/10 + 23/100 (33/100).

On Level: Finding Patterns

1. Have students solve several addition problems with the same digit in the numerator of both fractions, such as 3/10 + 3/100 and 8/10 + 8/100. Have students identify any patterns they notice, guiding them to recognize that the numerator over 10 always becomes the tens place in the numerator of the sum.
2. Display the problem *2/10 + 22/100.* Say, "This doesn't follow the pattern we found earlier because there are two digits over 100 instead of 1 digit. So, I can convert 2/10 to the equivalent fraction with a denominator of 100, or 20/100. Remember, I did not just add zeros to the top and bottom. I multiplied by 10/10 to find the equivalent fraction."
3. Explain, "Next, I add the numerators. I write the sum, 42, over the denominator."
4. Have students solve several more problems with two-digit numbers over 100 and identify any patterns they notice with this type of problem.

Enrichment: Thinking Critically

1. Display *4/10 + 12/100.* Ask, "Is the sum greater than or less than 1/2? I know that 4/10 is close to 1/2. I can think of it as 40/100. I only need 10 more to equal 1/2. Adding 12 will make it greater than 1/2. When I add the hundredths, I get 52/100, which is greater than 1/2."
2. Display *19/100 + 3/10.* Have students mentally decide whether the sum is greater than or less than 1/2, justify their answers, and then solve to check. (49/100)
3. Display *82/100 – 5/10.* Explain, "I can't subtract until the fractions have the same denominator. So, I can convert 5/10 to have a denominator of 100 by multiplying by 10/10. Now, I can subtract 82 – 50 and write the difference (32) over 100."
4. Have students practice subtraction with the following problems: 64/100 – 6/10 (4/100), 48/100 – 2/10 (28/100), and 9/10 – 57/100 (33/100).

Assess and Extend

Oliver says 5/10 + 2/100 is 7/100. Is he correct? Why or why not? If not, give the correct answer. (No, 52/100)

Name ______________________ Date ______________

Fractions with Denominators of 10 and 100

Using Models

Tell how many dimes and pennies are in each amount. Then, rewrite the dimes and pennies as fractions of a dollar. Finally, color in the hundredths board to match the amount and write it as a fraction of a dollar.

1. $0.56

________ dimes, ——

________ pennies, ——

——

2. $0.71

________ dimes, ——

________ pennies, ——

——

3. $0.60

________ dimes, ——

________ pennies, ——

——

4. $0.98

________ dimes, ——

________ pennies, ——

——

Add. Use two colors on the model to show the addition.

5. $\frac{3}{10} + \frac{2}{10} =$ ——

6. $\frac{4}{10} + \frac{6}{100} =$ ——

Name ______________________ Date ____________

Fractions with Denominators of 10 and 100

Finding Patterns

Solve.

1. $\frac{2}{10} + \frac{3}{10} =$ ____

2. $\frac{50}{100} + \frac{21}{100} =$ ____

3. $\frac{4}{10} + \frac{30}{100} =$ ____

4. $\frac{6}{10} + \frac{1}{100} =$ ____

5. $\frac{20}{100} + \frac{7}{10} =$ ____

6. $\frac{15}{100} + \frac{8}{10} =$ ____

7. $\frac{7}{10} + \frac{3}{100} =$ ____

8. $\frac{4}{100} + \frac{4}{10} =$ ____

9. $\frac{4}{10} + \frac{44}{100} =$ ____

10. $\frac{57}{100} + \frac{1}{10} =$ ____

11. $\frac{9}{100} + \frac{9}{10} =$ ____

12. $\frac{32}{100} + \frac{5}{10} =$ ____

13. $\frac{73}{100} + \frac{3}{10} =$ ____

14. $\frac{8}{10} + \frac{20}{100} =$ ____

15. Were you able to solve any problems mentally? Why or why not? Explain.

____

____

____

____

Name ______________________ Date ______________

Fractions with Denominators of 10 and 100

Thinking Critically

Solve.

1. $\frac{3}{10} + \frac{56}{100} =$ ____

2. $\frac{13}{100} + \frac{2}{10} =$ ____

3. $\frac{9}{10} - \frac{22}{100} =$ ____

4. $\frac{1}{100} + \frac{1}{10} =$ ____

5. $\frac{63}{100} - \frac{5}{10} =$ ____

6. $\frac{85}{100} - \frac{7}{10} =$ ____

7. $\frac{47}{100} + \frac{4}{10} =$ ____

8. $\frac{6}{10} - \frac{23}{100} =$ ____

9. $\frac{7}{10} - \frac{68}{100} =$ ____

10. $\frac{2}{10} + \frac{89}{100} =$ ____

Look at each problem. Without solving, write *C* for correct or draw an *X* on the incorrect answers. Then, justify your answer.

11. $\frac{8}{10} - \frac{8}{100} = \frac{7}{10}$

____

____

12. $\frac{55}{100} - \frac{5}{10} = \frac{5}{100}$

____

____

13. $\frac{34}{100} + \frac{3}{10} = \frac{37}{100}$

____

____

14. $\frac{2}{10} + \frac{42}{100} = \frac{62}{100}$

____

____

15. $\frac{41}{100} - \frac{1}{10} = \frac{31}{100}$

____

____

16. $\frac{7}{100} + \frac{3}{10} = \frac{10}{100}$

____

____

Money, Money, Money!

Materials: sharpened pencil, paper clip, dry-erase markers

To play: Players take turns. Use the sharpened pencil and paper clip to spin each spinner and find out how many dimes and pennies you get on each turn. State each amount as a fraction and add them to get a fraction out of 100. For example, if you spin 1 dime and 8 pennies, you would say "1/10 plus 8/100 equals 18/100." Then, color that amount in on the hundredths board. Use the boards to decide who has more "money" and circle the winner. Repeat for all four rounds.

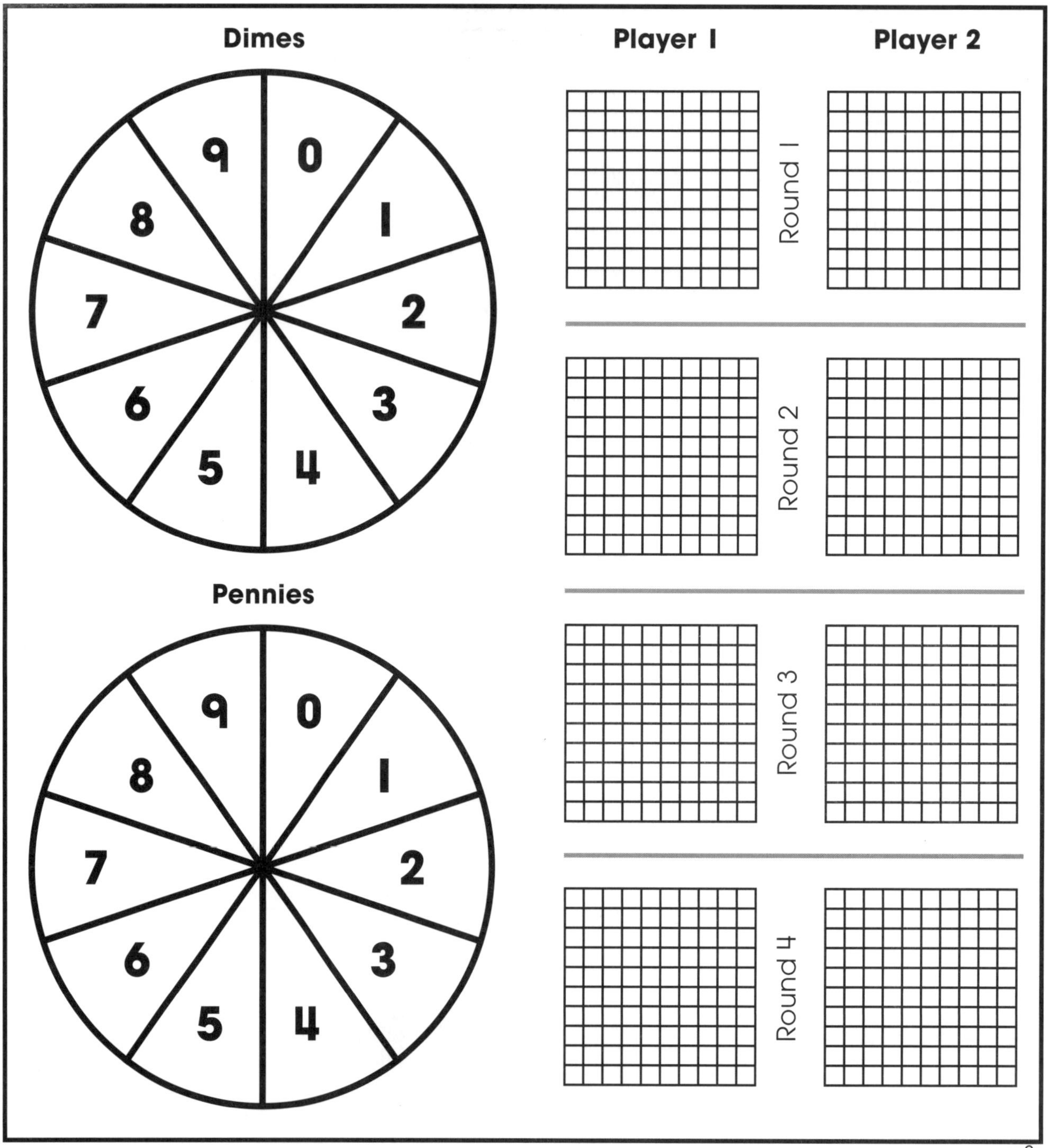

To prep: Copy on card stock for durability. Laminate so students can use dry-erase markers. Cut off these directions before copying.

Understanding Decimals

Essential Question

How are fractions and decimals related?

Warm-Up/Review

Pass out index cards programmed with fractions and whole numbers. Play music as students walk around. When the music stops, have them pair up with someone with the opposite type of number. Partners should multiply their numbers and discuss how the product is a multiple of the fraction. Repeat.

Mini-Lesson

Materials: play money, laminated place value mats

1. Hold up a $1 bill. Explain, "I want to give half of this dollar to a friend. How much should I give him?" Record *1/2* and *$0.50* on the board.
2. Ask, "How many pennies is that? How many dimes? How would you write each as a fraction of the whole?" Record 50/100 and 5/10 on the board. Explain, "All of these amounts are different ways of representing the same amount of money."
3. Point out the decimal representation. Explain, "Like fractions, decimals are a way of showing parts smaller than a whole number. You often see decimals with money. The numbers after the decimal represent amounts that are less than a whole dollar. The numbers to the left of the decimal represent whole dollars." Give several examples and have students identify the whole amount and the partial amount in each one.
4. Draw and label a place value chart from ones to hundreds. Add the decimal and two unlabeled columns to the right. Explain, "Place value includes whole numbers and parts of a number. The place values to the right of the decimal follow the same rules. Multiply by 10 when moving left. Divide by 10 when moving right. Dividing 1 into 10 gives you tenths." Label the tenths column. "Dividing tenths into 10 gives you hundredths." Label the hundredths column. Draw tenths and hundredths models as a visual if needed.
5. Divide students into pairs. Give each pair a random amount of coins (less than $1) and have them record the amount as a fraction and as a decimal on the place value mat.

Math Talk

Describe how tenths and hundredths are related to place value.

How can you convert __ to a fraction? Decimal?

Define *decimal* in your own words.

Journal Prompt

Ray has $0.56. He says he has 56 tenths of a dollar. Is he correct? Why or why not?

Materials

laminated tenths and hundredths grids
dry-erase markers
laminated tenths number lines, unlabeled
laminated place value mats with tenths and hundredths

Workstations

Activity sheets (pages 119–121)
Decimal Four-in-a-Row (page 122)
Money, Money, Money! (page 116)

Guided Math

Remediation: Using Multiple Representations

1. Give each student a tenths grid. Say different tenths, such as 1/10, 4/10, and 7/10. Have students record the fraction and color the grid to match. Guide students through writing the decimal form for each.
2. Repeat step 1 with the hundredths grid, using the same fractions. Explain, "Each column is worth 1 tenth. You are showing the same number and coloring the same columns, but the grid shows the smaller divisions within each tenth." Guide students to record each fraction as an equivalent fraction over 100 and as a decimal. Emphasize that 0.1 and 0.10 represent the same amount, but you say them differently (one-tenth vs. ten-hundredths) and the hundredths represent smaller pieces.
3. Then, repeat step 1 with the hundredths grid to represent numbers such as 56/100 and 28/100. Ask, "How many tenths are in this number? Hundredths?" Emphasize the place value by pointing to the digit in the decimal as well as the columns vs. the individual blocks.

On Level: Converting Between Fractions and Decimals

1. Have students label a number line from 0 to 1 with fractions on the top. Then, explain, "Just like you count from 0 to 10, you count tenths using the same count order: one-tenth, two-tenths, three-tenths . . ." Work with students to label the decimals correctly along the bottom.
2. Point out the fractions and their equivalent decimals. Ask students to identify the decimal forms of several fractions, and vice versa.
3. Then, have students erase the number line. Ask, "How would we show 15/100 on the number line? What tenths is it between?" Model finding the benchmarks (1/10, or 10/100 and 2/10, or 20/100) and labeling the first and last ticks on the number line. Then, model counting between 10 and 20, and labeling the fractions along the top. Explain, "It can be helpful to think of money: 15 cents is 1 dime and 5 pennies, so it is greater than 1/10, but less than 2/10."
4. Repeat steps 1 and 2 to label and identify the related decimals. Then, have students erase and redo the number line to identify decimals between other tenths such as 0.81, 0.36, and 0.72.

Enrichment: Using Place Value

1. Have students record *800* on their place value mats. Then, have them record the quotients of 800 ÷ 10, 80 ÷ 10, 8 ÷ 10, and 0.8 ÷ 10, giving guidance as needed. Discuss the pattern they see (dividing by 10 moves the digit right one place).
2. Repeat step 1 with 0.4, multiplying by 10 at each step. Discuss the pattern they see (multiplying by 10 moves the digit left one place).
3. Repeat steps 1 and 2 with different numbers, such as 450, 32, 0.6, and 0.27.
4. Ask, "How is multiplying by 10 different from multiplying by 10/10 to create an equivalent fraction?" (Multiplying by 10 increases the number, while multiplying by 10/10 makes an equal number, because it is the same as multiplying by 1.) Demonstrate by multiplying 0.2 by 10 and by 10/10 to demonstrate the difference in the products. (2 and 0.20)

Assess and Extend

Rewrite *60/100* as a decimal. Rewrite *0.34* as a fraction. How would you change 1.34 to a fraction?

Name ______________________ Date ____________

Understanding Decimals

● Using Multiple Representations

Find the number of tenths or hundredths in each model. Write the total as a fraction and as a decimal.

1. 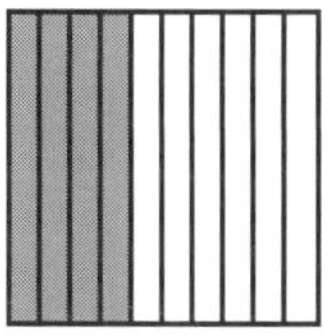

Fraction: ____________

Decimal: ____________

2. 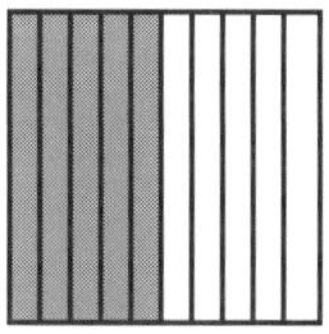

Fraction: ____________

Decimal: ____________

3. 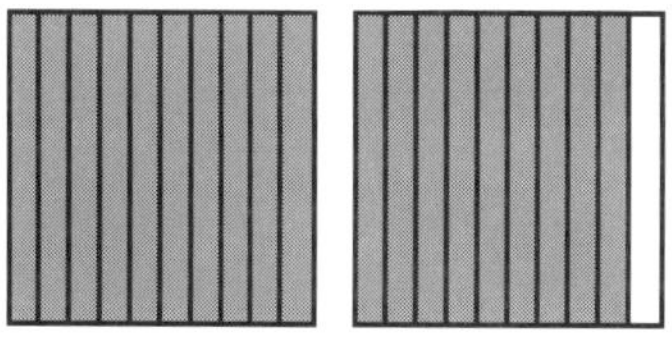

Fraction: ____________

Decimal: ____________

4. 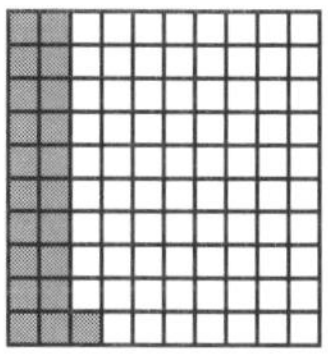

Fraction: ____________

Decimal: ____________

5. 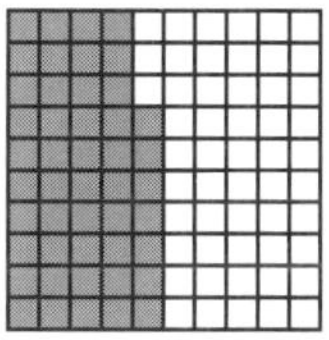

Fraction: ____________

Decimal: ____________

6. 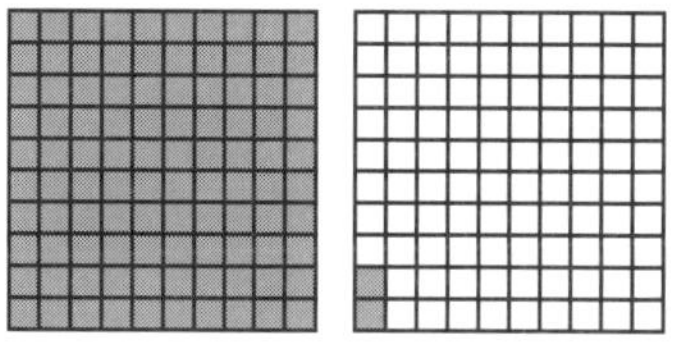

Fraction: ____________

Decimal: ____________

Shade the model to match the fraction or decimal. Then, write the equivalent fraction or decimal.

7. 0.7

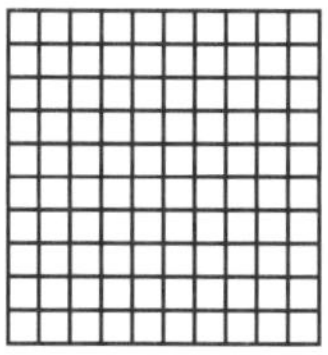

____

8. $\frac{70}{100}$

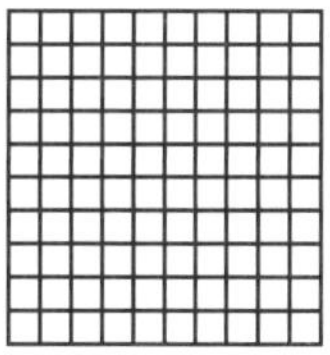

____

9. 0.57

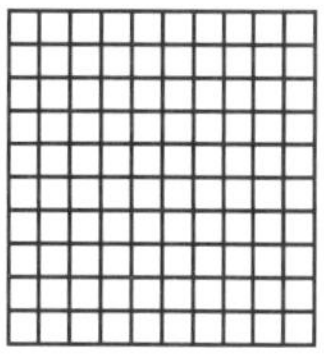

____

10. $\frac{13}{100}$

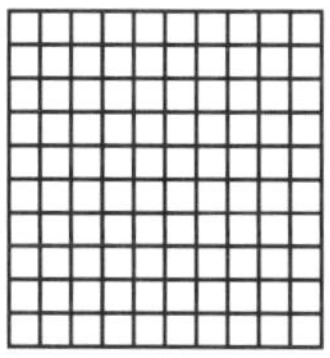

____

11. $\frac{8}{10}$

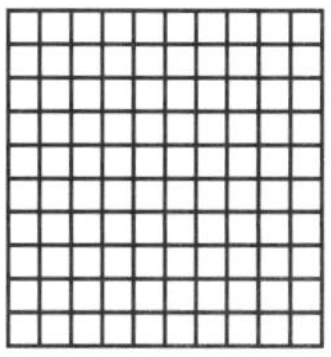

____

12. 0.62

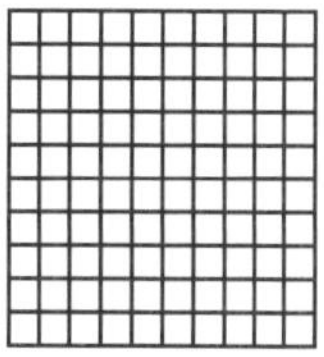

____

Name ______________________ Date ______________

Understanding Decimals

Converting Between Fractions and Decimals

Rewrite each fraction as an equivalent decimal.

1. $\frac{4}{10}$ =

2. $\frac{88}{100}$ =

3. $3\frac{25}{100}$ =

4. $6\frac{5}{10}$ =

5. $4\frac{1}{10}$ =

6. $9\frac{30}{100}$ =

Rewrite each decimal as an equivalent fraction.

7. 0.6 ______________

8. 0.5 ______________

9. 0.91 ______________

10. 0.07 ______________

11. 1.23 ______________

12. 4.8 ______________

Write the equivalent fraction or decimal.

13. $\frac{65}{100}$ __________

14. 6.9 __________

15. $2\frac{12}{100}$ __________

16. 0.21 __________

17. $7\frac{34}{100}$ __________

18. $\frac{99}{100}$ __________

19. 16.08 __________

20. 300.24 __________

21. 25.04 __________

22. $25\frac{34}{100}$ __________

23. $75\frac{2}{100}$ __________

24. 4.3 __________

Name ____________________ Date ____________

Understanding Decimals

Using Place Value

Use what you know about place value to multiply and divide each number.

1. 1.2 × 1,000 = ________

1.2 × 100 = ________

1.2 × 10 = ________

1.2 × 1 = ________

1.2 ÷ 1 = ________

1.2 ÷ 10 = ________

2. 0.23 × 1,000 = ________

0.23 × 100 = ________

0.23 × 10 = ________

0.23 × 1 = ________

0.23 ÷ 1 = ________

0.23 ÷ 10 = ________

3. 30.7 × 100 = ________

30.7 × 10 = ________

30.7 × 1 = ________

30.7 ÷ 1 = ________

30.7 ÷ 10 = ________

30.7 ÷ 100 = ________

4. 546 × 100 = ________

546 × 10 = ________

546 × 1 = ________

546 ÷ 1 = ________

546 ÷ 10 = ________

546 ÷ 100 = ________

Multiply each number by 10 and $\frac{10}{10}$.

5. 0.4 × 10 = ________

$0.4 \times \frac{10}{10}$ = ________

6. 0.9 × 10 = ________

$0.9 \times \frac{10}{10}$ = ________

7. 2.7 × 10 = ________

$2.7 \times \frac{10}{10}$ = ________

8. 1.2 × 10 = ________

$1.2 \times \frac{10}{10}$ = ________

Decimal Four-in-a-Row

Materials: sharpened pencil, paper clip, two colors of dry-erase markers

To play: Players take turns. Use the sharpened pencil and paper clip to spin the spinner twice. Use the numbers you spun in any order to create a decimal in the space beside the hundredths chart. For example, if you spin 2 and 3, you can make 0.23 or 0.32. Each player has three zeros that they can use during any turn to replace one of their digits. Once a 0 is used, a player should color one of the circles below their section. After making a decimal, the player should convert it to a fraction in the space provided and use their marker to color that space on the hundredths chart. The first player to get four in a row wins.

Player 1

0 0 0

Player 2

0 0 0

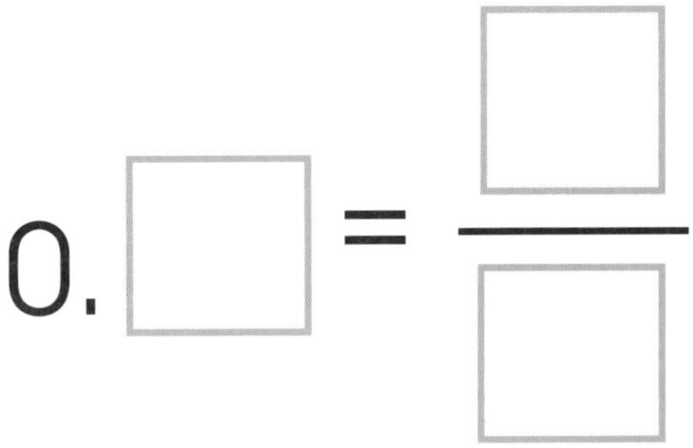

0.01	0.02	0.03	0.04	0.05	0.06	0.07	0.08	0.09	0.10
0.11	0.12	0.13	0.14	0.15	0.16	0.17	0.18	0.19	0.20
0.21	0.22	0.23	0.24	0.25	0.26	0.27	0.28	0.29	0.30
0.31	0.32	0.33	0.34	0.35	0.36	0.37	0.38	0.39	0.40
0.41	0.42	0.43	0.44	0.45	0.46	0.47	0.48	0.49	0.50
0.51	0.52	0.53	0.54	0.55	0.56	0.57	0.58	0.59	0.60
0.61	0.62	0.63	0.64	0.65	0.66	0.67	0.68	0.69	0.70
0.71	0.72	0.73	0.74	0.75	0.76	0.77	0.78	0.79	0.80
0.81	0.82	0.83	0.84	0.85	0.86	0.87	0.88	0.89	0.90
0.91	0.92	0.93	0.94	0.95	0.96	0.97	0.98	0.99	1.00

To prep: Copy on card stock for durability and laminate so students can use dry-erase markers. Cut off these directions before copying and laminating.

Comparing Decimals

Essential Question

How is comparing decimals the same as and different from comparing whole numbers?

Warm-Up/Review

Place students in pairs. Give each pair a set of dice. Have students roll the dice to create 4-digit numbers. Then, have students compare to find the larger number. Repeat several times.

Mini-Lesson

1. Write *$16.02* and *$14.99* on the board. Ask, "Which amount would you rather have? Why?" Guide students to understand that they used the whole numbers (16 and 14) to make their decision. Ask, "Did it matter that 99¢ is greater than 2¢? Why not?" Repeat several times with larger amounts.
2. Write *562.3* and *601.89* on the board. Have students identify the larger number. If students struggle, model adding the 0 in the hundredths place in 562.3 and adding dollar signs. Explain, "Just like in comparing whole numbers and amounts of money, you look at the largest place value first. Here, 6 hundreds is greater than 5 hundreds, so 601.89 is greater."
3. Have students compare 61.2 and 61.20. Record the numbers on a place value chart. Emphasize that the 0 is a placeholder. Because 2 tenths and 20 hundredths are equivalent, the numbers are equal.
4. Repeat step 3 with 28.9 and 28.09. Explain that 9 tenths, or 90 hundredths, is greater than 9 hundredths, so 28.9 is greater.
5. Give students several more pairs of decimals to compare independently. Address any misconceptions, encouraging students to use a place value chart to align and compare decimals easily.

Math Talk

How do you know that number is greater?

Can you draw a model to justify your answer?

Explain how place value helps you compare these decimals.

Journal Prompt

Which prize would you rather win: $410 or $399.99? Why?

Materials

laminated number lines
dry-erase markers
large and small tenths grids

Workstations

Activity sheets (pages 125–127)
Comparison War (page 128)
Money, Money, Money! (page 116)

Guided Math

Remediation: Using a Number Line

1. Give each student a number line and display the decimals *5.6* and *7.8*. Ask, "Which two benchmark whole numbers are these decimals between?" (5 and 10, or 0 and 10) Have students use those benchmarks to create a number line with whole numbers.
2. Have students place each decimal on the number line, explaining that they don't have to be exact. Knowing that 5.6 is a little over halfway between 5 and 6, and 7.8 is closer to 8 is good enough. Guide students to look at the number line and identify the larger number. State, "5.6 is closer to 0 than 7.8. So, 7.8 is greater than 5.6." Record the comparison with a symbol.
3. Repeat with several more decimal pairs, guiding students to look at the whole number to compare before involving the decimal. Encourage students to identify and use benchmark numbers to mentally consider each number before comparing.

On Level: Justifying Comparisons

1. Have students compare 42.3 and 74.3. Then, have students explain how they found their answer. Explain and model each strategy, such as using place value, lining up the decimal and comparing the whole numbers first, using a number line, or drawing a model.
2. Next, have students compare 18.4 and 19.04. Students should justify their answer by using one of the strategies explained in step 1. Have students share their method with a partner. Then, challenge students to justify their comparison using a different method.
3. Repeat step 2 with several more pairs of decimals, including 501.56 and 501.6; and 92.1 and 92.10.

Enrichment: Identifying the Whole

1. Write *0.5* and *0.5* and ask students to compare the decimals.
2. Then, show a pizza with eight slices. Ask, "Would you rather have 0.5 of a slice, or 0.5 of a pizza?" Explain, "With the pizza example, these decimals are not equal." Color in half of a slice of pizza. Color in half of the pizza with a second color. Say, "Understanding what you are comparing is important when comparing numbers."
3. Show a large tenths grid and a smaller tenths grid. Color in 0.3 on the large grid. Color in 0.4 on the smaller grid. Ask, "Can we compare 0.3 and 0.4? Why not?" (No, because they are from different wholes.)
4. Say, "Tia used 4.75 yards of fabric to make curtains. Seth used 4.8 yards of the same fabric to make a costume. Who used more fabric? What are we comparing? (Amount of fabric used) Is it the same type of fabric? (Yes) Does it matter what they made with the fabric? (No)" Have students compare the decimals and record the comparison using a symbol.

Assess and Extend

Which is larger: 903.56 or 905.81? How do you know?

Name ______________________ Date ____________

Comparing Decimals

Using a Number Line

Write the missing decimals.

1.

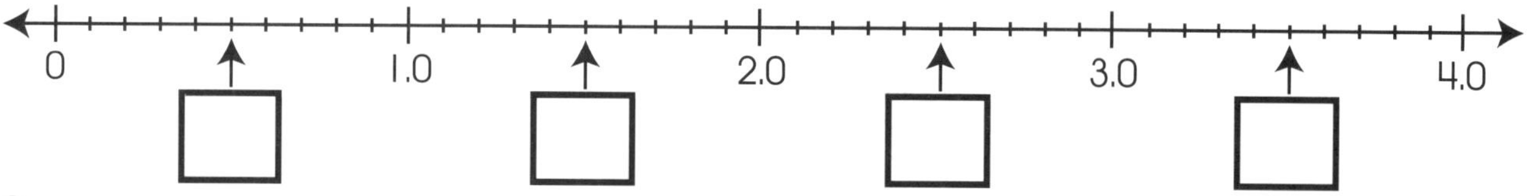

2.

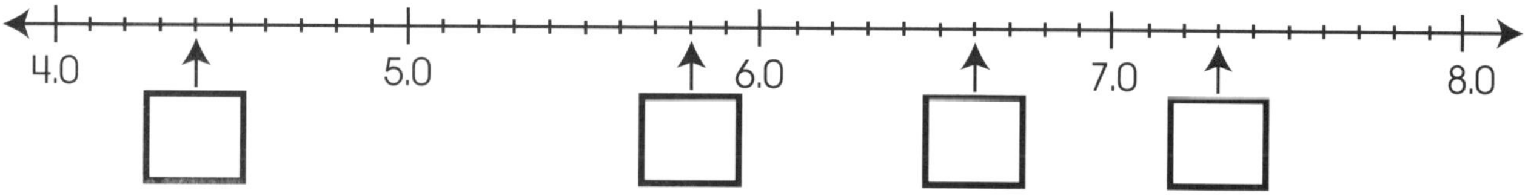

Write the numbers in order from least to greatest.

3. 2.0 0.5 1.0 1.5

4. 2.5 1.5 2.0 3.0

5. 3.0 3.5 2.5 0.5

6. 3.5 2.5 5.5 4.5 4.0

Use <, >, or = to compare.

7. 1.2 ◯ 1.8

8. 2.2 ◯ 1.9

9. 6.5 ◯ 6.50

10. 4.7 ◯ 7.4

Name ______________________ Date ______________

Comparing Decimals

Justifying Comparisons

Use <, >, or = to compare.

1. 0.6 ◯ 0.4	**2.** 0.1 ◯ 0.5	**3.** 0.23 ◯ 0.03
4. 0.6 ◯ 0.9	**5.** 0.06 ◯ 0.60	**6.** 0.4 ◯ 0.7
7. 22.31 ◯ 22.18	**8.** 1.4 ◯ 1.7	**9.** 5.6 ◯ 5.8
10. 0.72 ◯ 0.27	**11.** 0.25 ◯ 0.52	**12.** 0.7 ◯ 0.3
13. 9.4 ◯ 9.9	**14.** 4.7 ◯ 4.2	**15.** 34.93 ◯ 49.04

Name ______________________________ Date ______________

Comparing Decimals

▲ Identifying the Whole

Write *Y* if you can compare the numbers and *N* if you cannot. If you write *Y*, use <, >, or = to compare.

1.

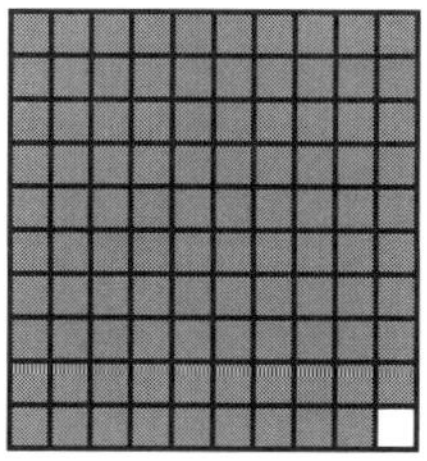

◯

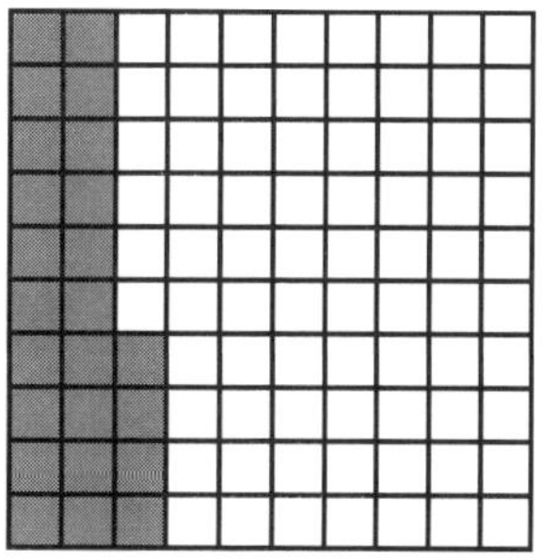

____

2. Mr. Irving's class ate 0.62 of the pizzas. ◯ Mrs. Lang's class ate 0.4 of the pizzas. ________

3. Cole drank 0.78 of a liter of water. ◯ India drank 0.7 of a liter of lemonade. ________

4.

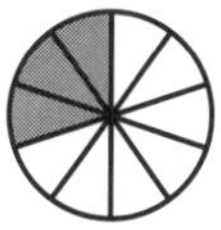

◯

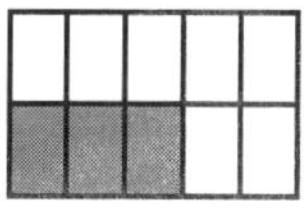

____

Use <, >, or = to compare.

5. 3.4 ◯ 4.5 **6.** 6.01 ◯ 2.06 **7.** 5.01 ◯ 5.09

8. 3.02 ◯ 2.03 **9.** 0.567 ◯ 0.563 **10.** 56.001 ◯ 56.01

11. 3.003 ◯ 3.003 **12.** 5.9 ◯ 5.09 **13.** 6.01 ◯ 2.06

14. 1.456 ◯ 1.665 **15.** 8.076 ◯ 8.076 **16.** 2.798 ◯ 2.709

Comparison War

To play: Shuffle the cards and deal half of the deck facedown to each player. Each player should place their deck facedown in front of them. Players flip over their top card at the same time. The player with the greatest decimal takes both cards and places them facedown at the bottom of her deck. If the decimals are equal, both players place two cards from their deck facedown and a third card faceup. The player with the greatest decimal takes all eight cards. Play until one player has all of the cards, or until time is up (in which case, the player with the most cards wins).

0.1	0.24	0.16	0.6	0.70
0.32	0.88	0.77	0.27	0.22
0.79	0.35	0.8	0.89	0.83
0.4	0.40	0.7	0.11	0.10
0.5	0.80	0.38	0.57	0.64
0.13	0.61	0.60	0.75	0.46

To prep: Copy on card stock for durability. Cut apart the cards and place in a center with the directions. Discard these directions. To make multiple sets, copy on different colors of card stock.

Converting Measurements

Essential Question

What is a system of measurement, and how are units related?

Warm-Up/Review

Program index cards with different units, such as *meters, liters, gallons,* etc. Give each student a card. Challenge students to find other students with similar measurements. Have each group name their group, give their criteria for membership, and identify what their units are used to measure.

Mini-Lesson

Materials: metersticks, yardsticks, 12-in. rulers, measuring cups, clocks

1. Place students in small groups and give each group a meterstick to look at. Write *1 m = ____ cm* on the board. Have students look at the meterstick to answer the question. (100)
2. Challenge students to figure out how many centimeters are in 2, 5, 6, and 10 meters. (200, 500, 600, 1,000) Then, have groups work together to come up with a rule for converting meters to centimeters. Encourage students to think of conversion in terms of multiplication. ($m \times 100 = cm$)
3. Next, challenge groups to solve the problem *4 m + 50 cm = ____ cm.* (450) Allow groups to share their answers and the strategies they used to find the answer.
4. Repeat steps 1–3 to practice converting other common measurements, such as customary length, capacity, and time.

Math Talk

How is that unit related to __? Is it larger or smaller?

Can you think of a time you might need to convert between __ and __?

Explain in your own words how to change from __ to __.

Journal Prompt

Wyatt's dad measured the top of the windows as 7 feet from the floor. At the fabric store, they measure fabric in yards. Explain how Wyatt can use his dad's measurement to figure out how many yards of fabric he should buy.

Materials

copies of measurement units list (see below)
scissors
blank paper
glue

Workstations

Activity sheets (pages 131–133)
Conversion River Run (page 134)

Guided Math

Remediation: Using Models to Convert

1. Give each student a list of measurement units and have students cut them apart. Then, work with students to organize the units by what they measure (length, weight, capacity, etc.) and by customary and metric. If necessary, review the difference between customary and metric units.
2. Next, have students sort the units from smallest to largest within each group and glue each group to the blank paper. Review the simple conversion amounts, such as 100 cm = 1 m, 12 in. = 1 ft., 1,000 mL = 1 L, 60 min. = 1 hr., etc., and have students record them beside each group to create a reference page.
3. Ask, "How many feet are in 8 yards?" Model drawing a rectangle to represent the total length. Draw lines to divide the rectangle into 8 sections. Say, "I know each yard is 3 feet, so I can write 3 in each section. Then, I can add or multiply 3 times 8 to find the total. There are 24 feet in 8 yards."
4. Guide students through drawing bar diagrams to solve the following conversions: 5 m = __ cm (500); 3 L = __ mL (3,000); 6 hr. = __ min. (360)

On Level: Using a Table

1. Explain that students can use charts to find patterns and convert measurements. Draw a 2-column chart and label the columns *kilometers* and *meters*. Say, "One kilometer is equal to 1,000 meters." Record *1* and *1,000* on the chart. Continue filling in the chart for 2 meters, 3, 4, etc.
2. Ask, "What do you notice about kilometers and meters?" (as kilometers increase by 1, meters increase by 1,000; kilometers times 1,000 equals the meters; etc.) Guide students to find a multiplication sentence to describe the conversion.
3. Say different amounts of kilometers, and have students use the chart to convert it to meters.
4. Repeat steps 1–3 with other unit pairs, such as inches and feet, feet and yards, liters and milliliters, hours and minutes, etc.

Enrichment: Solving Measurement Problems

1. Say, "Raul ran 2 miles last week. His sister ran 7,500 feet. Who ran farther? How much farther?"
2. Have students identify the important numbers (2 miles, 7,500 feet) and what they are solving for (who ran farther, and by how much). Emphasize including the units with the important numbers. Point out how the numbers can't be compared until they are in the same unit.
3. Explain, "I know there are 5,280 feet in 1 mile. So, I can multiply 2 by 5,280 to find out how many feet Raul ran. (10,560) He ran more than his sister, since 10,560 is greater than 7,500. Now, I can subtract his sister's distance from his to find out how much farther he ran." (3,060 ft.)
4. Have students use conversion to solve the following problem: *Fluffy drank 1,200 milliliters of water. Sunny drank 1,800 milliliters of water. Pogo drank 900 milliliters of water. Did the dogs drink more or less than 3 liters of water?* (more, 3,900 mL > 3,000 mL)

Assess and Extend

Convert *2 m + 60 cm* to centimeters. (260 cm) Explain how you solved the problem.

Name ______________________ Date ____________

Converting Measurements

Using Models to Convert

Give the equivalent for each measurement. Use a model if needed.

1. 3 ft. = __________ in.

2. 3 yd = __________ ft.

3. 10 km = __________ m

4. 6 km = __________ m

5. 10 ft. = __________ in.

6. 5 yd. = __________ ft.

7. 5 m = __________ cm

8. 70 m = __________ cm

9. 3 hr. = __________ min.

10. 2 L = __________ mL

11. 10 hr. = __________ min

12. 4 L = __________ mL

Use >, <, or = to compare.

13. 2 m ◯ 200 cm

14. 4 m ◯ 50 cm

15. 1 m ◯ 150 cm

16. 3 km ◯ 3 m

17. 12 ft. ◯ 4 yd.

18. 1 mi. ◯ 1,700 ft.

19. 62 in. ◯ 5 ft.

20. 72 in. ◯ 24 yd.

21 3 L ◯ 300 mL

22. 5,000 mL ◯ 5 L

23. 120 min. ◯ 3 hr.

24. $2\frac{1}{2}$ hr. ◯ 200 min.

Name ______________________ Date ____________

Converting Measurements

Using a Table

Complete a table for each set of conversions. Then, use the table and the patterns you notice to convert or compare the measurements.

1.

meters	centimeters

2. 1,000 cm = ____________ m

3. 8 m = ____________ cm

4. 1 m ◯ 150 cm

5. 30 cm ◯ 3 m

6.

yards	feet	inches

7. 4 yd. = ____________ in.

8. 48 ft. = ____________ yd.

9. 11 ft. ◯ 100 in.

10. 5 yd. ◯ 15 ft.

11.

liters	milliliters

12. 3 L = ____________ mL

13. 10,000 mL = ____________ L

14. 6 L ◯ 600 mL

15. 2,500 mL ◯ 3 L

16.

hours	minutes

17. 5 hr. = ____________ min.

18. 360 min. = ____________ hr.

19. 400 min. ◯ 4 hr.

20. 2 hr. ◯ 150 min.

Name ______________________ Date ____________

Converting Measurements

▲ Solving Measurement Problems

Solve each problem.

1. Brad read for 2 hours and 45 minutes. Brooke read for 200 minutes. Who read the longest?

2. Amira has 250 inches of ribbon. She uses 6 yards for a project. How many inches of ribbon does she have left?

3. A bridge has a weight limit of $2\frac{1}{2}$ tons. The delivery truck weighs 6,250 pounds fully loaded. Can the truck safely cross the bridge?

4. Felipe is making orange juice. If he has 2 gallons of juice, how many 1-cup servings can he pour?

5. The sugar cookie has 3,000 milligrams of sugar in it. Is that more or less than the oatmeal cookie, which has 2 grams of sugar?

6. The new lion at the zoo weighed 47 ounces when it was born. The zoo said an average lion cub weighs 3 pounds at birth. Was the new lion cub average, or was it above or below average? By how much?

7. Carla has a piece of yarn that measures 18 centimeters. Her brother Dion has a piece of yarn that is 275 millimeters long. Who has the longer piece of yarn? How much longer is it?

8. Four fourth-graders competed in a running long jump contest. But, some distances were recorded in feet, while others were recorded in inches. Use the chart to figure out who placed first, second, third, and fourth in the contest.

Ansley	11 ft. 9 in.	**Jawan**	140 in.
Nora	139 in.	**Reid**	11 ft. 4 in.

Conversion River Run

Materials: 2 or 3 sets of number cards 0–9, 1 counter per player

To play: Place the counters on Start. Players take turns. Shuffle the conversion cards and the number cards and place each set in a stack facedown. Player 1 draws one conversion card and two number cards. Use the first number card drawn in the tens place, and the second in the ones place to create a two-digit number. Then, use that number to complete the conversion on the conversion card. If correct, move forward 1 space. If not, lose a turn. Reshuffle the sets of cards as needed. The first player to reach Finish wins.

kilometers to meters	meters to centimeters	centimeters to millimeters	kilograms to grams	liters to milliliters	miles to yards	miles to feet	yards to feet	yards to inches	feet to inches
pounds to ounces	pints to cups	quarts to cups	gallons to cups	quarts to pints	gallons to pints	gallons to quarts	hours to minutes	hours to seconds	minutes to seconds

To prep: Copy on card stock for durability. Cut the cards out and place in a center with the game board and other materials. Discard these directions.

Area and Perimeter

Essential Question

How are area and perimeter related?

Warm-Up/Review

Give students rulers and have them measure their desktops to find the area and perimeter. (Use math textbook covers instead if students use large shared tables instead of individual desks.)

Mini-Lesson

Materials: graph paper

1. Give each student a sheet of graph paper. Explain that each square on the paper is 1 unit tall by 1 unit wide. Remind students that *perimeter* measures the distance around the outside of a shape.
2. Draw a 5 x 1 rectangle. Explain, "If you start at one corner of this rectangle and walk all the way around it along the border, how far would you walk?" Count the outside units of the rectangle and show how they add up to 12. Then, show how the formula finds the same perimeter ($P = (2 \times l) + (2 \times w)$).
3. Have students draw all other rectangles they can find with a perimeter of 12. Allow students to share, and record the dimensions of each rectangle. (5 x 1, 4 x 2, 3 x 3)
4. Next, ask students to count the squares inside each rectangle. Remind students that *area* is the space inside the rectangle. It is written in square units because you are counting the entire square as a unit. Find and record the area for the 5 x 1 rectangle. Model counting the squares. Then, show how the formula finds the same area ($A = l \times w$).
5. Have students find the areas of the remaining rectangles. Allow students to share, and have them give the related multiplication sentence for each rectangle.
6. Continue finding the area and perimeter of other rectangles, including rectilinear figures.

Math Talk

How did you find the area/perimeter?
How would your method change for a square? Why?
How are area and perimeter the same? Different?
Is there another strategy you can use?

Journal Prompt

A 35-square-foot rug covers the floor in a room. The room is 7 feet long. How wide is it? How do you know?

Materials

index cards
graph paper
markers

Workstations

Activity sheets (pages 137–139)
Room Designer (page 140)

Guided Math

Remediation: Finding Area and Perimeter

1. Give each student an index card. Reinforce the difference between area and perimeter by having students write *perimeter* repeatedly around the border of the card, and write *area* large enough to fill the inside space. Explain, "Perimeter measures the distance around a shape. Area measures the space a shape covers." Have students record the definitions in their own words on the backs of their cards.
2. Give each student graph paper. Have them draw a rectangle with a width of 8 and a length of 6. Students should trace the perimeter in blue marker, and solve for the perimeter in blue. (28 units) Then, have students color the inside of the shape red, and solve for the area in red. (48 sq. units)
3. Remind students of the formulas for solving for area and perimeter and the units for each. If desired, have students add the formulas and units to the backs of their index cards.
4. Give students several more rectangles with varying dimensions to solve for area and perimeter. Encourage students to move from counting spaces to using the formulas.

On Level: Finding Missing Measurements

1. Give each student graph paper. Tell them to draw a rectangle with an area of 24 square units.
2. Allow students to share the dimensions of their rectangles as well as their strategy for finding a rectangle with the correct area. List the dimensions of each rectangle. (1 x 24, 2 x 12, 3 x 8, 4 x 6) Ask, "What do you notice about the dimensions?" (They are all the factors of 24.)
3. Ask, "Which rectangle would I be talking about if I said it had an area of 24, and a width of 3? What is the length? How do you know?" Explain that because $A = l \times w$, you can use the known factors of a number to find the missing factor. Direct students to look at the problem as an unknown factor problem: "What number times this equals the area?"
4. Ask, "What is the length of a rectangle with an area of 36 and a width of 4?" (9) Allow students to use their graph paper as needed, but encourage them to move towards using multiplication facts. Repeat with several more rectangles and squares with missing side lengths.

Enrichment: Area and Perimeter of Irregular Figures

1. Draw an irregular figure with multiple sides and angles on graph paper. A good example is a block letter *E*. Ask students to determine the area and perimeter of the shape.
2. Draw a similar irregular figure on plain paper. Label a few of the sides but not all of them. Ask, "What do you need to know to find the perimeter of this shape? How can the given measurements help you determine the missing ones?" Help students add, subtract, and compare the known measurements to calculate all of the side lengths and determine the perimeter of the shape.
3. Now, ask, "How can we find the area?" Show students how to divide irregular figures into rectangular chunks. Find the areas of the smaller sections and add them together to find the total area of the irregular figure.
4. Challenge students to draw their own irregular figures, label only a few sides, and trade with partners to solve for perimeter and area.

Assess and Extend

Virginia's book is 12 inches tall and 8 inches wide. Mason's book is 10 inches tall and 9 inches wide. How do the areas of their books compare? Perimeters? (Virginia: $A = 96$ sq. in., $P = 40$ in.; Mason: $A = 90$ sq. in., $P = 38$ in.)

Name ______________________ Date ______________

Area and Perimeter

Finding Area and Perimeter

Find the area and the perimeter of each rectangle.

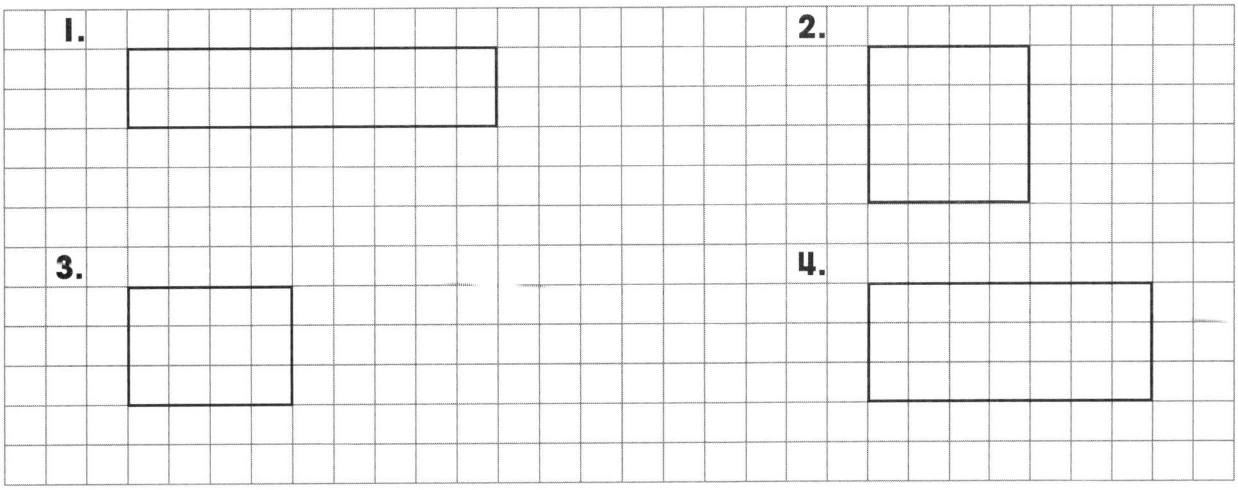

1. Area = ____________ square units

   Perimeter = ____________ units

2. Area = ____________ square units

   Perimeter = ____________ units

3. Area = ____________ square units

   Perimeter = ____________ units

4. Area = ____________ square units

   Perimeter = ____________ units

5.

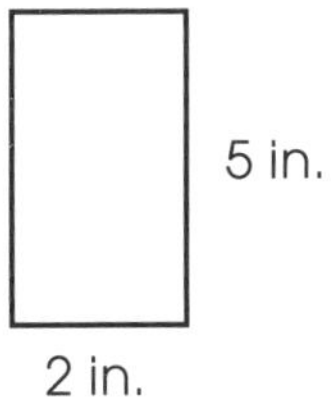

Area = ______________________

Perimeter = ______________________

6.

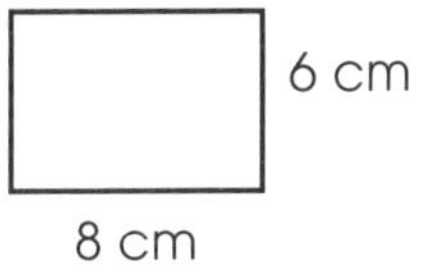

Area = ______________________

Perimeter = ______________________

7.

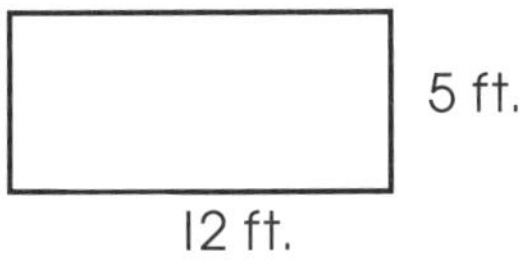

Area = ______________________

Perimeter = ______________________

8.

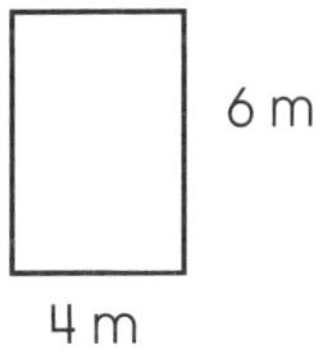

Area = ______________________

Perimeter = ______________________

Name ____________________ Date ____________

Area and Perimeter

Finding Missing Measurements

Find the missing measurement for each rectangle.

1. 3 cm

A = 15 square cm

length = ____________

2. 9 mm

A = 36 square mm

width = ____________

3. 2 in.

A = 8 square in.

width = ____________

4.

A = 49 square ft.

width = ____________

length = ____________

5. 8 cm

A = 80 square cm

length = ____________

6. 7 m

A = 35 square m

width = ____________

7. 4 in.

A = 24 square in.

length = ____________

8. 8 mm

A = 56 square mm

length = ____________

9.

A = 36 square m

width = ____________

length = ____________

10. 6 ft.

A = 54 square ft.

width = ____________

Name ______________________ Date ______________

Area and Perimeter

▲ Area and Perimeter of Irregular Figures

Find the area of each figure.

1.

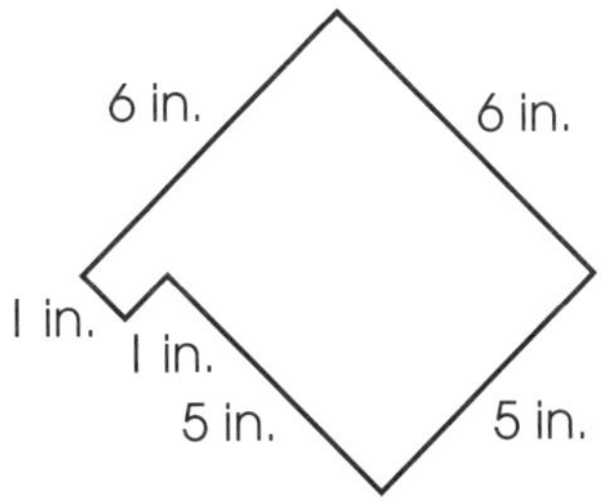

A = ______________

2.

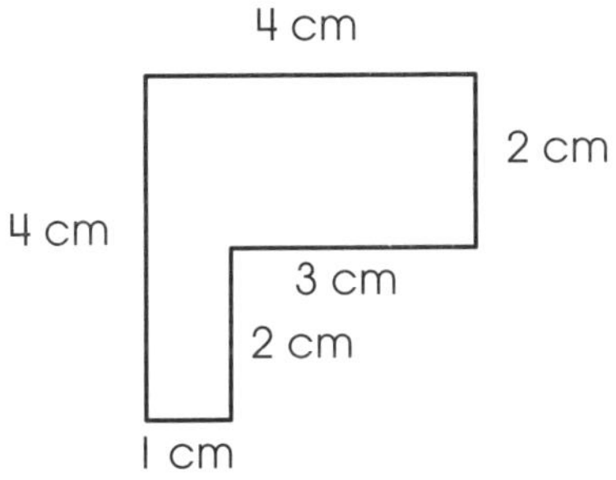

A = ______________

3.

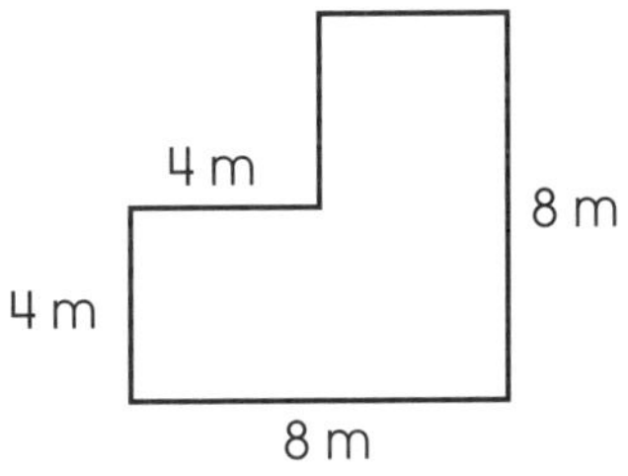

A = ______________

4.

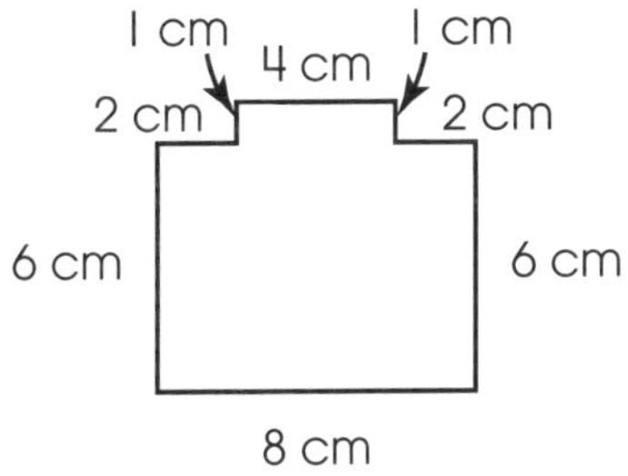

A = ______________

5.

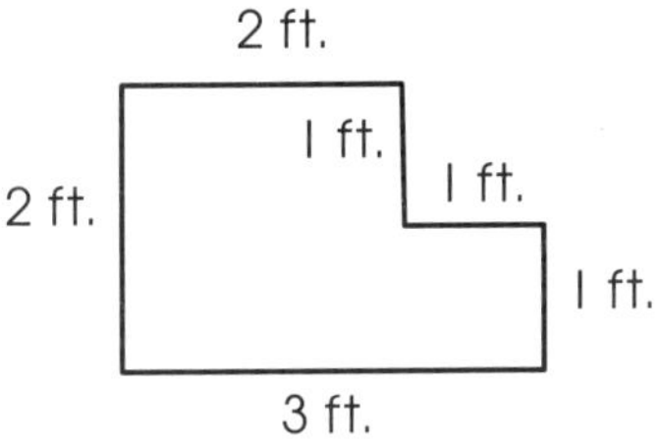

A = ______________

6.

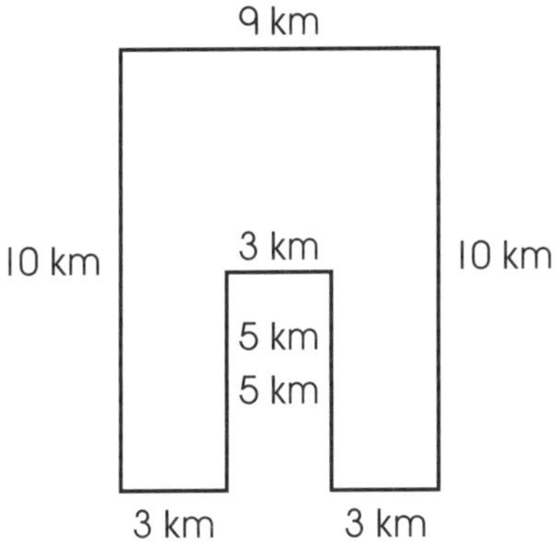

A = ______________

7.

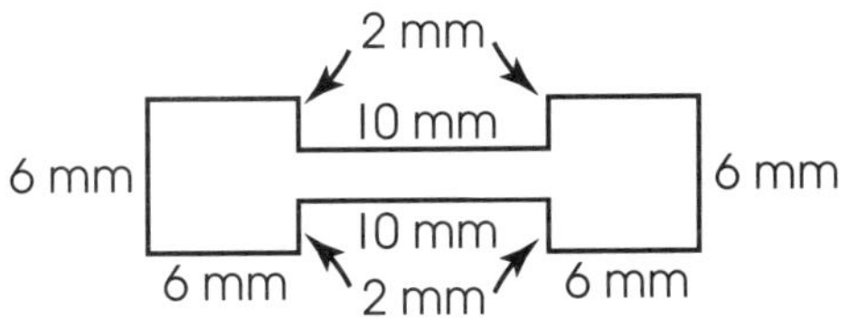

A = ______________

8.

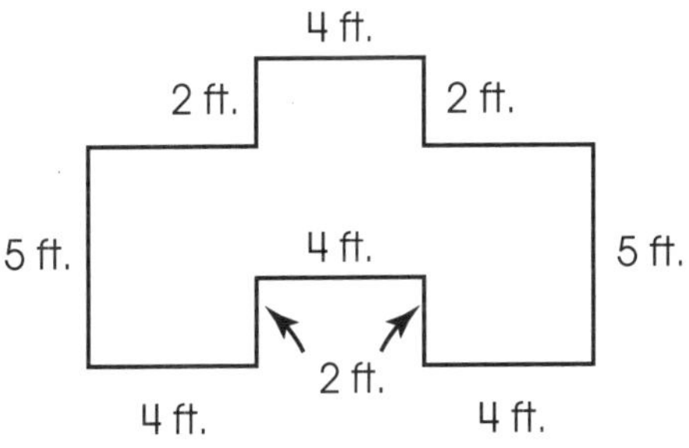

A = ______________

Room Designer

Materials: 1 die

To play: Roll the die. The number you roll is the type of room you will design. Use the grid to create the room. Pretend you are looking at the room from the ceiling. Draw borders and add furniture and decorations. Then, use the room to answer the questions.

 bedroom	 classroom	 library
 living room	 restaurant	 den/ playroom

1. What is the perimeter of your room? ____________________

The area? ____________________

2. Which piece of furniture takes up the most space? ____________________

The least? ____________________

3. How much flooring would you need to buy? ____________________

4. How much floor space is left empty? ____________________

5. Choose two pieces of furniture. Name each one and give the area and perimeter of each.

______________ $A =$ ______________ $P =$ ______________

______________ $A =$ ______________ $P =$ ______________

Working with Line Plots

Essential Question

What types of information are best shown on a line plot?

Warm-Up/Review

Give students laminated blank number lines and dry-erase markers. Challenge students to make each of the following number lines: with a non-zero start; with a scale of 5; from 0 to 100; etc.

Mini-Lesson

Materials: rulers, sticky notes, laminated number lines, dry-erase markers

1. Have students measure their pencils to the nearest quarter inch and write the length on their sticky notes. Ask who has the shortest and the longest pencils, and record those amounts on the board. Explain, "A line plot would show this data well because our data is numbers, not categories, and we want to show frequency, or how often a data point occurs."
2. Review the main parts of a line plot (*number line, title, axis label*, and *data points*). Draw a blank line plot on the board. Say, "First, we determine what section of the number line best fits the data. We can look at the lowest and highest data points and use those as boundaries."
3. Guide students to use the highest and lowest numbers and complete the number line. Explain that amounts that do not have any data still need to be shown so that the number line is unbroken.
4. Have students add their sticky notes to the line plot. Then, replace the sticky notes with Xs. Emphasize the importance of lining up the Xs horizontally. Ask questions such as: "Which length occurs the most? The least? How many students have pencils longer than __?" etc.
5. Have students work with a partner to measure all of the writing utensils in their desks and create a new line plot on the blank number lines.

Math Talk

What are your benchmarks? Why?
What do these represent?
Give one true statement about the line plot and explain how you know.
Can we leave out this number on the number line? Why not?

Journal Prompt

Brianna wants to graph how much snow fell each hour during a blizzard. Is a line plot the best choice? Why or why not? If not, which type of graph would be better?

Materials

colored fraction rods
blank laminated line plots
dry-erase markers
rulers
paper strips
scissors

Workstations

Activity sheets (pages 143–145)
Line Plot Creator (page 146)

Guided Math

Remediation: Concrete Line Plots

1. Choose a random assortment of colored fraction rods. Have students sort the rods by length and place the groups in order from shortest to longest. Then, guide students to place each group in order by length, placing the rods horizontally so they clearly show frequency.
2. Say, "Using the actual objects makes the line plot large and difficult to read. So, mathematicians use an *X* to represent each object. But, we need to know what the *X* represents, so first we need to measure each rod and label the group." Measure a rod from each group to the nearest half-inch and label the line plot. Then, replace each rod with an *X*.
3. Point out the marks on a ruler and explain how a ruler is like a number line. When plotting items by length, students can use the ruler to help create a line plot.
4. Give each student a random set of rods and have them repeat steps 1 and 2. Encourage students to use the ruler and skip the step of making the concrete line plot when they are ready.

On Level: Creating and Interpreting Line Plots

1. Give each student a random assortment of colored fraction rods and a ruler. Have students measure the length of each rod to the nearest quarter of an inch and record the measurements.
2. Model creating a line plot to show the data. Point out the highest and lowest numbers, mark them, and mark the measurements in between. Then, plot your data. Have students repeat with their line plots and data.
3. Then, ask students to use your line plot to answer the following questions: "Which length was most common? Least common? How many rods measured longer than 2 inches? Which length occurred only twice?" etc. Have students use the line plot to justify their answers. Then, have students answer the same questions with their line plots and data.

Enrichment: Working with Data

1. Have each student measure 3 random colored fraction rods to the nearest eighth of an inch. Pool the students' data and have each student use the data to create a line plot, with guidance as necessary.
2. Ask, "How many rods did we measure in all?" Model counting the Xs to find the answer. Then, model finding the answers to the following questions: "What is the difference between the shortest and longest rods we measured? Is the total length of all of the rods greater than 3 inches more or less than 1 foot? What would the total length be if we laid all of the rods end to end?"
3. Give each student a paper strip and scissors. Have students cut their strips into 10 pieces of varying lengths. Then, have students measure their strips to the nearest eighth of an inch and plot the data on a line plot. Finally, have students use their line plots to answer the questions in step 2.

Assess and Extend

Measure the spines of the books in your desk to the nearest half-inch. Then, create a line plot to show the data. Write a true statement about the data.

Name ______________________ Date ____________

Working with Line Plots

● Concrete Line Plots

Use each set of data to complete a line plot.

1. Kasey looked through her grandmother's baking cookbook to see how much sugar is used in the recipes. She recorded how many cups of sugar were called for in each recipe.

$\frac{1}{2}$	$\frac{1}{2}$	1	1	$\frac{1}{2}$
2	$\frac{1}{2}$	$1\frac{1}{2}$	1	$\frac{1}{2}$

2. The students in Mr. Park's class recorded their shoe sizes.

$3\frac{1}{2}$	$4\frac{1}{2}$	4	4	5	3	$5\frac{1}{2}$	$4\frac{1}{2}$
5	$4\frac{1}{2}$	$3\frac{1}{2}$	$4\frac{1}{2}$	4	4	$4\frac{1}{2}$	5

Name ____________________ Date ____________

Working with Line Plots

Creating and Interpreting Line Plots

Use the data to complete a line plot. Then, use the line plot to answer the questions.

Leo's class grew aloe plants. At the end of the month, they measured the heights of the plants in inches.

$2\frac{1}{4}$	2	2	$2\frac{1}{4}$	$2\frac{1}{2}$	$2\frac{3}{4}$	$2\frac{1}{4}$	3
$1\frac{3}{4}$	2	$2\frac{3}{4}$	$2\frac{1}{2}$	$2\frac{1}{4}$	2	$2\frac{1}{4}$	$2\frac{1}{2}$

1. How tall was the shortest plant? ____________ The tallest? ____________

2. Which height was the most common? ____________

3. How many plants were shorter than $2\frac{1}{2}$ inches? ____________

4. How many plants were at least 2 inches tall? ____________

5. Which height occurred exactly three times? ____________

6. Which measurements only had one plant with that height? ____________

7. How many plants did the class measure? ____________

Name ______________________ Date ____________

Working with Line Plots

▲ Working with Data

Use the data to complete a line plot. Then, use the line plot to answer the questions.

Coach Ramirez wants to know how much water his players drink during each game. He measured in cups.

$3\frac{1}{4}$	3	3	$2\frac{3}{4}$	$2\frac{1}{2}$	$3\frac{1}{2}$	$3\frac{1}{4}$
3	2	$3\frac{1}{4}$	$2\frac{3}{4}$	3	$3\frac{1}{4}$	$3\frac{1}{4}$

1. Which amount was the most common? ____________

Least common? ____________

2. How many players are on the team? How do you know? ____________

____

3. Coach Ramirez wants his players to drink at least 3 cups each game. How many players drank enough during this game? ____________

4. How much water did his team drink in all? ____________

5. If Coach brought 3 gallons of water to the game, how much does he have left? (*Hint:* There are 16 cups in a gallon.) ____________

Line Plot Creator

Materials: 1 die

Directions: Create and label the line plot using the fractions given. Roll the die 10 to 20 times. Record each roll on the line plot. Give the line plot a title. Then, use the data to answer the questions.

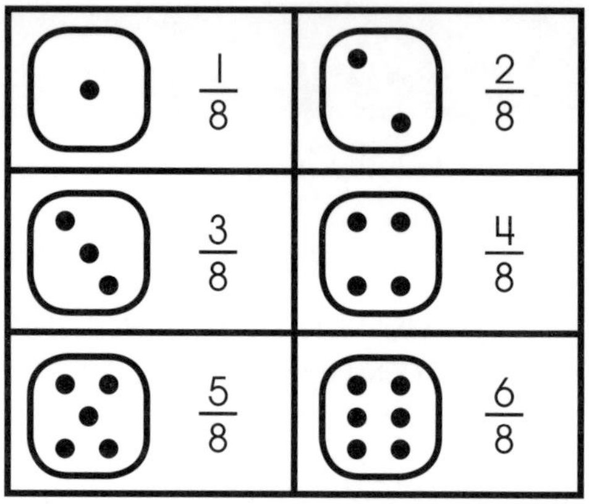

Each eighth represents 1 slice.
A pizza has 8 slices.

____

Title

1. Which amount of slices was the least common?	**2.** Which amount of slices was the most common?
3. How many people ate 2 slices?	**4.** How many people ate more than 4 slices?
5. How many people ate pizza? How do you know?	**6.** How many whole pizzas were eaten? How many slices were left over?

Understanding Angles

Essential Question

What are angles, and how are they measured?

Warm-Up/Review

Have students stand beside their desks and face the front of the room. Say, "Turn one-half turn to the left, turn one-quarter turn to the right," etc., and have students turn the corresponding amount to face a different direction.

Mini-Lesson

Materials: small paper plates (enough for each student to have two)

1. Remind students about the warm-up activity. Ask, "What would I say if I wanted you to turn less than a quarter turn?"
2. Explain, "Just like a circle can be divided into halves, fourths, sixths, eighths, etc., it can continue being divided into much smaller pieces." Point out the clock, and have students figure out how many equal sections it is divided into. (60)
3. Give each student two paper plates. Have them color the face of one plate and leave the other plate blank. Then, fold each plate in half twice to find the center, and cut a straight line from the edge to the center point. Finally, place the blank plate on top of the other with the cuts aligned, and start turning the bottom plate so it slides over the cut line and they are locked together. It should create a colored wedge that can be made larger or smaller.
4. Say, "Mathematicians call the section of a circle an angle. Angles can be large or small." Demonstrate with a set of plates. Point out the vertex (the center of the plates) and each ray that forms the angle (the two cut edges). Have students label each part on their plates. Explain that a circle is divided into 360 equal sections to make it easier to describe the size of an angle. Help students mark the benchmark angles on their plates. (0°, 90°, 180°, 270°, 360°)
5. Have students use the plates to make certain angles, such as an angle larger than 90°, or *an angle between 180° and 270°*.

Math Talk

How are angles related to circles?
What type of angle is this? How do you know?
How is this related to fractions of a circle?

Journal Prompt

Is the corner of your paper an angle? Why or why not?

Materials

chenille stems
pony beads
paper plate angles from the mini-lesson (page 147)
pattern blocks
sticky notes

Workstations

Activity sheets (pages 149–151)
Angles Puzzle (page 152)

Guided Math

Remediation: Forming Angles

1. Give each student two chenille stems and a pony bead. Remind students that an angle is formed by two rays with a common endpoint. Have students form each chenille stem into a ray by making an arrow shape on one end. Then, have students join the rays using the pony bead as a common endpoint (twist the ends together for a permanent join).
2. Explain, "Like the hands of a clock move in a circle when they turn, the rays turn around a circle too. The space in between the rays is the angle." If needed, have students place the angle on top of their paper plate angles to show the colored space and make the angle more visible.
3. Say, "The vertices in polygons are all angles too." Give students pattern blocks and have them use their chenille stem angle to identify and model the angles in each shape.
4. Explain, "Anywhere two lines meet can form one or more angles." Have students explore the room to find several more angles and share what they found.

On Level: Types of Angles

1. Give each student two chenille stems and a pony bead. Have students form an angle using the steps described in step 1 above.
2. Explain, "Mathematicians classify angles into categories by how large or small they are. Angles less than 90° are called *acute angles.* Angles that measure exactly 90° are called *right angles.* Angles that are between 90° and 180° are called *obtuse angles.*" Have students identify 90° and 180° on their paper plate angles. If desired, define *straight angles* (180°), *reflex angles* (181°–359°), and a *full rotation* (360°).
3. Say different angle types and have students model each with their chenille stem angles. Point out that the corner of a paper is a good benchmark for right angles. Give each student a sticky note to help them draw and identify right angles.
4. Then, have students identify and categorize angles around the room.

Enrichment: Estimating Angle Measures

1. Display a right angle. Ask students to estimate how many degrees it is and explain their thinking.
2. Ask, "What would an angle that is 85° look like? How do you know? What about a 95° angle?" Lead students to understand that those angles would be slightly smaller and slightly larger than a right angle.
3. Explain that 45 is exactly halfway between 0 and 90, so an acute angle that measures 45° is halfway between 0° and 90°. Have students draw a 45° angle. Then, challenge students to draw a 30° angle and explain their thinking. Encourage students to use known angle measures to estimate angle measures.
4. Draw several more angles and have students give an estimated measure for each.

Assess and Extend

Identify three angles in the room. Explain how you know each is an angle.

Name ______________________ Date ______________

Understanding Angles

Forming Angles

Label the parts of an angle.

1.

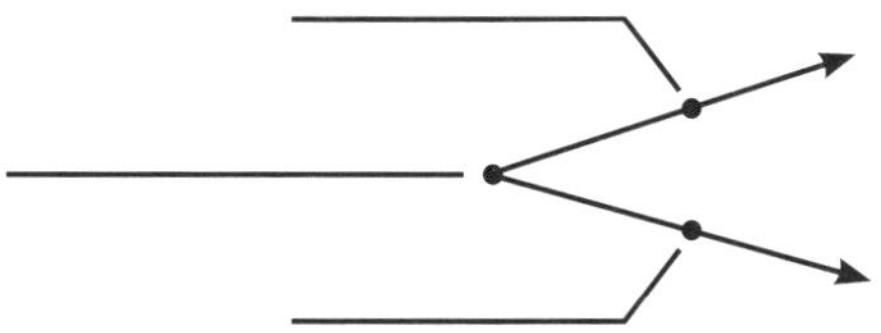

Use a ruler to complete each angle.

2.

3.

4.

Color or highlight the angles in each polygon. Write how many angles each polygon has.

5.

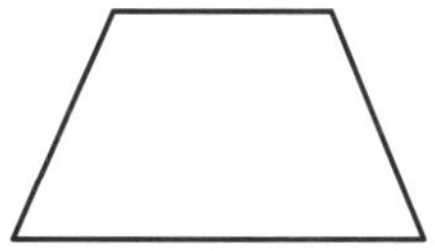

____

6.

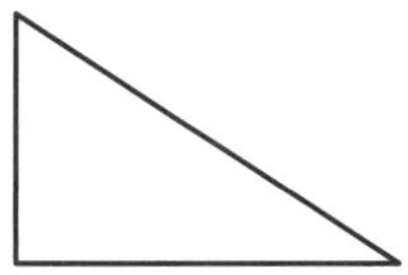

____

7.

____

8.

____

9.

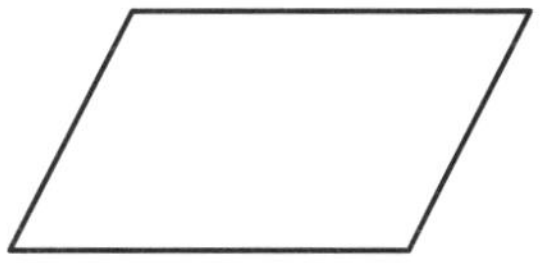

____

10.

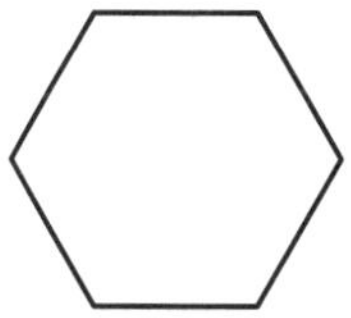

____

Name ______________________ Date ____________

Understanding Angles

Types of Angles

Identify each angle as *acute, right,* or *obtuse.*

1.
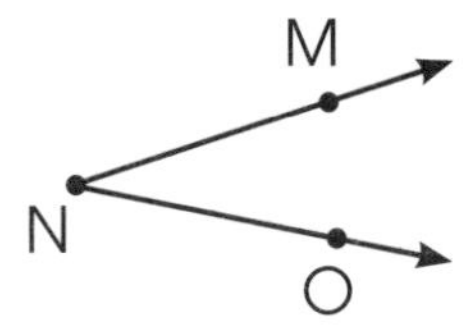

____

2.

____

3.
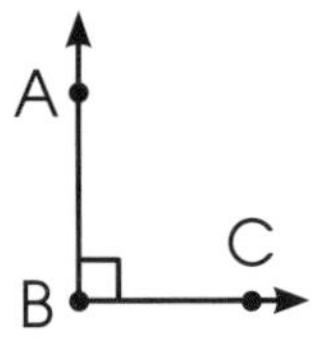

____

4.
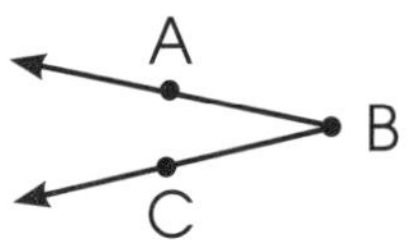

____

5.
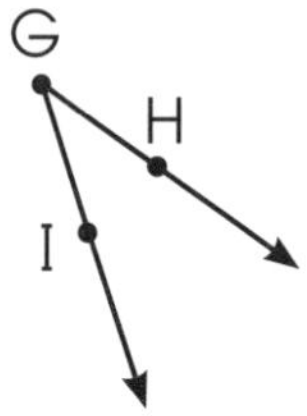

____

6.

____

7.
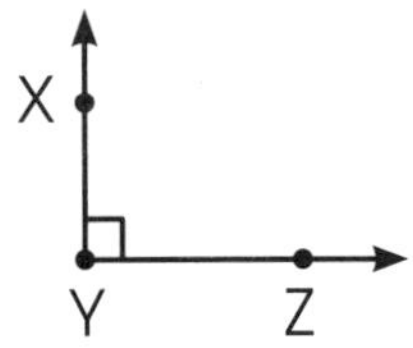

____

8.
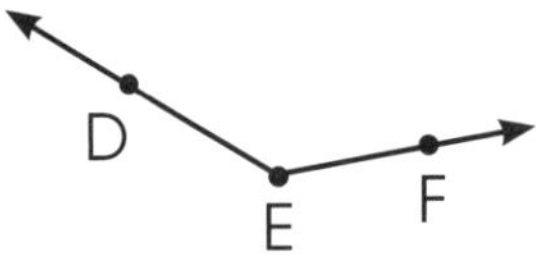

____

9.
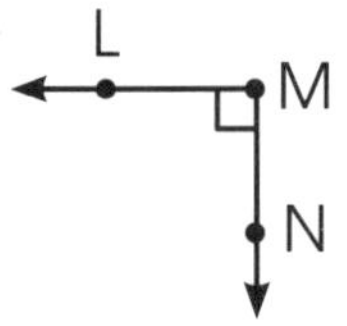

____

10.

____

11.
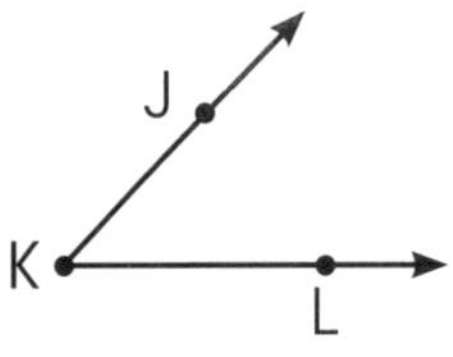

____

12.
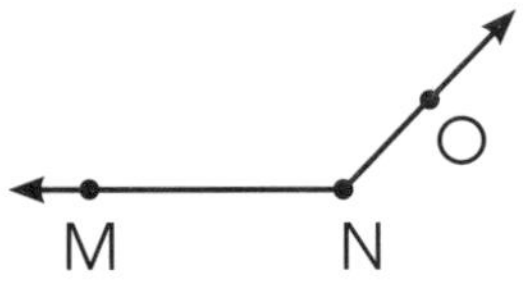

____

Name ____________________ Date ____________

Understanding Angles

▲ Estimating Angle Measures

Estimate the measure of each angle.

1.

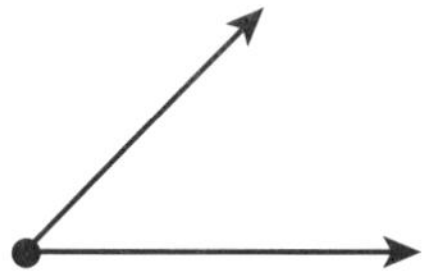

____

2.

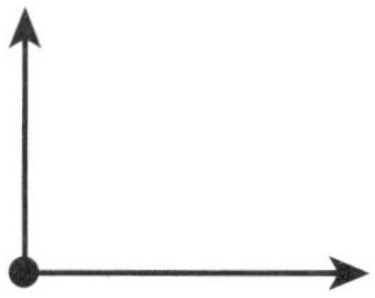

____

3.

____

4.

____

5.

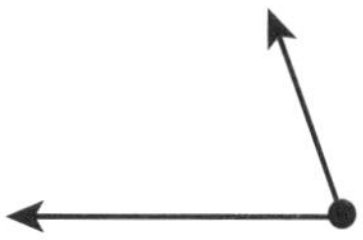

____

6.

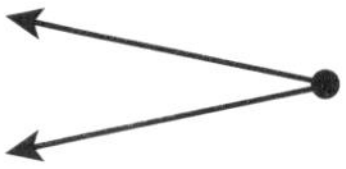

____

7.

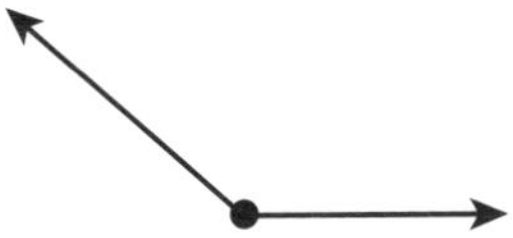

____

8.

____

9.

____

Sketch an angle to match each angle measure. Do not use a protractor.

10. 45°

11. 130°

12. 10°

Angles Puzzle

To play: Assemble the puzzle by matching the question or prompt on one piece to the answer on another piece. The answers are always on the top of each piece. When complete, the puzzle should form a full circle with no gaps and no pieces left over.

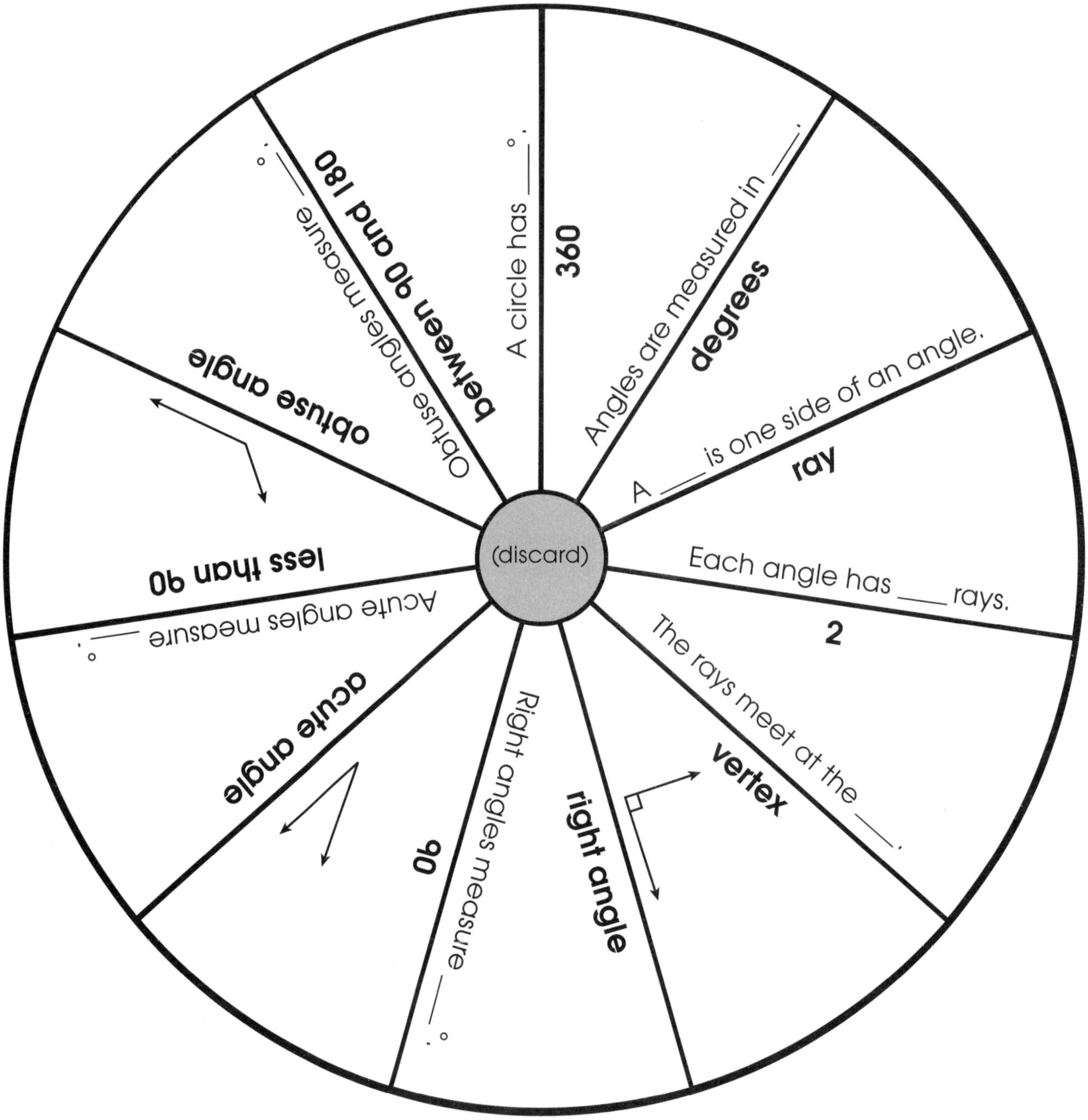

To prep: Copy on card stock for durability. Copy on different colors of card stock to create multiple copies. Cut out the puzzle pieces. Discard the center piece. Place in a center with the directions.

Measuring Angles

Essential Question

How does an angle's measure relate to the fraction of a circle it represents?

Warm-Up/Review

Have each student draw a polygon on a sticky note and exchange with a partner. Have the partner categorize each angle in the polygon. Then, have a third student check it.

Mini-Lesson

Materials: protractors, worksheet with unmeasured angles, sticky notes

1. Review acute, right, and obtuse angles. Explain that those categories are useful for talking about angles, but angles can be measured more accurately.
2. Remind students that there are 360 degrees in a circle. If needed, have students refer to the paper plate angles they created earlier (see page 147). Say, "Angles are measured by the exact amount of degrees they have turned in the circle. So, a 38° angle has turned through 38 out of the 360 degrees in the circle."
3. Give each student a protractor. Explain that this tool is a special ruler for measuring angles. Point out the tick marks, the 0 starting point, the 180 ending point, the semicircular shape, and the larger tick marks for benchmark numbers.
4. Model using the protractor to measure an angle. Emphasize placing the endpoint in the circle at the bottom and aligning one ray with the line at the bottom. Model using the straight edge to extend the ray if needed. If desired, explain to students how to use a sticky note to quickly and easily extend a ray.
5. Guide students to use the protractor to measure several angles on the worksheet. Then, have students work with partners to complete the sheet.

Math Talk

How is the measurement you found related to the fraction of a circle?

Explain what a *degree* is in your own words.

How is a protractor similar to and different from a straight ruler?

Journal Prompt

What angle do the hands make when the clock shows 2:00? (60°) How do you know?

Materials

plastic straw coffee stirrers
chenille stems (cut into 1" pieces)
blank angles
graph paper
black markers
protractors

Workstations

Activity sheets (pages 155–157)
Stained Glass Angles (page 158)

Guided Math

Remediation: Using Protractors

1. Have students place a piece of chenille stem halfway in the end of a coffee stirrer. Then, place the other end through the hole on a protractor and bend it so the coffee stirrer lays flat against the top of the protractor.
2. Give students an angle to measure. Guide them to place the endpoint under the hole (the chenille stem) and align the bottom ray. Then, have students move the coffee stirrer so it aligns with the other ray. Read the measurement.
3. Give students several more angles to measure using the protractor. Encourage students to measure without the stirrer as they become more comfortable using a protractor.

On Level: Using Estimates

1. Give students a sheet of graph paper. Have them write their name in large blocky letters on the graph paper and trace over it with a black marker. Then, have students identify the angles in each letter in their name by drawing a semicircle near the vertex of each.
2. Explain that you can use known benchmark angles, like 45°, 90°, and 180°, to estimate an angle's measure or to check a measurement. Ask, "What would an angle that is 85° look like? How do you know? What about a 95° angle?" Lead students to understand that those angles would be slightly smaller and slightly larger than a right angle.
3. Have students estimate the measure of each angle in their name and record it near the angle. Then, have them measure each angle and use their estimate to judge whether they measured correctly.
4. Explain that keeping estimates in mind is very helpful when trying to decide which set of numbers to use on a protractor. If you know an angle should be close to 45°, then a measure of 130° is obviously incorrect.

Enrichment: Drawing Angles with a Given Measure

1. Say, "You can also use a protractor to draw an angle with a given measure." Model drawing a 55° angle. Use the straight edge to create a ray and mark the endpoint. Then, line the ray and endpoint up, as when measuring an angle. Draw a mark at 55°, and use the straight edge of the protractor to connect the endpoint to the mark.
2. Then, guide students through the steps to create their own 55° angle.
3. Have students draw angles of 65°, 100°, 80°, 175°, and 20°.
4. Then, have students switch papers and use a protractor to measure and check their partner's angles.

Assess and Extend

Give students a page with a large uppercase *A*. Have students identify an angle in the letter and measure it. For a challenge, find and measure all of the angles.

Name ____________________________ Date ______________

Measuring Angles

● Using Protractors

To use a protractor to measure an angle, follow these steps:

1. Find the dot, hole, or intersecting lines along the straight edge on the bottom of the protractor.

2. Place the dot, hole, or intersecting lines over the vertex of the angle.

3. Rotate the protractor so that the 0 mark on the straight edge lines up with one ray of the angle.

4. Find the point where the second ray of the angle intersects the numbered edge of the protractor. If the angle does not extend far enough to intersect the numbered edge, use the protractor as a straight edge to extend the ray. Then, realign the protractor.

5. Read the number that is written on the protractor at the point of intersection. This is the measure of the angle in degrees.

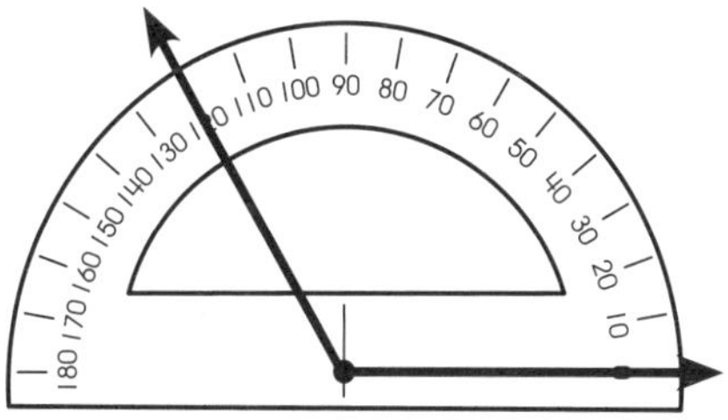

Use a protractor to measure each angle. Then, identify each angle as *acute, right,* or *obtuse.*

1.

________°, ____________

2.

________°, ____________

3.

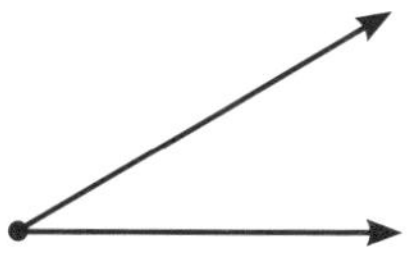

________°, ____________

4.

________°, ____________

5.

________°, ____________

6.

________°, ____________

Name ______________________________ Date ______________

Measuring Angles

Using Estimates

Estimate each angle measure. Then, use a protractor to measure the angle.

1. 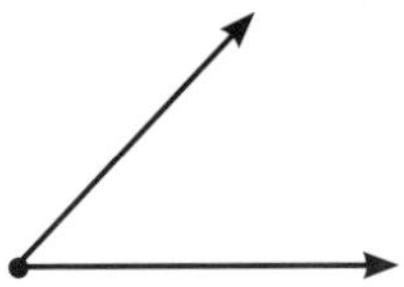

Estimate: ______________

Actual: ______________

2. 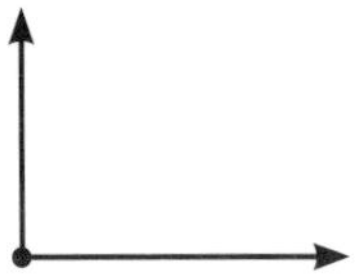

Estimate: ______________

Actual: ______________

3. 

Estimate: ______________

Actual: ______________

4. 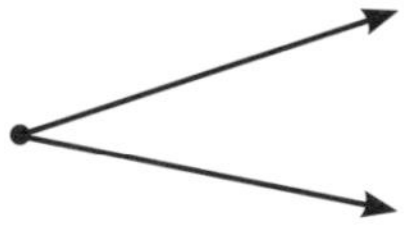

Estimate: ______________

Actual: ______________

5. 

Estimate: ______________

Actual: ______________

6. 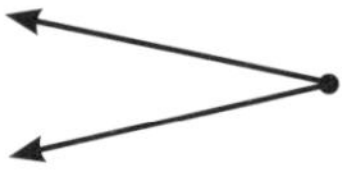

Estimate: ______________

Actual: ______________

7. 

Estimate: ______________

Actual: ______________

8. 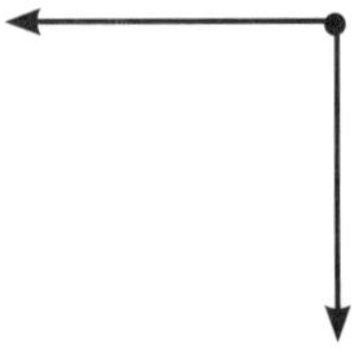

Estimate: ______________

Actual: ______________

9. 

Estimate: ______________

Actual: ______________

10. 

Estimate: ______________

Actual: ______________

11. 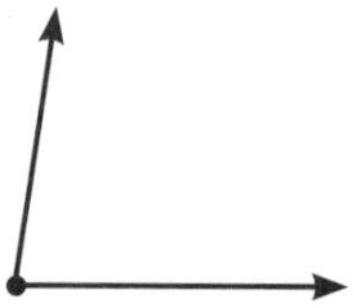

Estimate: ______________

Actual: ______________

12. 

Estimate: ______________

Actual: ______________

Name ______________________ Date ____________

Measuring Angles

▲ Drawing Angles with a Given Measure

Use a protractor to draw an angle with the given measure.

1. 15°	**2.** 30°
3. 100°	**4.** 85°
5. 45°	**6.** 120°
7. 60°	**8.** 175°

Stained Glass Angles

Materials: protractor; sticky notes; crayons, colored pencils, or markers

To play: Find a section you want to color. Use a protractor to measure each angle in the section. To extend a ray without drawing on the design, align the sticky edge of a sticky note with the ray. Label each angle with its measure. Once you have found all of the angles, color the section. Continue until all sections have been colored in. If desired, use graph paper and a ruler to make your own design to measure and color.

Additive Angle Measures

Essential Question

How are angle measures related, and how can that help me solve problems?

Warm-Up/Review

Have students use rulers to draw triangles. Then, students should use protractors to find the measure of each angle in the triangle.

Mini-Lesson

Materials: rulers, blank paper

1. Have students use a ruler to draw a line extending from one corner of their paper. The line can go in any direction. Then, have students find the measure of the two angles they created (using the edges of the page as the two outer rays).
2. Have students add the two angle measures together and share their answer. Then, have students repeat step 1 with a different corner and a line at a different angle. Ask students to identify what they notice (the sum of the two angles is equal to the total angle, or the 90° corner of the paper).
3. Then, have students repeat steps 1 and 2 using the sides of their paper instead of corners. They should draw a line extending from the straight edge in any direction so that the straight edge of the paper forms the two outer rays of the two angles. Those angles should equal 180° when added together, which equals the measure of the straight angle that is the edge of the paper.
4. Explain, "Like fractions, angles can be composed and decomposed. A 26° angle is equal to 26 1-degree angles added together. So, you can add and subtract angle measures to find missing measures."
5. Draw a 120° angle on the board with a 55° angle inside bisecting it. Challenge students to find the missing angle measure. (65°)

Math Talk

How can you relate this to the measure of a circle (360°) and the benchmark angles within it?

Why can you add and subtract angles?

How can this help you solve real-world problems?

Journal Prompt

Describe at least two different ways you can decompose an angle measuring 70°.

Materials

laminated angles (punch holes over the vertices)
chenille stems
brass paper fasteners
protractors
sticky notes (optional)
scissors
rulers
copies of triangles
scissors

Workstations

Activity sheets (pages 161–163)
On the Mark (page 164)

Guided Math

Remediation: Decomposing Angles

1. Give each student a laminated angle, and have them use a protractor to measure the angle.
2. Have each student twist the end of a chenille stem around the base of a brass paper fastener. They should place the fastener through the hole at the vertex of their angle and fasten it to create a moveable ray that bisects the angle.
3. Have students bisect the angle in any way and use a protractor to find the measures of the two angles created by the chenille stem ray. (If needed, use sticky notes to hold the unattached end in place while measuring.) Then, have them add the measures to find the total.
4. Have students repeat step 2 several times with different bisecting angles. Discuss what students notice about the addends and the sum each time (the sum is always the same).

On Level: Finding Missing Angle Measures

1. Have students use a ruler to draw two straight lines in an X shape. The lines can cross at any angle. Then, students should find the measures of all four angles.
2. Ask students what they notice about the angle measures. (Opposite angles are equal.) Then, have students explore and add the four pairs of adjacent angles together. Ask if they notice any patterns. (Each adjacent pair should equal 180°.) Point out that like in the mini-lesson, each pair of angles shares a straight line as a ray. If necessary, use a sheet of paper to cover the other line and focus on each pair separately.
3. Draw a straight angle (180°) with a 95° angle bisecting it. Challenge students to use what they know to find the missing angle measure. (85°)

Enrichment: Angles in Triangles

1. Give students a triangle. Have them measure all three angles in the triangle and then add the angle measures together. Repeat with other triangles. Ask students what they notice.
2. Explain that the angle measures in a triangle always add to 180°. Give students another triangle and have them measure and label the angles. Then, have them cut the triangle out and tear off each corner. Discard the center. Arrange the corners (points together) to create a straight angle (see diagram).

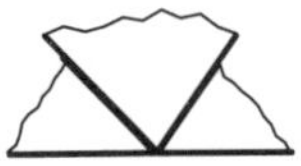

3. Say, "Because the angles in a triangle always equal 180°, we can use that information to find a missing angle in a triangle." Display a triangle with an unknown angle measure. Model adding the known angles and subtracting the sum from 180° to find the missing angle measure.
4. Have students practice finding unknown angle measures in several different triangles.

Assess and Extend

A tree is growing at an angle next to the base of a wall. It makes an angle of 15° with the wall. What angle does it make with the ground? (75°) Justify your answer.

Name ______________________________ Date ______________

Additive Angle Measures

● Decomposing Angles

Find the measure of the missing angle. Use what you know to complete the related addition sentence below each angle.

1.

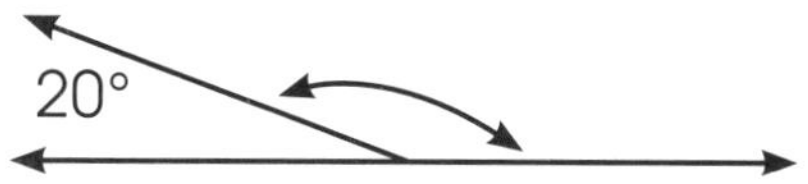

_______° + _______° = 180°

2.

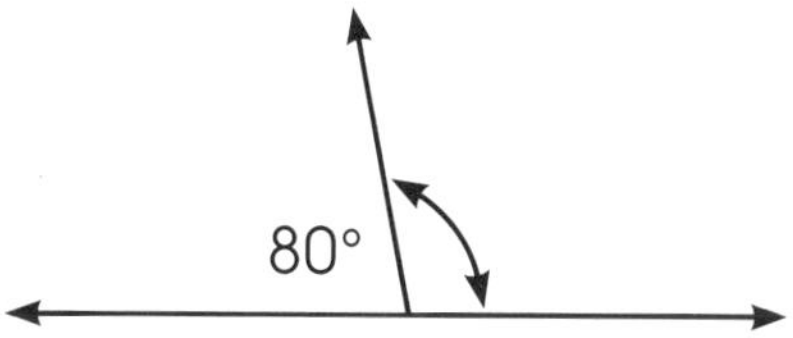

_______° + _______° = 180°

3.

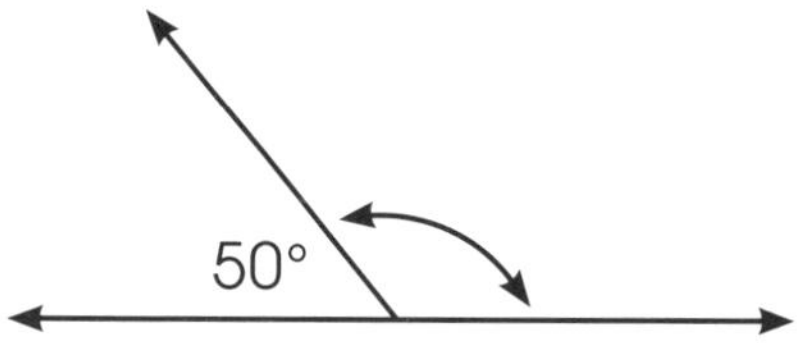

_______° + _______° = _______

4.

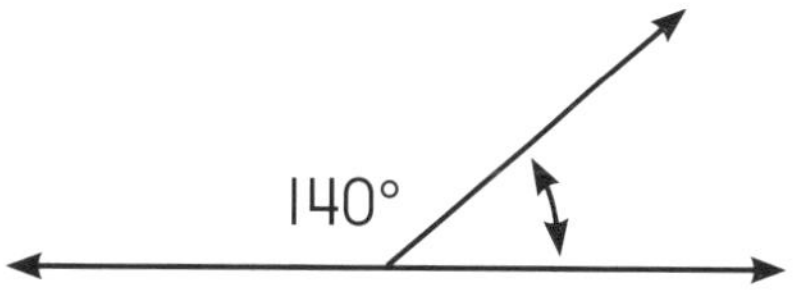

_______° + _______° = _______

5.

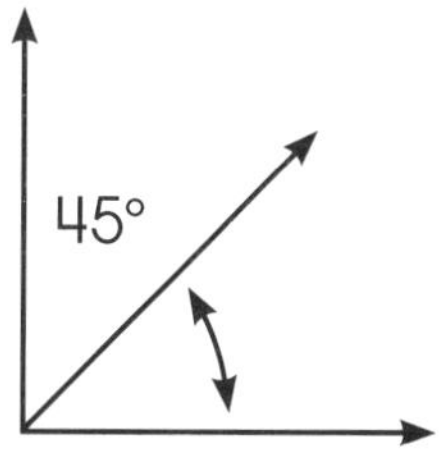

_______° + _______° = _______

6.

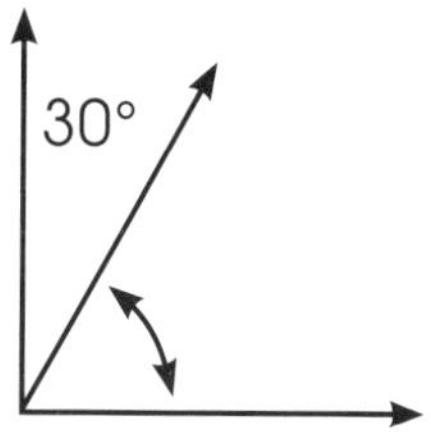

_______° + _______° = _______

7.

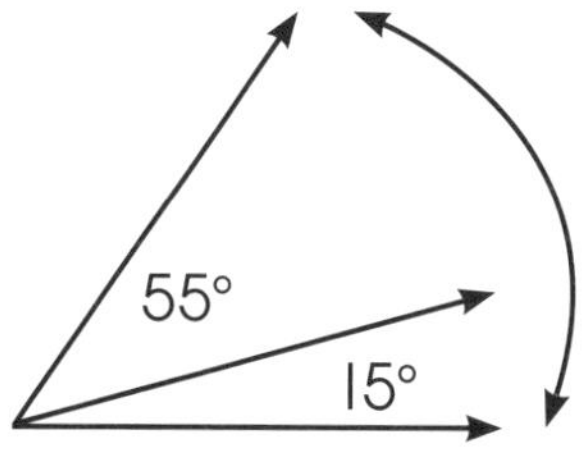

_______° + _______° = _______

8.

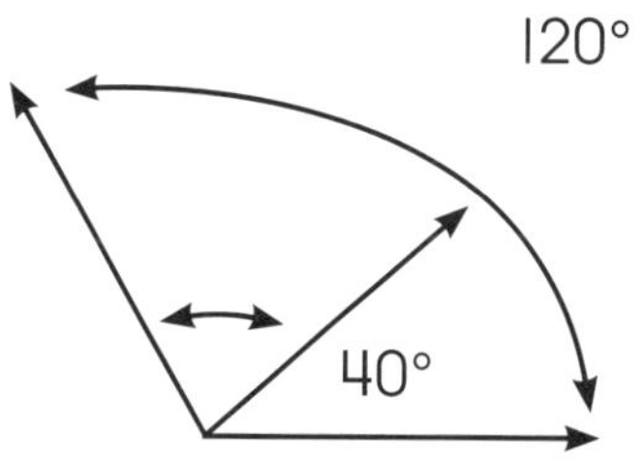

_______° + _______° = _______

Name ____________________ Date ____________

Additive Angle Measures

Finding Missing Angle Measures

Find the measure of the missing angle and record it on the line.

1.

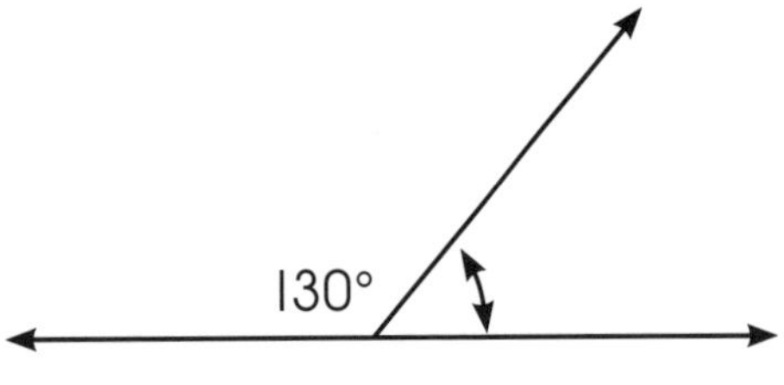

____

2.

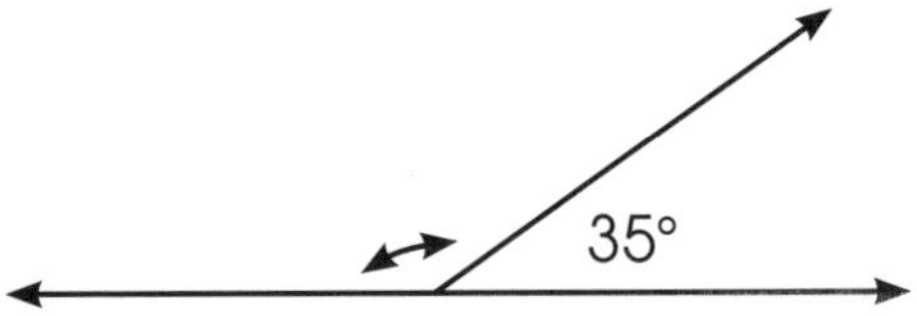

____

3.

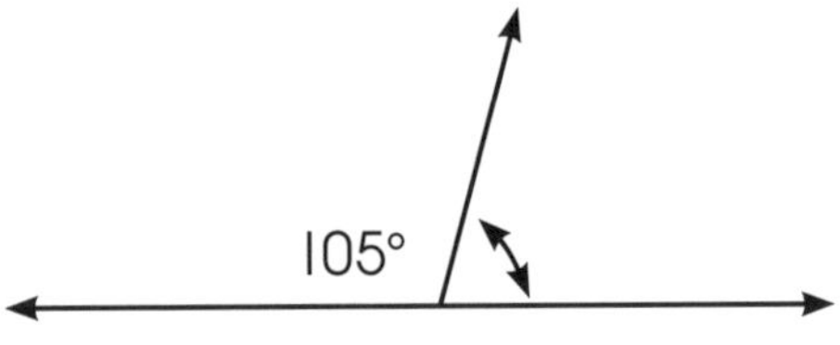

____

4.

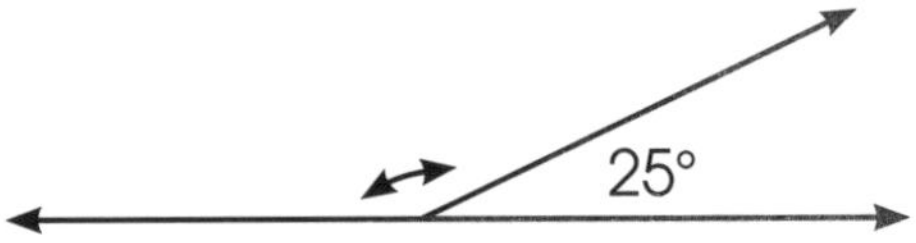

____

5.

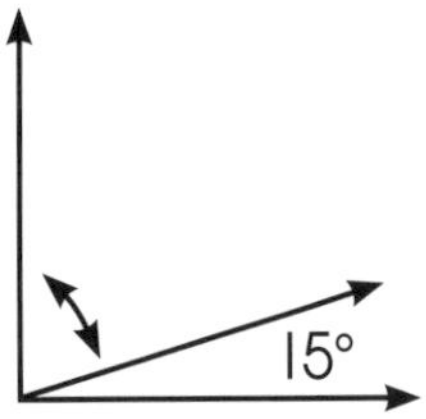

____

6.

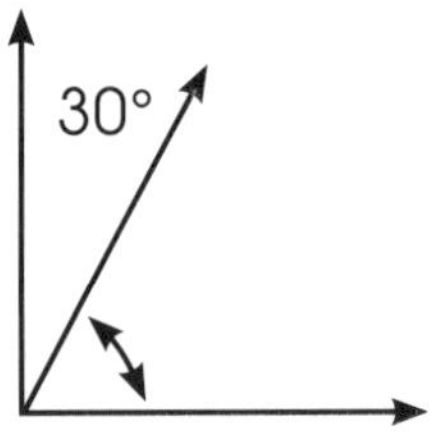

____

7.

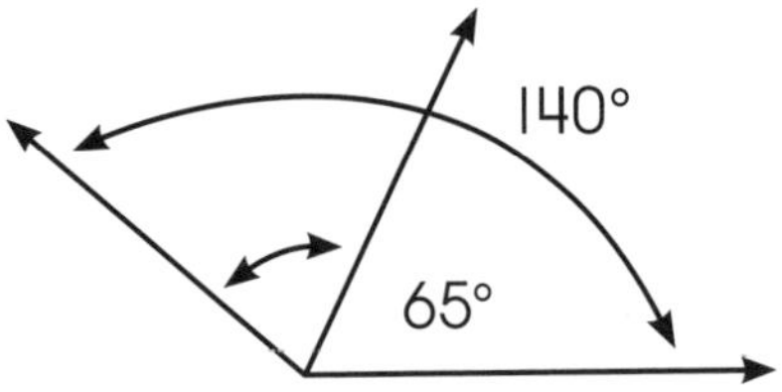

____

8.

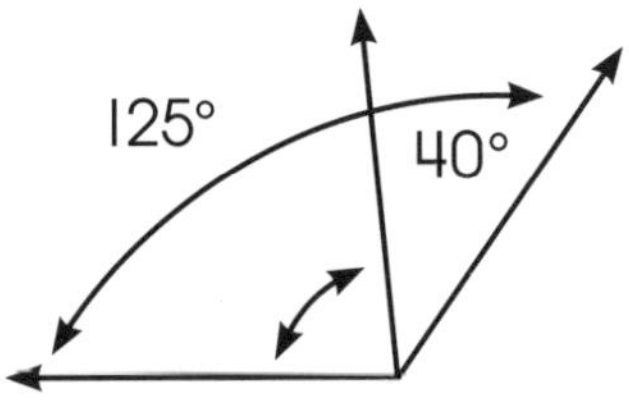

____

9.

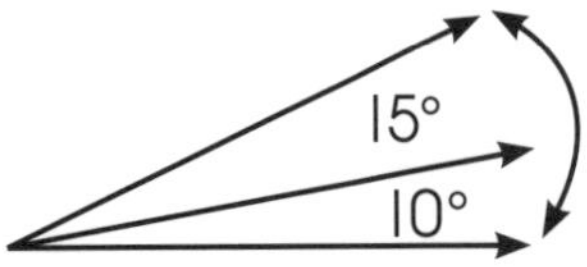

____

10.

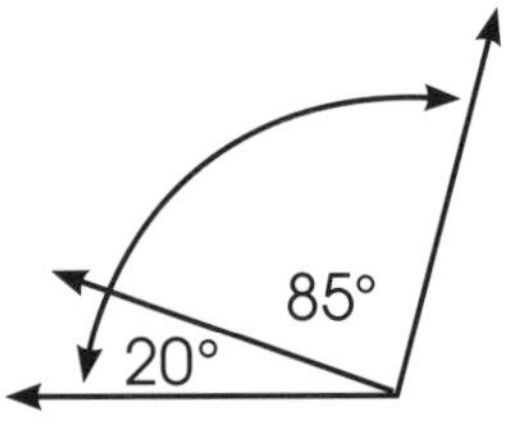

____

Name ______________________ Date ______________

Additive Angle Measures

Angles in Triangles

Find the missing angle measure in each triangle.

1.
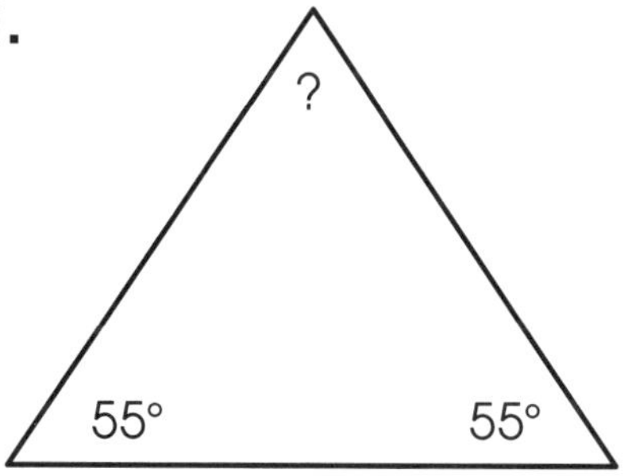

____

2.
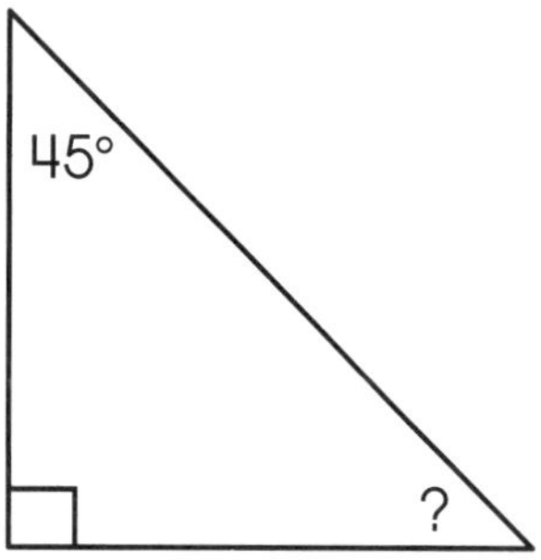

____

3.
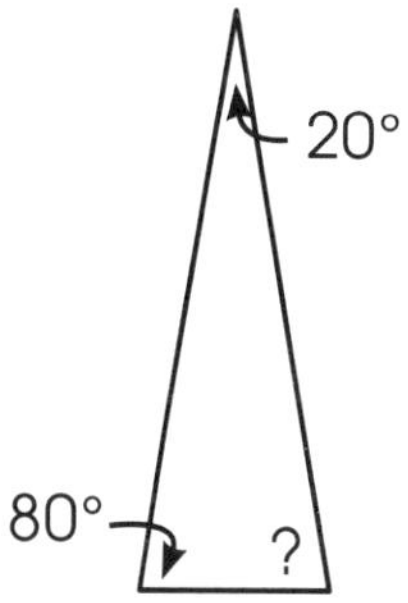

____

4.
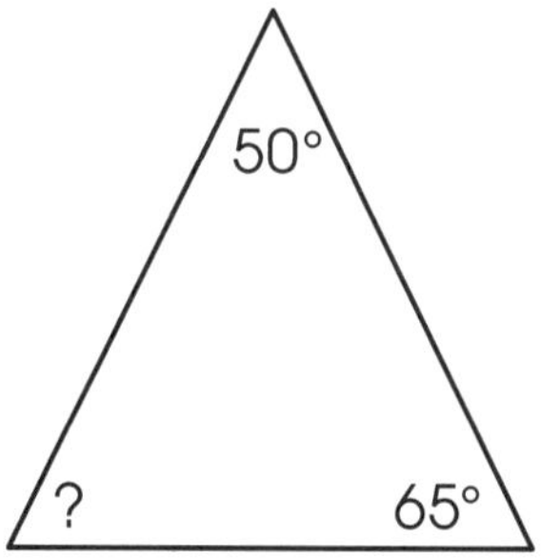

____

5.
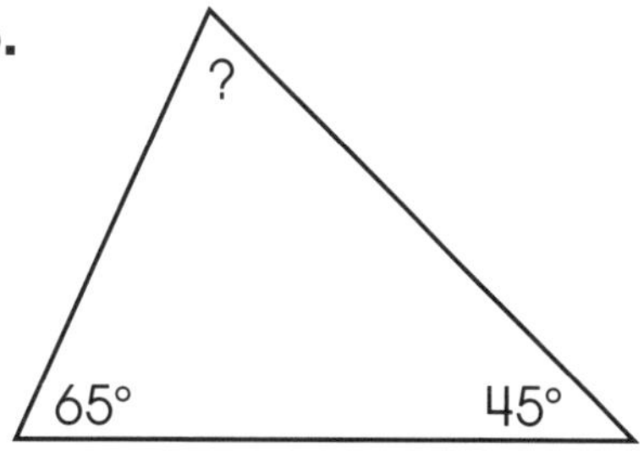

____

6.
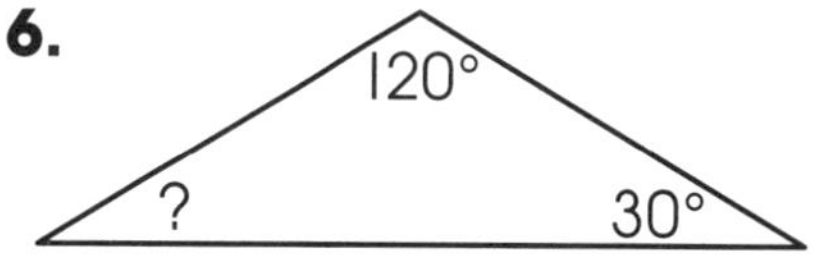

____

7.
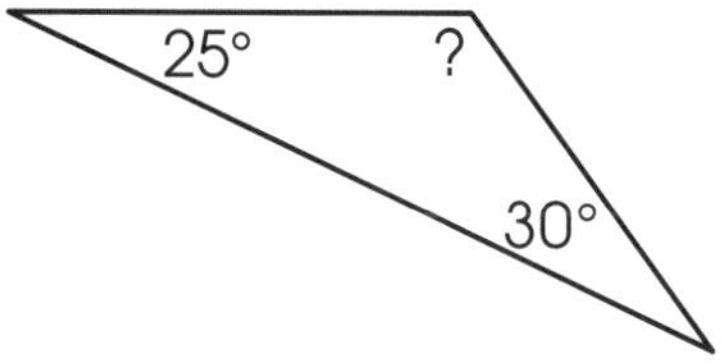

____

8.
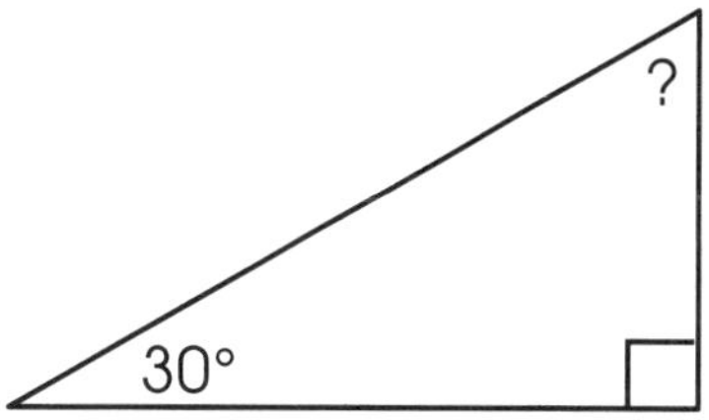

____

9.
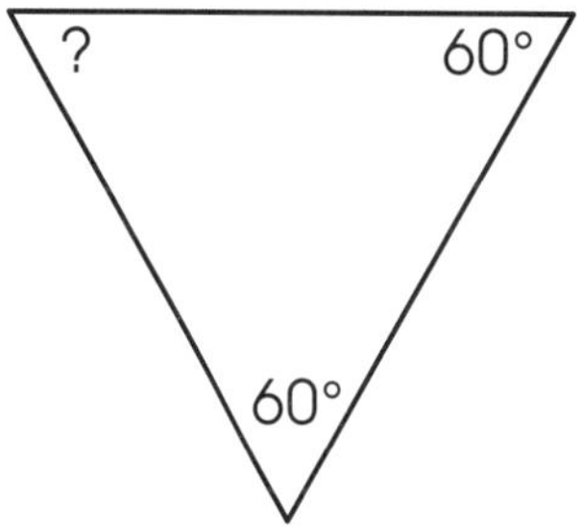

____

On the Mark

Materials: dry-erase marker, ruler

To play: Shuffle the cards and place them facedown in a draw pile. Decide on a goal angle from 80° to 180°. Record it in the goal space. Choose a card from the draw pile. Choose the angle you would like to use and mark it on the target. Repeat with two more cards. Find the total measure of the three angles. Did you get close to the goal without going over? If playing with a partner, keep the same goal angle for each player's turn during a round. The player who gets the closest without going over wins the round.

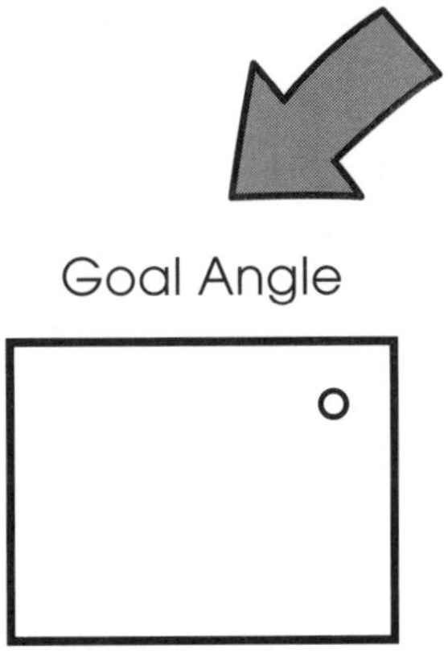

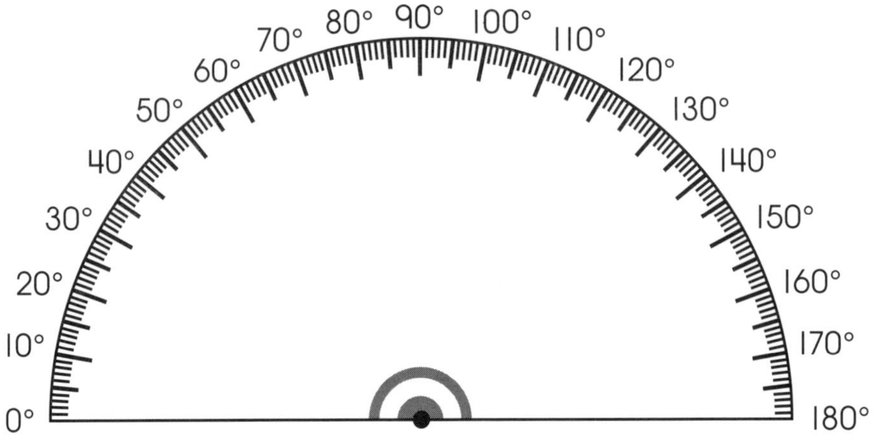

11° / 94°	34° / 77°	123° / 26°	29° / 71°	47° / 83°	52° / 88°
58° / 97°	23° / 104°	18° / 63°	39° / 99°	9° / 76°	55° / 82°
24° / 90°	16° / 68°	53° / 75°	61° / 44°	14° / 79°	28° / 66°

To prep: Copy on card stock and laminate for durability and use with dry-erase markers. Cut apart the angle cards and place in a resealable bag. Discard these directions. Place the cards, directions, and game mat in a center.

Geometric Figures

Essential Question

What are polygons composed of?

Warm-Up/Review

Review polygon attributes. Assign partners. Say the name of a polygon, and have partners go back and forth saying different attributes of that polygon until they can't think of any more. Repeat as time allows.

Mini-Lesson

Materials: sheets of paper; masking or painter's tape; highlighters, markers, or crayons

1. Give each student a sheet of paper and have them fold it in half lengthwise, then in half twice width-wise. When the paper is unfolded, it should have eight boxes. Have students label the top-left box *Geometric Figures.*
2. Draw and define each figure on the board (point, line, line segment, ray, angle, parallel lines, perpendicular lines). Have students record each term in a new box, draw a picture, and write the definition in their own words. After defining similar terms (line and line segment, parallel and perpendicular lines, etc.), have students compare and contrast the figures with a partner.
3. Give each student a length of masking tape. Allow students to place their tape on the board or the floor in any orientation. After all students have added their tape to the same area, it should look like a web of tape.
4. Have students identify geometric figures in the tape and label them. Challenge the class to find at least one example of each type of geometric figure.
5. Then, have students write their names in block letters on a sheet of paper, turning their paper and overlapping letters as desired. (*Note:* the name probably won't be readable, and that is to be expected.) Students should use highlighters, markers, or crayons and repeat step 4 with their name drawings.

Math Talk

How are these figures the same? How are they different?

How do these figures relate to the polygons you know?

How can these figures help you better understand and group polygons?

Journal Prompt

Write a statement that is always true, a statement that is sometimes true, and a statement that is never true about geometric figures.

Materials

uncooked spaghetti
clay or play dough
graph paper
dry-erase boards
dry-erase markers

Workstations

Activity sheets (pages 167–169)
Lines, Points, and Angles
Four-in-a-Row (page 170)

Guided Math

Remediation: Concrete Geometric Figures

1. Give each student access to uncooked spaghetti and clay. Have students follow along and make each geometric figure as you do.
2. Roll a ball of clay and explain, "This is a point. It represents a location." Display a piece of spaghetti and say, "This is a line segment. It is a path between two points." Add a ball of clay to each end of the spaghetti. Help students understand that the points are the ends of that line segment. Continue using spaghetti and clay balls (or clay triangles for representing continuing lines) to model and define *line*, *ray*, and *parallel* and *perpendicular lines.*
3. Then, challenge students to build each geometric figure as you say it. Allow students to share their creations and compare and contrast them. For example, line segments may be different lengths, or a ray might be part of a larger line.

On Level: Geometric Figures in Polygons

1. Give each student a sheet of graph paper. Ask students to draw a rectangle on the paper. Explain that what they think of as "sides" are actually line segments. Have students identify and label each line segment.
2. Say, "These line segments are parts of four lines." Point out how the lines on the graph paper continue past the rectangle. It is because the lines intersect that they create the rectangle. Explain that the corners, or where the lines intersect, are points. Have students identify and label each point.
3. Work with students to identify and label the sets of parallel and perpendicular lines and relate them to the four right angles.
4. Repeat with several more common shapes, such as triangles, trapezoids, and octagons.
5. Then, challenge students to create polygons with certain attributes, such as *a quadrilateral with only one set of parallel sides*, or *a triangle with a right angle.*

Enrichment: Using Geometric Vocabulary

1. Review the new vocabulary. Say each term and have students sketch it or write a short definition. Use this time to correct any misconceptions.
2. Use the vocabulary to give them step-by-step directions to draw shapes on their dry-erase boards. For example, say, "Draw a shape that is made of 4 line segments." Students may not all draw the same shape. Then, give another direction: "This shape has 4 right angles." Students should revise their shapes to reflect the new information. Continue until all of the attributes have been given. Check students' drawings to see if they drew the correct shape.
3. If time allows, place students in pairs and have them repeat step 2. Students should take turns and switch who gives clues and who draws each time.

Assess and Extend

Draw a picture using only points, lines, line segments, rays, and parallel and perpendicular lines. Use each geometric figure at least once. Label an example of each figure.

Name ______________________________ Date ______________

Geometric Figures

Concrete Geometric Figures

Identify each figure as a *line, ray, line segment,* or *points.*

1.

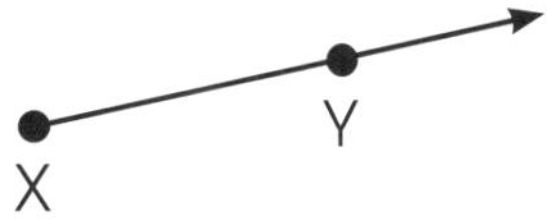

____

2.

____

3.

____

4.

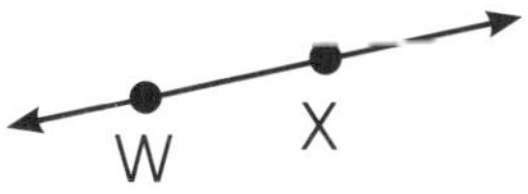

____

5.

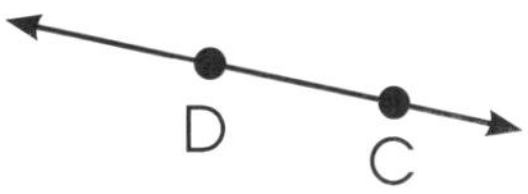

____

6.

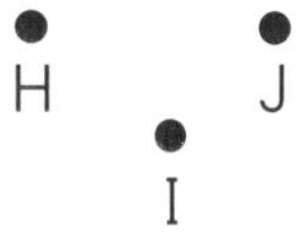

____

7.

____

8.

____

Identify each set of lines as *parallel* or *perpendicular* lines.

9.

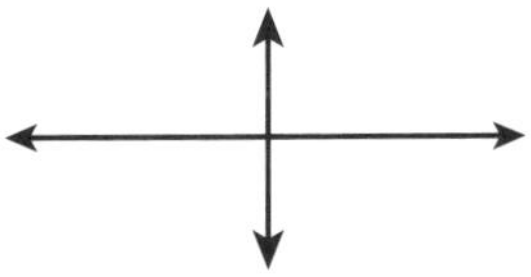

____

10.

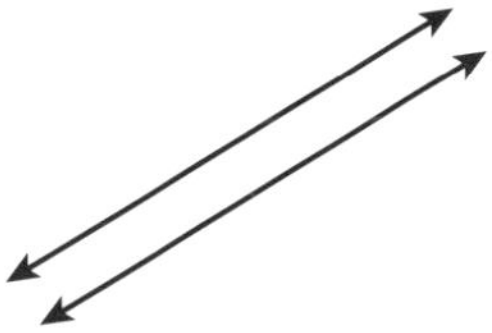

____

Name ______________________ Date ______________

Geometric Figures

Geometric Figures in Polygons

Use the figures to the right to answer each set of questions. Use the key below to help name each figure.

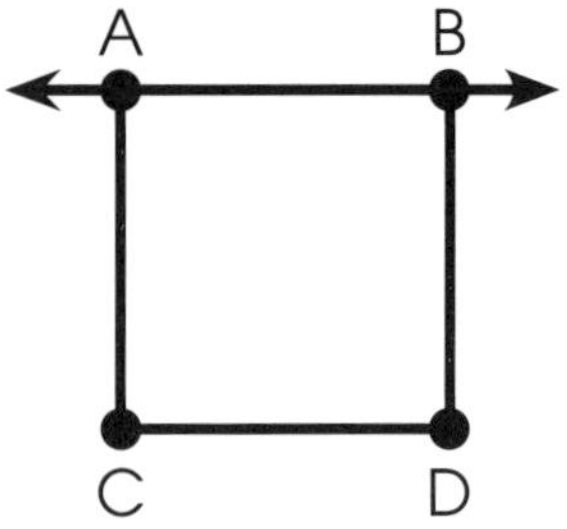

point A	● A	line AB	$\overleftrightarrow{AB}$
line segment CD	$\overline{CD}$	ray AB	$\overrightarrow{AB}$

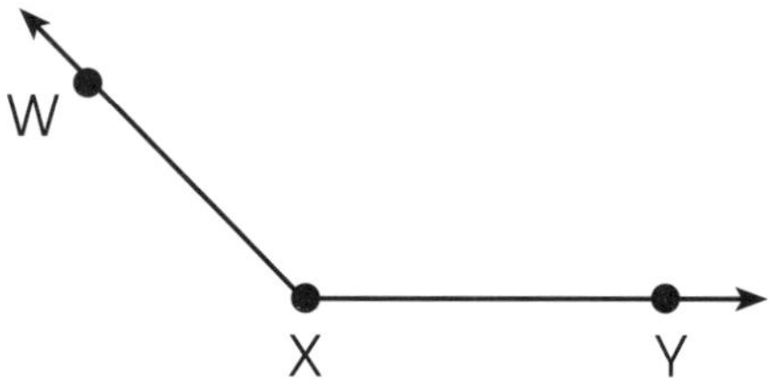

1. Name this figure. ______________________

2. Name the points. ______________________

3. Name the rays. ______________________

4. Name a line segment. ______________________

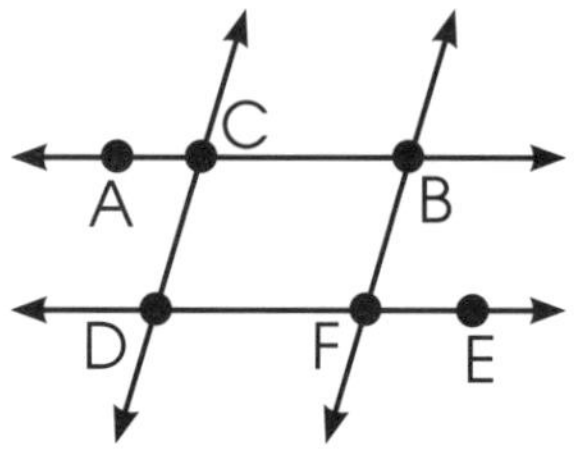

5. Name four points. ______________________

6. Name two parallel lines. ______________________

7. Name two line segments. ______________________

8. Name the figure formed by the four lines. ______________________

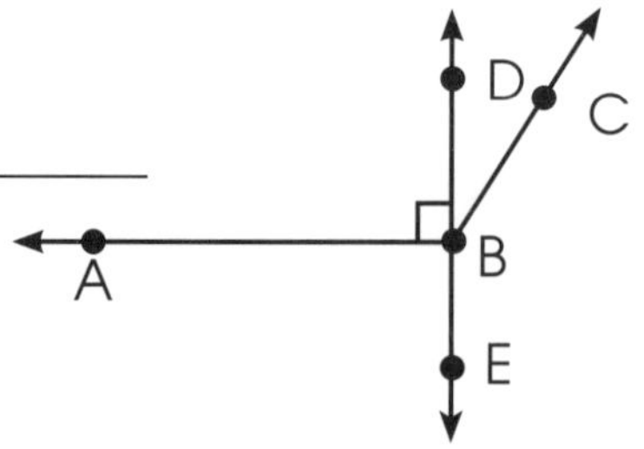

9. Name three points. ______________________

10. Name the two perpendicular lines. ______________________

11. Name two line segments. ______________________

12. Name four rays. ______________________

Name ______________________ Date ______________

Geometric Figures

Using Geometric Vocabulary

Follow each set of directions to complete the correct geometric figure.

1. Draw two perpendicular rays that share an endpoint.	**2.** Draw a line segment with three points on it.
3. Draw three parallel lines.	**4.** Draw two parallel lines. Then, draw a line perpendicular to the parallel lines.
5. Draw two parallel rays.	**6.** Draw a line intersecting a ray.
7. Draw two lines with two points on each line. Draw a line segment connecting the lines.	**8.** Draw a rhombus made from four intersecting lines.

Lines, Points, and Angles Four-in-a-Row

Materials: 1 die, two different colors of counters

To play: Players take turns. Roll the die. Use the key to identify your geometric figure and place your counter on a matching geometric figure. If a marker is already on a space, you may not place a marker on the same space. If there are no more matching geometric figures on the board, you lose your turn. The first player with four markers in a row wins.

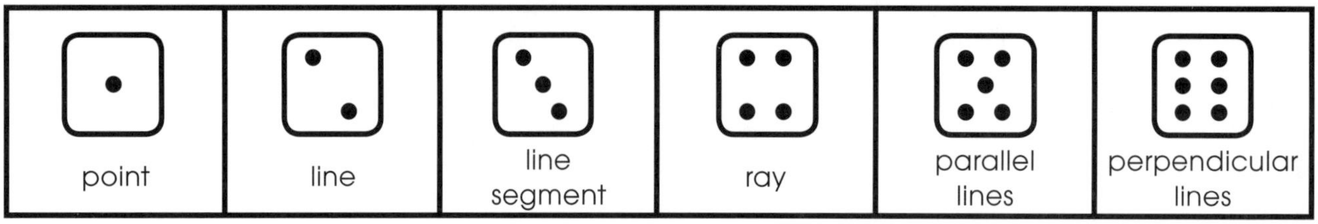

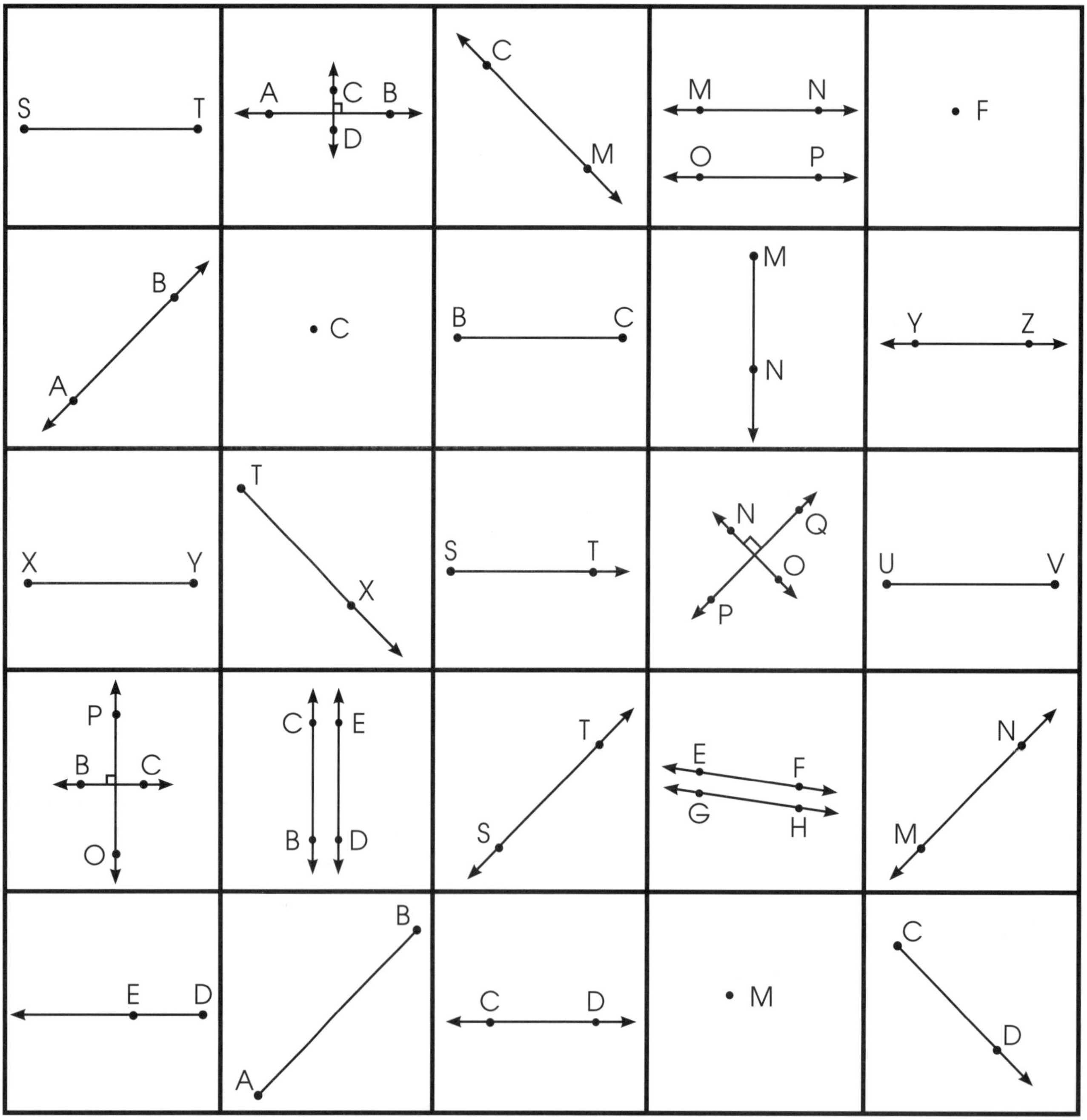

Classifying Shapes

Essential Question

In what ways can polygons be sorted and grouped?

Warm-Up/Review

Say polygon riddles, such as, "I am a quadrilateral. I have one right angle and one set of parallel sides. What am I?" Have students guess the polygon. (trapezoid) Repeat as time allows.

Mini-Lesson

Materials: assorted polygons drawn on half-sheets of paper (enough for each student to have one), copies of sheets with all polygons shown, scissors, index cards

1. Give each student a polygon card. Say attributes, such as "one set of parallel lines," "at least one right angle," or "has obtuse angles." Students whose polygon matches the attribute should stand at the front of the room.
2. Discuss how the set of polygons at the front of the room all have the attribute in common, though they may not share other attributes. Point out that some students remained standing at the front of the room as attributes changed. Have students explain why. Explain that classifying shapes by attributes can help you gain a better understanding of individual polygons as well as larger groups of polygons, such as quadrilaterals.
3. Place students in small groups. Give each group a sheet with polygons and have them cut the polygons apart. Then, groups should work together to sort and arrange all of the polygons in a way that makes sense to them. Have them use the index cards to label the groups. Students should use all polygons in their arrangement.
4. Allow groups to share their groups and reasoning.

Math Talk

How are these polygons the same? How are they different?

What would you name this set of polygons? Why?

Give a true statement in your own words about this set of polygons.

Journal Prompt

Defend or disprove this statement: *All squares are rectangles, but not all rectangles are squares.*

Materials

polygon cards (or copies of polygons for students to cut into cards)
dry-erase boards
dry-erase marker

Workstations

Activity sheets (pages 173–175)
Design Challenge (page 176)

Guided Math

Remediation: Identifying Attributes

1. Give each student a set of polygon cards. As a group, come up with a list of important attributes to look for, such as *number of sides, number of angles, sides of the same length, parallel lines, perpendicular lines*, and *acute, right*, and *obtuse angles*.
2. Guide students through setting up a chart with the attributes listed across the top and the polygons along the left side.
3. Looking at one polygon at a time, guide students to complete the chart for each polygon. (*Note:* Some categories may be yes/no, while others require an amount.)
4. Once the chart is complete, help students use it to find all of the polygons with given attributes, such as a 4-sided polygon with 2 sets of parallel sides.

On Level: Diagramming Attributes

1. Have students draw 3 large overlapping circles to form a triple Venn diagram. Review the geometric figures from the previous lesson (page 165). Have students choose 3 attributes (such as *1 right angle, parallel lines*, and *4 sides*) and label each circle with one of the attributes.
2. Have students write the names of the polygons that fit into each category inside the circles. Polygons that fit into more than one category should be written inside the overlapping sections. Write polygons that don't fit any categories outside of the circles.
3. Have students continue making diagrams with other attributes. Let students share their diagrams when they are complete.

Enrichment: Thinking Critically about Polygons

1. Choose a secret polygon. Draw it on a dry-erase board and place it so the shape is hidden from students.
2. Allow students to ask yes/no attribute questions to guess the shape. For example, "Does it have parallel sides?" "Does it have a right angle?" etc. Once a student volunteers the correct answer, have her justify her guess using the attribute information. Ask clarifying questions, such as, "A rhombus also has 4 equal sides, so why isn't it a rhombus?" etc.
3. Place students in pairs and allow them to repeat steps 1 and 2 with their partner. Students should take turns choosing the shape and asking the questions.

Assess and Extend

Explain how a square and a rhombus are similar and different, using attributes and correct vocabulary.

Name ______________________ Date ______________

Classifying Shapes

Identifying Attributes

Draw lines to connect the polygons that match each attribute to the center dot.

1. has at least one set of parallel sides

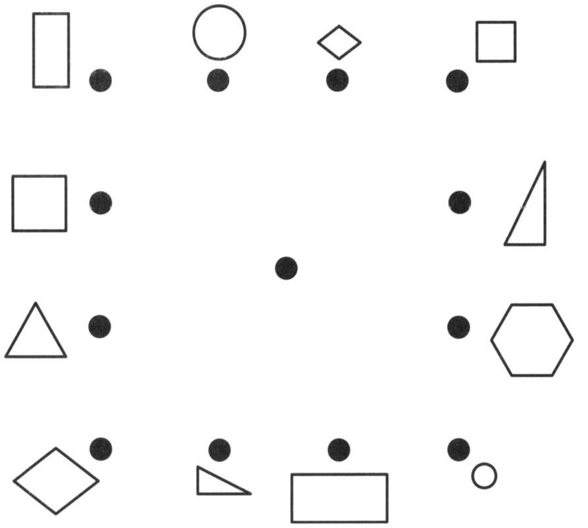

2. has one or more right angles

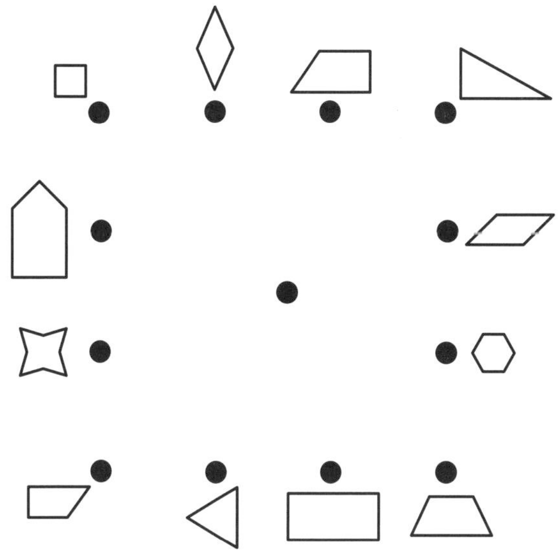

3. all sides are equal lengths

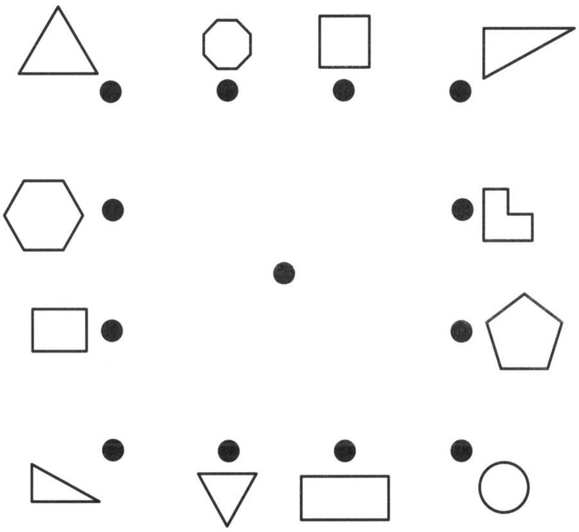

4. has obtuse angles

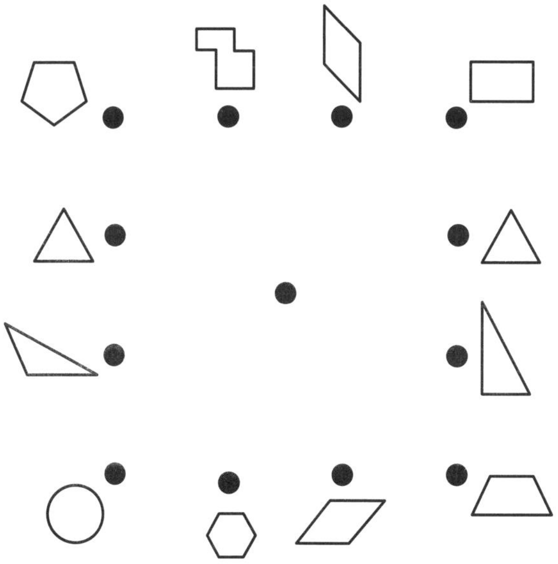

Name ______________________ Date ____________

Classifying Shapes

Diagramming Attributes

Complete each diagram by writing the corresponding letters in the correct section.

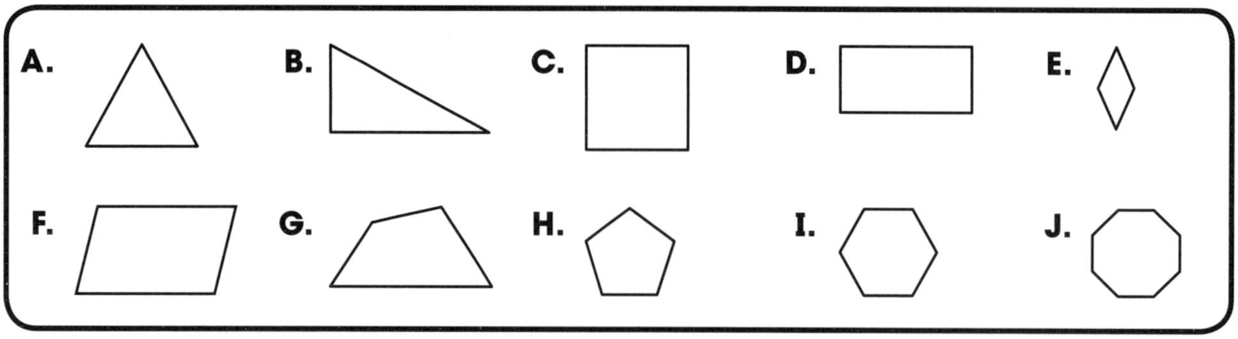

1. Quadrilateral Has Obtuse Angles

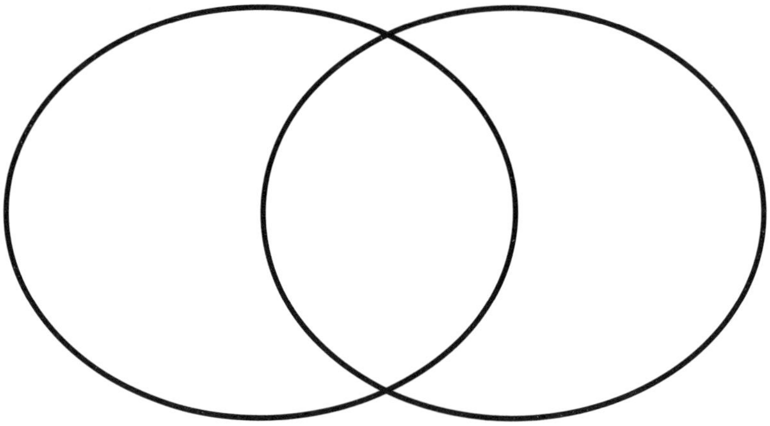

2. Quadrilateral Has Right Angles

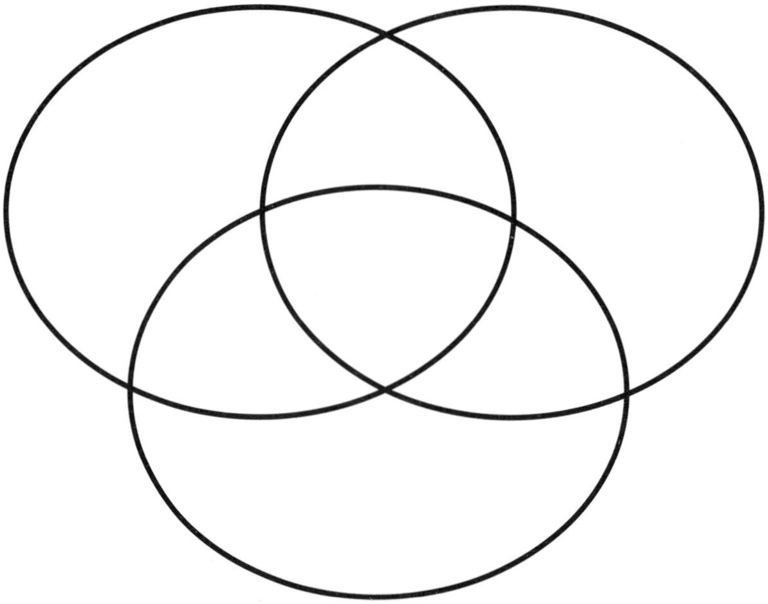

Has Two or More Sets of Parallel Sides

Name ______________________________ Date ______________

Classifying Shapes

▲ Thinking Critically about Polygons

Cut out the shapes. Use the clues to place the shapes correctly. Then, glue the shapes in place. *Hint:* Record the attributes of the shape in each square as you discover them. Then, find a shape that matches only that space.

Each student in Mrs. Abbot's class chose a different polygon for a math project. Mrs. Abbot lost the sheet that told her which student was using which polygon. Help her recreate her chart.

- All students in row 2 have quadrilaterals.
- No students in group A have shapes with right angles.
- All of the students in group D have shapes with 2 or more sets of parallel sides.
- The students in row 1 all have shapes with more than 4 sides.
- The students in 1B and 2B both have shapes with 4 right angles.
- The student in 1D has the shape with the most sides in the class.
- The student in group D was the only one in row 3 that doesn't have a triangle.
- The students in 1D and 3D have shapes with at least 6 obtuse angles.
- The student in 3B has a shape with equal sides.
- The student in 1A has a shape with exactly 5 sides.
- The student in 2D has the only shape in group D without all equal sides.

	A	B	C	D
1				
2				
3				

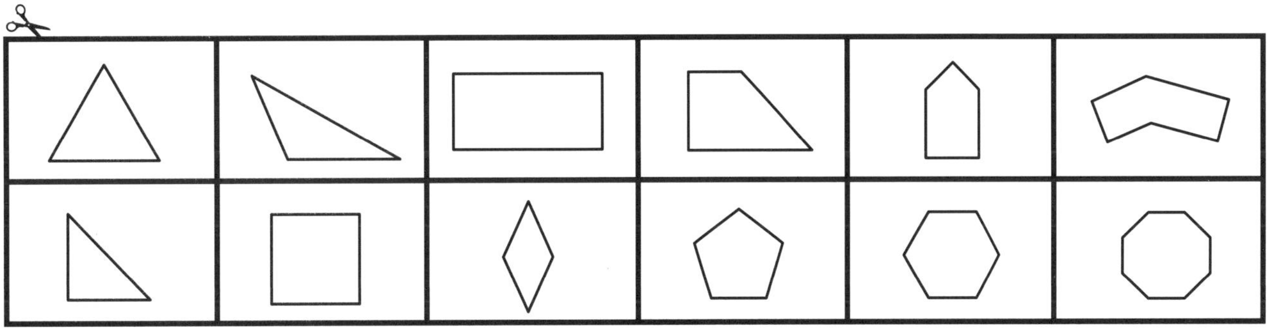

Design Challenge

Materials: pattern blocks and tangrams

To play: Use more than one pattern block or tangram to complete each challenge. Record the card letter and trace your solution in a math journal or on a separate sheet of paper. For a challenge, see if you can come up with more than one solution for each card.

A symmetrical figure composed of only polygons with right angles **A**	A figure composed of only polygons with equal sides **B**
A figure with a set of parallel sides and no right angles **C**	A symmetrical figure formed without quadrilaterals **D**
A right triangle composed of smaller shapes **E**	A figure with no right angles composed of smaller shapes **F**
A symmetrical figure composed of 10 of the same shape **G**	A nonsymmetrical figure composed of an even amount of two different shapes **H**

To prep: Copy on card stock and laminate for durability. Cut apart the cards and discard these directions. Place the cards, directions, pattern blocks, and tangrams in a center.

Symmetry

Essential Question

What are lines of symmetry?

Warm-Up/Review

Assign each student a polygon, or give each student an index card with a polygon on it. Say different attributes, such as "equal sides," "has a right angle," etc. Students should stand if their polygon has that attribute and stay seated if it doesn't.

Mini-Lesson

Materials: paper, scissors, copies of popular logos

1. Provide partners with a sheet of paper. Ask students to work together to fold the paper in half. Allow pairs to share the different ways they folded the paper.
2. Discuss how students knew they had folded the paper exactly in half (the sides matched up, it was equal, the two sides are the same, etc.). Explain that this is called *symmetry*.
3. Have students unfold the paper and observe the fold line. Explain that the fold line represents the line of symmetry because it is the line where everything on one side is the exact match of the other side. Discuss how there were different folding methods, so the paper has more than one line of symmetry.
4. Have students use the scissors to cut the paper so it is not symmetrical anymore. Allow pairs to share how they cut their papers and why they are no longer symmetrical. For a further challenge, have partners then work together to make the paper symmetrical again.
5. Provide partners with a copy of a popular logo. Explain that many popular logos are symmetrical, while others are not. Have the pairs identify whether or not their logo is symmetrical, and if so, draw the line or lines of symmetry. Allow pairs to share and discuss any misconceptions as a class.

Math Talk

What do you mean by *equal*?
Can a shape have more than one line of symmetry? Why or why not?
How do you know the shape is/is not symmetrical?

Journal Prompt

Choose at least four different polygons. Draw and label them. Tell whether each polygon is symmetrical, and describe why or why not.

Materials

cutouts of shapes (star, heart, rectangle, square, etc.) and letters
mirrors
short lengths of string or yarn
pattern blocks

Workstations

Activity sheets (pages 179–181)
Balanced Blocks (page 182)

Guided Math

Remediation: Finding Symmetry

1. Place a star cutout on the table. Place a mirror on the line of symmetry and have students observe the reflection. Remove the mirror and ask students what was reflected and how it relates to the whole shape. (It shows the matching half.)
2. Explain, "The star is symmetrical because half of it matches the other half." Fold the star in half to demonstrate. "This shape is symmetrical because two halves have the same size and shape."
3. Ask, "But, if I fold it in half another way, does it create halves that match in size and shape?" Fold the star in half a different way and show how the halves don't match. "Folding this way does not create symmetry."
4. Place a piece of string on the fold line that created symmetry. Define it as the line of symmetry. Ask if the star has more than one line of symmetry. (No)
5. Give students additional shapes and have them use the mirrors or folding to find the line(s) of symmetry. They should place their strings to demonstrate each line of symmetry.

On Level: Identifying Symmetry

1. Review symmetry. Hold up a square cutout and fold it in half to show that it has symmetry. Demonstrate that a square has several lines of symmetry as you fold along different lines.
2. Provide each student with several cutout letters, a mirror, and a piece of string. Explain how students can use the mirror to find symmetry, or that they can fold letters to find it.
3. Have students explore each of their letters to identify whether each one is symmetrical or not. As they identify the symmetry of each letter, have them place their letters in *Symmetrical* or *Not Symmetrical* piles.
4. After students are done, review each shape with the group and correct any misconceptions. Work as a group to further identify the letters that have more than one line of symmetry.

Enrichment: Creating Symmetry

1. Have students create a design using several pattern blocks.
2. Give students mirrors and have them hold the mirror beside their design, so the reflection shows a symmetrical design. Challenge students to use the reflection to add to their original design to create a larger, symmetrical design. Encourage them to use their mirrors to periodically check their design and make sure it is symmetrical.
3. Give each student a string and have them place it on a different student's design to identify the line of symmetry.
4. Have students repeat the activity with a partner, where one student creates a design, and their partner must create the symmetrical half.

Assess and Extend

Identify three classroom items that have symmetry and three items that do not. Challenge: Identify how many lines of symmetry a circle has. (infinite lines of symmetry)

Name ______________________________ Date ______________

Symmetry

Finding Symmetry

Circle the figure in each row that shows symmetry.

1.

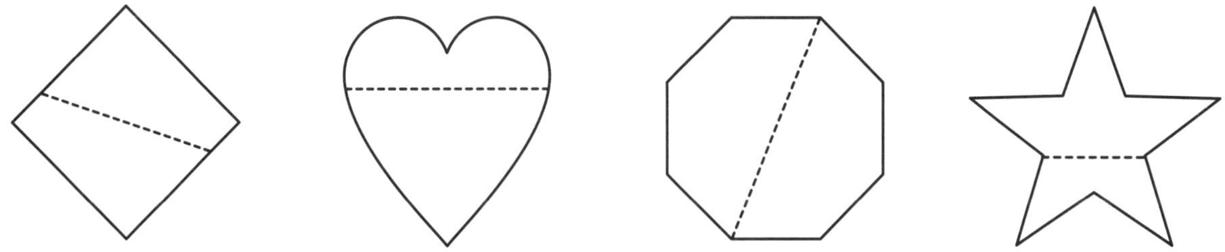

2.

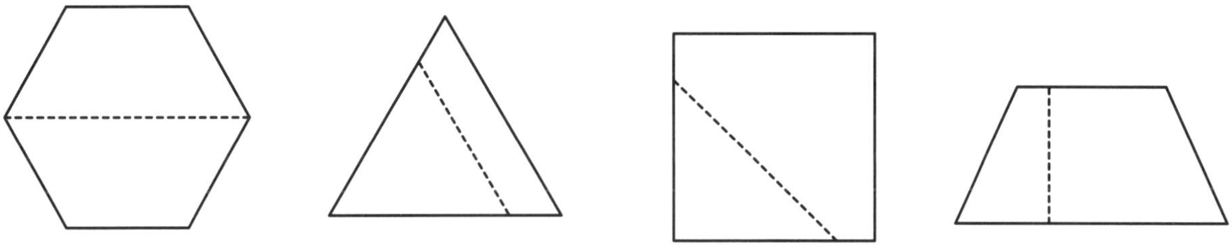

3.

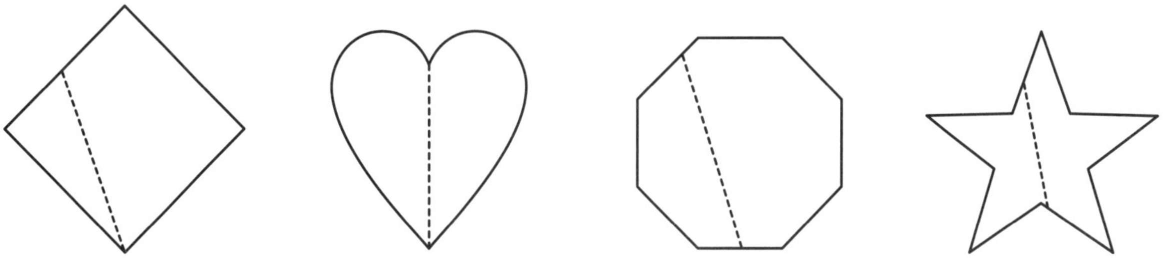

4.

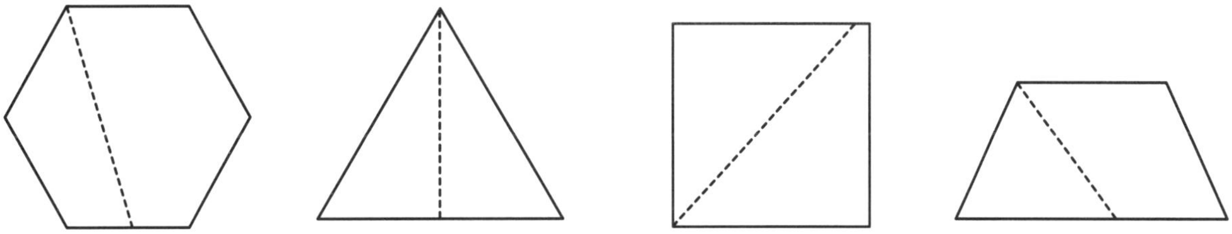

Draw two lines of symmetry on each figure.

5.

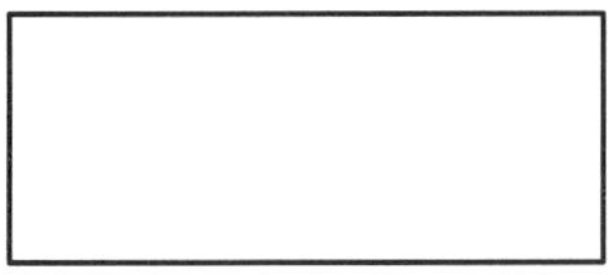

6.

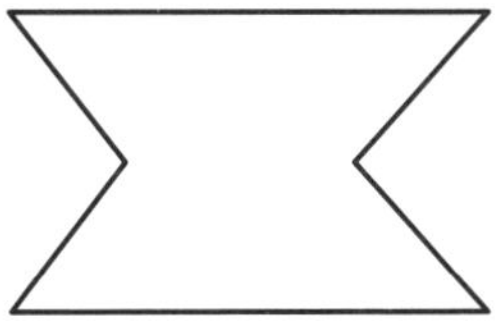

7.

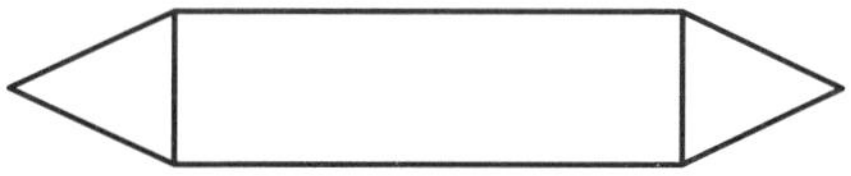

Name ____________________ Date ____________

Symmetry

Identifying Symmetry

Is each figure symmetrical? Write *yes* or *no*. If yes, draw the line or lines of symmetry.

1. 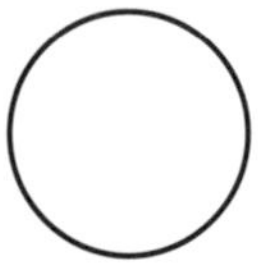 ____________

2. 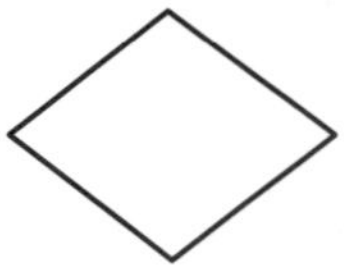 ____________

3.  ____________

4.  ____________

5. 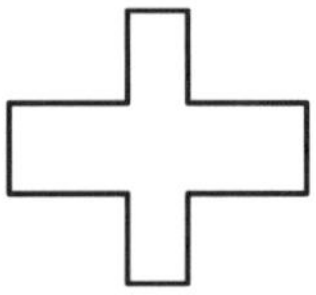 ____________

6.  ____________

7.  ____________

8.  ____________

9.  ____________

10.  ____________

11. 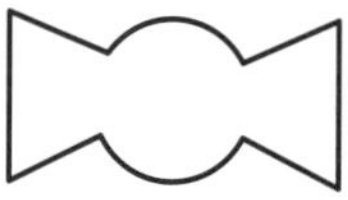 ____________

12. 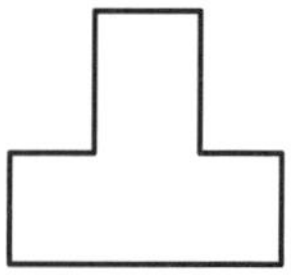 ____________

13.  ____________

14.  ____________

15.  ____________

16. 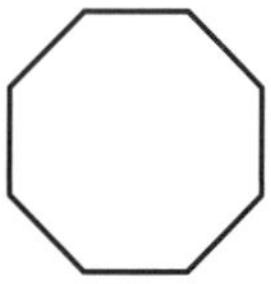 ____________

Draw all of the lines of symmetry on each figure.

17. 

18. 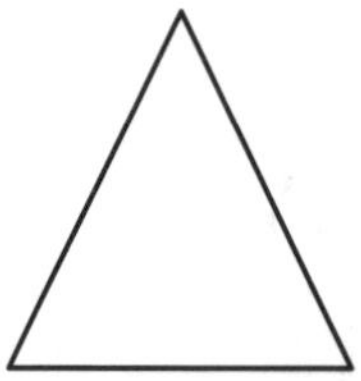

19. 

20. 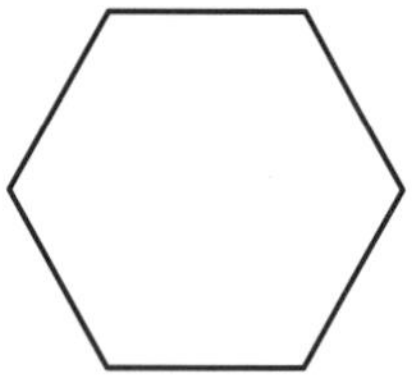

Name ______________________ Date ____________

Symmetry

▲ Creating Symmetry

Complete each shape so it is symmetrical across the dashed line.

1.

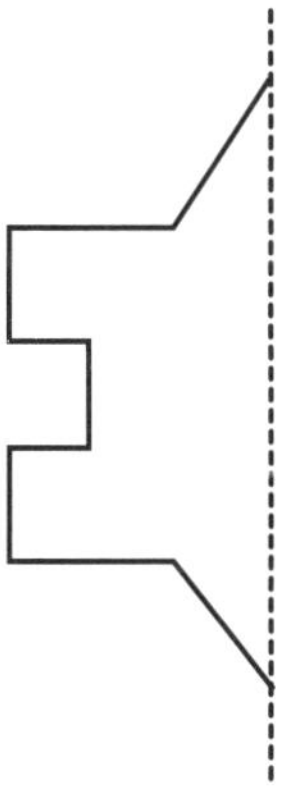

2.

3.

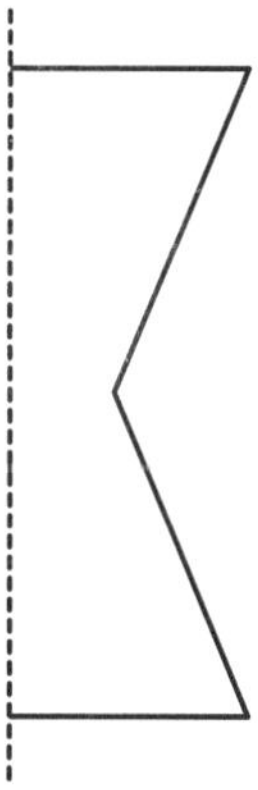

4.

5.

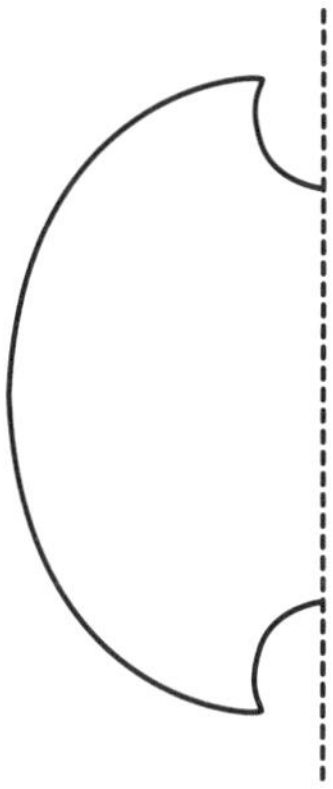

6.

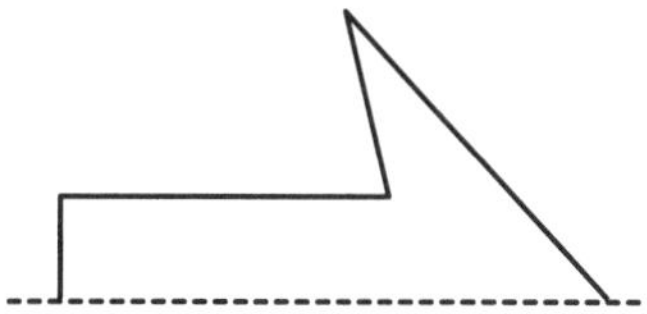

7.

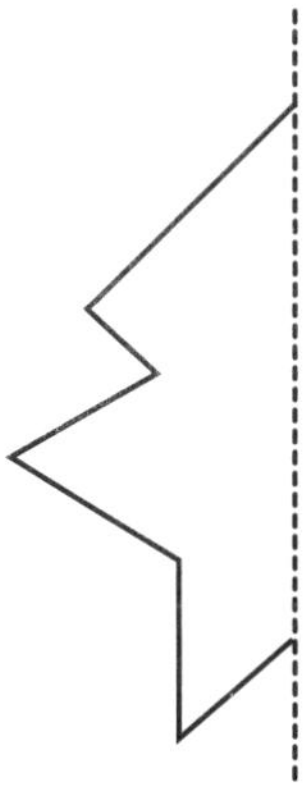

8.

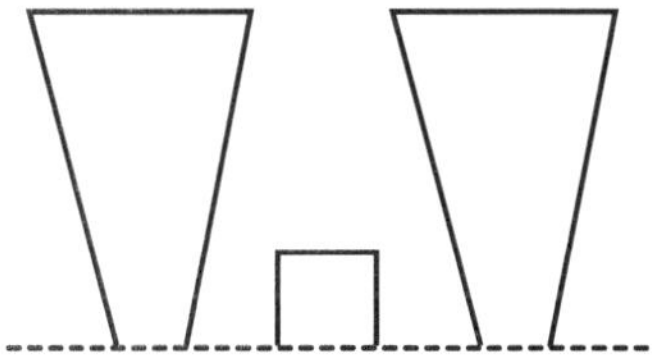

9.

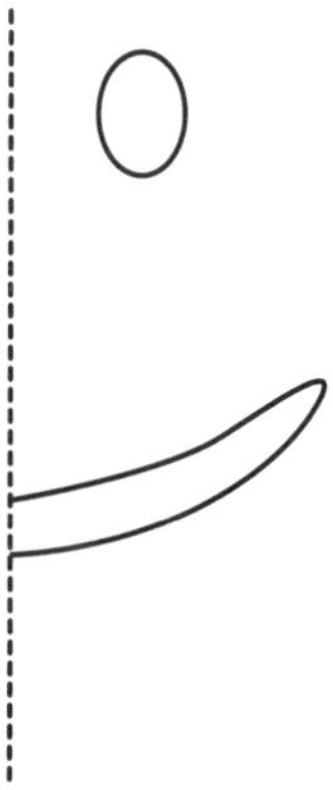

Balanced Blocks

Materials: dry-erase markers
To play: Shade in a pattern on one side of the line. Then, shade in a symmetrical pattern on the opposite side of the line. If playing with a partner, challenge them to draw the symmetrical pattern. Then, switch roles.

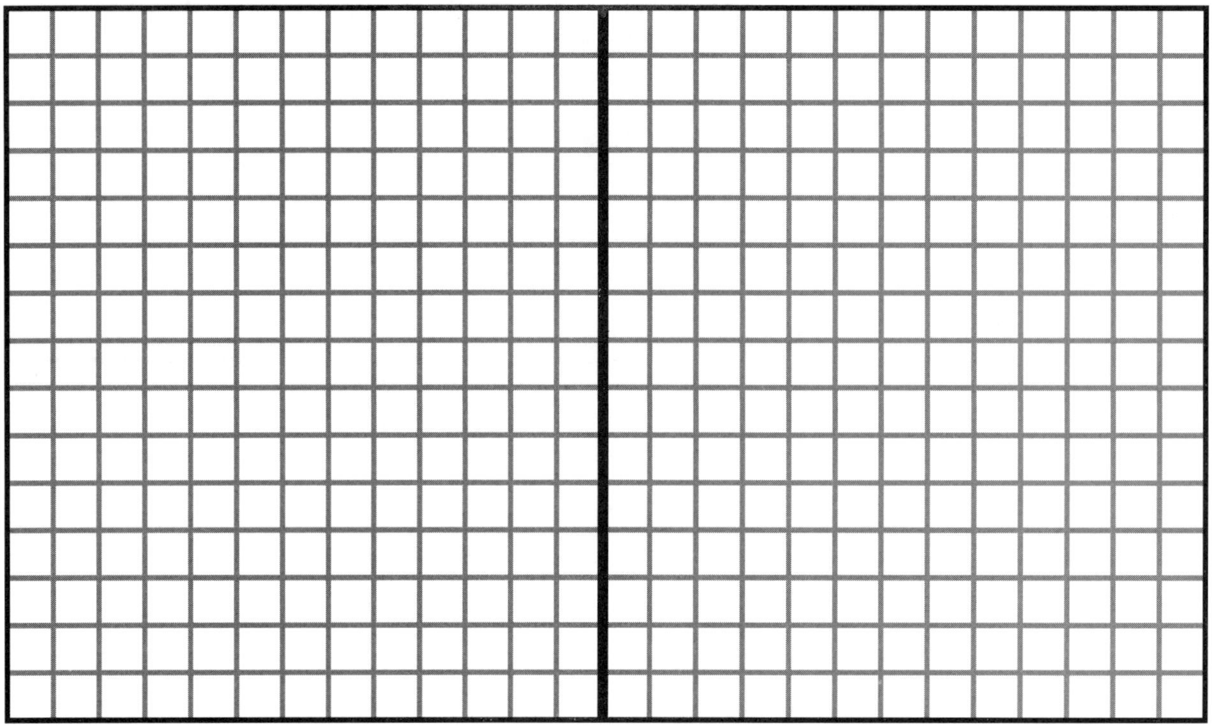

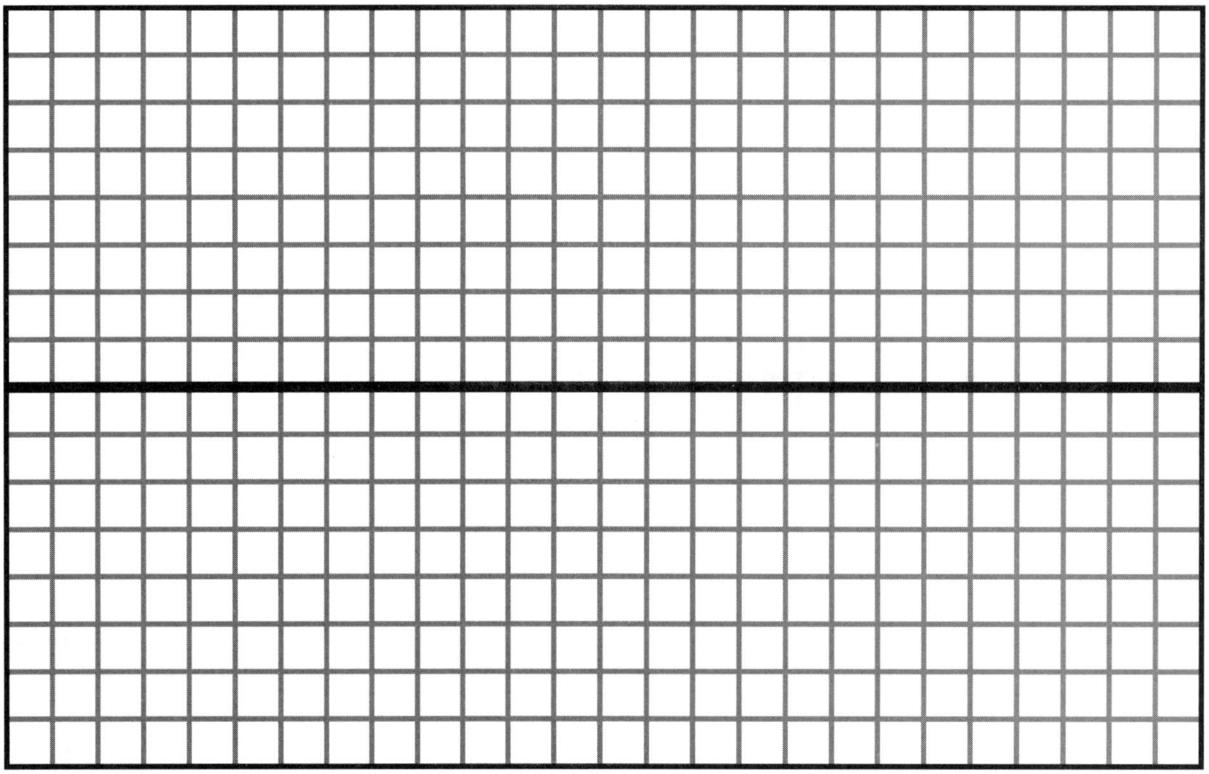

To prep: Copy on card stock and laminate for durability. Use with dry-erase markers. Place the game board and directions in a center.

Name ______________________________ Date ______________

hundred thousands	ten thousands	thousands	hundreds	tens	ones

Word Form

Expanded Form

Number of the Day

Divisible by . . .

2 3 4 5 6 7 8 9

Round to the

nearest ten ____________

nearest hundred ____________

nearest thousand ____________

highest place value ____________

Fraction of the Day

Model it.

Is it simplified?

☐ yes ☐ no

If not, simplify it.

☐ parts shaded

☐ equal parts in all

Place it on a number line.

Decompose it into the sum of unit fractions.

Roll a die. Multiply the fraction by that whole number.

___ × ☐ = ___

This fraction is

☐ greater than

☐ equal to

☐ less than

$\frac{1}{2}$.

Materials: 2 dice, 10 markers or counters (in two colors) per player

To play: Players take turns. Roll the dice and ______________________________. Cover the answer. You can "bump" the other player off of a space if there is only one counter on it. Once you place two counters on a space, it is yours and cannot be bumped. The player to use all of his or her markers first wins.

To prep: Complete the title with the skill. Fill in the spaces with possible answers. Complete the directions with instructions related to the skill that describe how students use the numbers they roll. For example, *multiply the numbers* or *add, then cover the number that is two less.* Cut these directions off before copying. If desired, copy on cardstock and laminate for durability. Place it in a station with the related materials.

____________________ Four-in-a-Row

Materials: ________ dice, two different colors of counters or markers

To play: Players take turns. ____
____. Place your marker on the answer. If a marker is already on a space, you may not place a marker on the same space. The first player with four markers in a row wins.

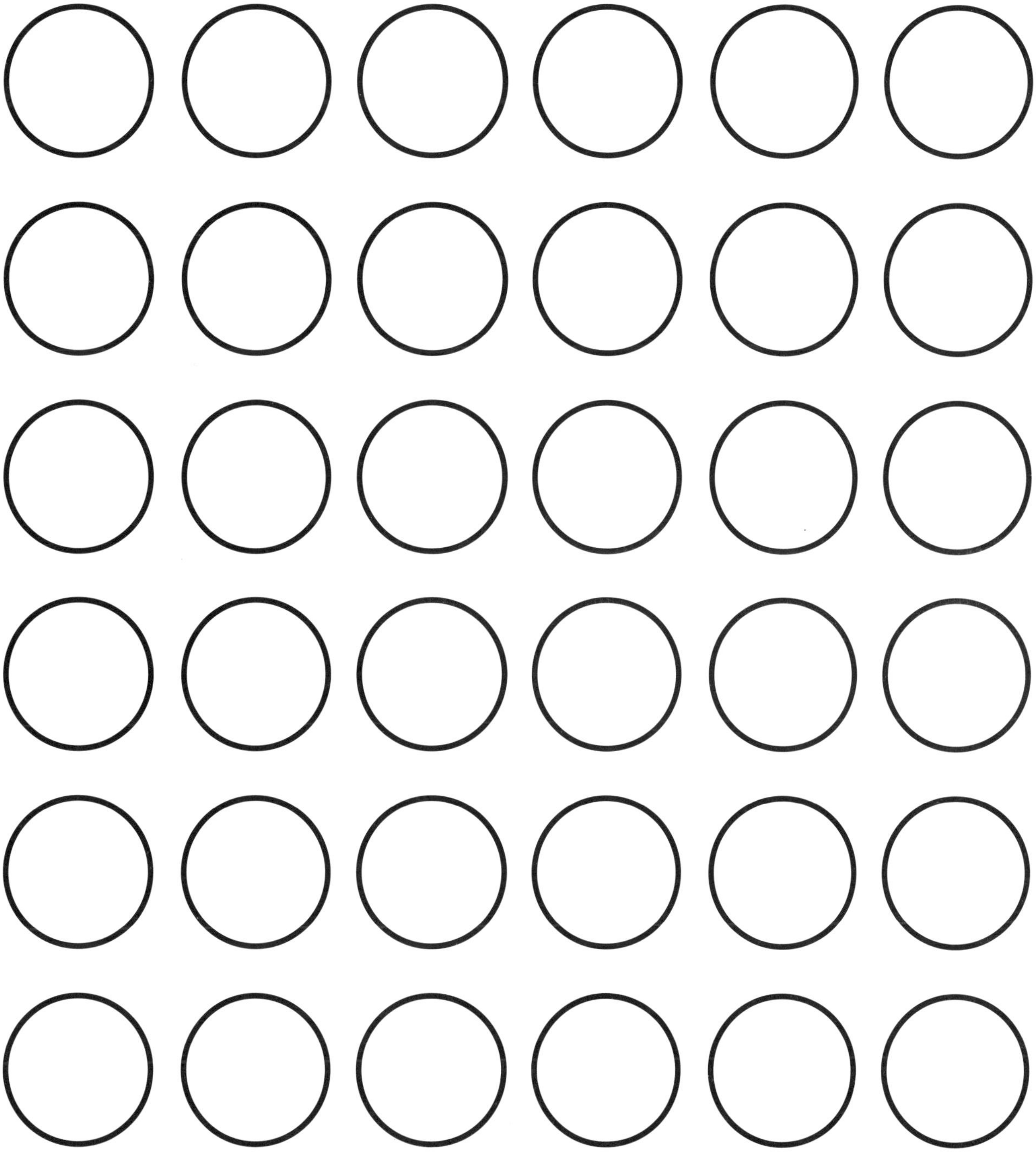

To prep: Fill in the circles with numbers. Place the numbers in random order and repeat numbers throughout. Fill in the number of dice needed in the Materials section. Complete the directions with instructions specific to the skill. For example, *roll two dice and add the numbers,* or *roll three dice, place the numbers in any order to create a three-digit number, and round it to the nearest ten.* Cut off these directions before copying. If desired, copy it on cardstock and laminate for durability. Place it in a station with the related materials.

____

Path Game

Materials: 1 die, 1 counter for each player

To play: Place the counters on Start. Players take turns. Roll the die. Move forward that many spaces. Solve the problem or follow the instructions on the space. If using cards, draw a card and solve the problem. If you answer correctly, stay on the space. If you answer incorrectly, return to your previous space. The first player to reach Finish wins.

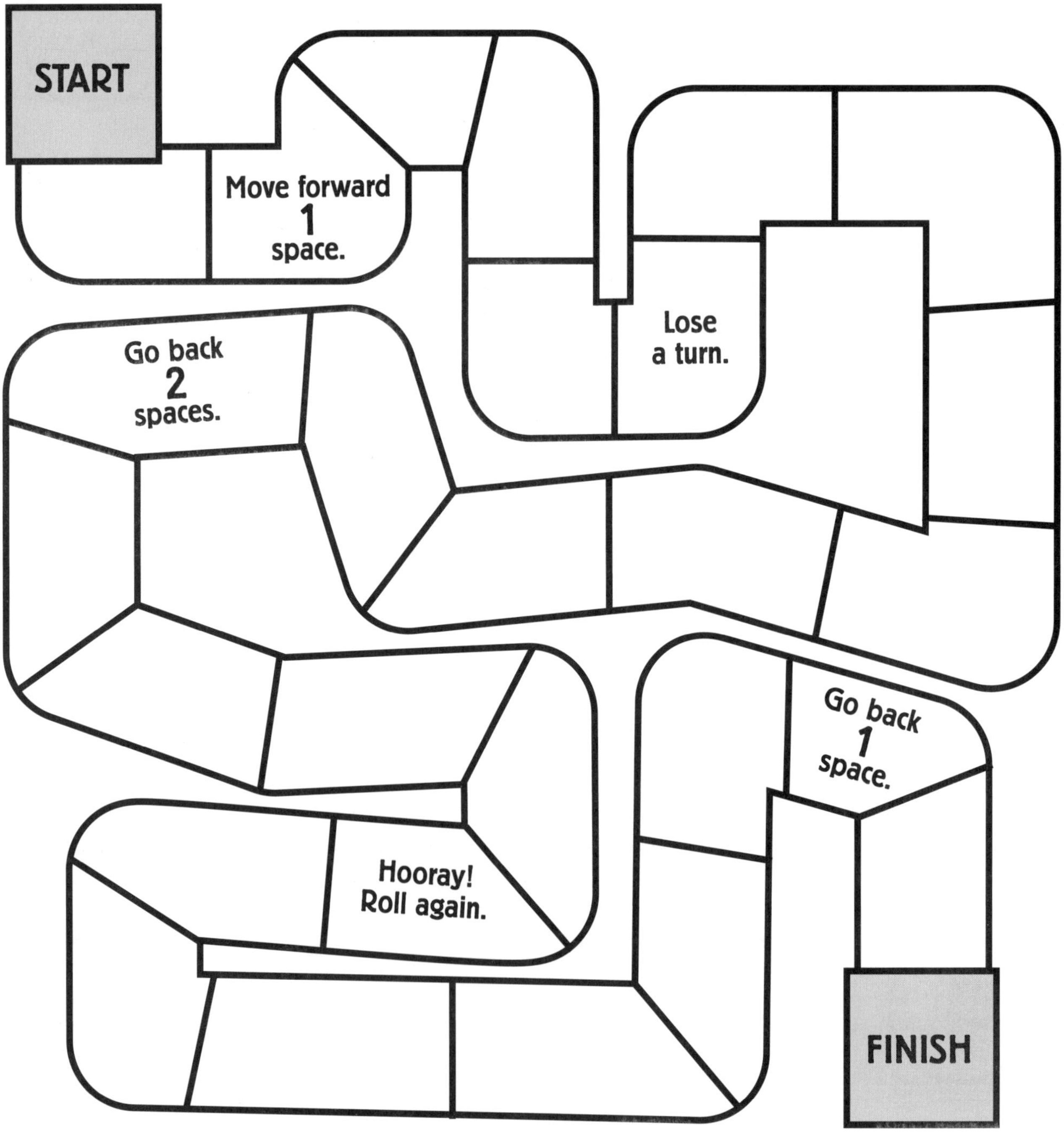

To prep: Fill in the title with a fun or skill-based name. If using cards, add them to the materials list and create cards with problems or prompts on cardstock or index cards. If not using cards, write problems directly on the blank spaces. Cut off these directions before copying. If desired, copy them on cardstock and laminate for durability. Place them in a station with the related materials.

____________________ Roll and Solve

Materials: 1 die

To play: Roll the die. Find the matching column and solve the bottom problem. Continue rolling and solving the next problem in each column until one column is complete. Color the winning animal. Continue to see which animals win second and third place.

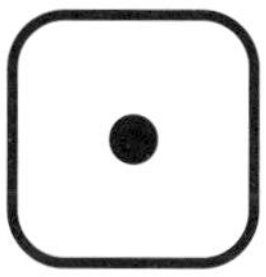					

To prep: Complete the title with the skill. Fill in the spaces below each animal with different problems. Cut off these directions before copying. If desired, copy it on cardstock and laminate for durability. Place it in a center with the related materials.

________________ Flip!

To play: Shuffle the cards. Place them all facedown. Players take turns. The first player flips over one card and ____ ____. If the player answers correctly, he may keep the card. If not, return the card facedown to the pile. Once all of the cards have been flipped, the player with the most cards wins.

To prep: Complete the title with the skill. Fill in the cards with numbers or other prompts, such as geometric figures, angles, or shapes. Complete the directions by telling how students should answer or solve the prompts on the cards. For example, *tell what type of angle is shown*, or *tell how many to add to make 10*. Copy the cards on cardstock for durability and laminate if desired. Place them in a center with the directions. You may include a spatula and paper plates with the activity for students to use when "flipping" the cards and maintaining their "keep" piles.

________________ Shut the Box

Materials: ________ dice, ________ counters or markers per person

To play: Cover all of the spaces on your board with markers. Players take turns. Roll the dice. ____

____

If it has already been uncovered, mark one of your strikes. After one player has gotten three strikes, the player who has removed the most markers wins. Or, the first player to remove all of the markers without getting three strikes wins.

- -

To prep: Complete the title with the skill. Fill in the spaces on each section with the possible answers. Both sections should have the same numbers. You do not have to fill in all of the spaces. Complete the materials section with the number of dice and counters needed. Complete the directions with instructions related to the skill that describe how students use the numbers they roll. For example, *double the number, then uncover the answer*, or *add, then uncover the sum*. Cut off these directions before copying. If desired, copy it on cardstock and laminate for durability. Place it in a station with the related materials.

Answer Key

Page 17
Check students' work. 1. 81 times; 2. 52 times; 3. 74 cars; 4. 4 balloons

Page 18
1. 136 tickets; 2. 10 packages; 3. Robin's cats, 3 oz.; 4. 296 pages; 5. 12 miles; 6. 42 kits

Page 19
1–5. Answers will vary.

Page 20
A. 6 copies; B. No, it would take 75 min. C. 54 wheels; D. 718 ft.; E. $10, 4 pencils; F. 60 apples; G. $181; H. 49 in.

Page 23
1. 1, 2, 4, 5, 10, 20; 2. 1, 2, 3, 6, 9, 18; 3. 1, 3, 9; 4. 1, 5, 25; 5. 1, 2, 3, 4, 6, 8, 12, 24; 6. 1, 7

Page 24
1. 7; 2. 8; 3. 6; 4. 7; 5. 5; 6. 7; 7. 36, 6, 3, 2, 18, 1; 8. 10, 2, 8, 5, 4; 9. 5, 1, 25; 10. 7, 2, 6; 11. 1, 2, 4, 7, 14, 28; 12. 1, 2, 3, 4, 5, 6, 10, 12, 15, 20, 30, 60; 13. 1, 2, 11, 22; 14. 1, 2, 4, 8, 16; 15. 1, 3, 9, 27

Page 25
1. 1, 3, 9; 2. 1, 2, 4, 8, 16; 3. 1, 2, 3, 6, 7, 14, 21, 42; 4. 1, 2, 3, 4, 6, 8, 12, 24; 5. 1, 2, 3, 4, 6, 9, 12, 18, 36; 6. 1, 7, 49; 7. 1, 3, 5, 15, 25, 75; 8. 1, 2, 3, 4, 6, 8, 12, 16, 24, 48

Page 29
1. 3, 6, 9, 12, 15, 18, 21, 24, 27; 2. 4, 8, 12, 16, 20, 24, 28, 32, 36, 40; 3. 6, 12, 18, 24, 30, 36, 42, 48, 54; 4. 7, 14, 21, 28, 35, 42, 49, 56, 63; 5. 8, 16, 24, 32, 40, 48, 56, 64, 72; 6. 9, 27, 36, 45, 54, 63, 72, 81; 7. Answers will vary.

Page 30
Check students' work.

Page 31
Answers will vary but may include: 1. 72 or 78; 2. 52 or 56; 3. 51, 57, 63, or 69; 4. none; 5. 60, 70, 80, or 90; 6. none; 7. 96, 99, or 102; 8. Answers will vary.

Page 35
1. 32, 38, 44, 50, 56; 2. Answers will vary. 3. 62, 68, 74; 4. 99, 96, 93, 90, 87, 84, 81, 78, 75, 72; 5. Answers will vary. 6. 69, 66, 63; 7. 95, 99, 103, 107, 111, 115, 119; 8. Answers will vary. 9. 123, 127, 131

Page 36
1. Check students' work. Answers will vary but may include: 2. 1, 4, 9, 16, 25, 36; 3. 1, +3, +5, +7, +9, +11; 4. 49, 64, 81; 5. Check students' work. Answers will vary but may include: 6. 4, 6, 8, 10, 12; 7. +2, The two squares added alternate between top and bottom. 8. Check students' work. Answers will vary.

Page 37
1. 1, 4, 9, 16, 25, 36, 49, 64, 81, 100; 2. 3, 5, 7, 9, 11, 13, 15, 17, 19; 3. Answers will vary. 4. Check students' work. 4, 9, 16 = 6 + 10, 25 = 10 + 15, 36 = 15 + 21; 5. Answers will vary.

Page 41
Check students' work. 1. 4,000 + 200 + 90 + 4; 2. 9,000 + 300 + 60 + 5; 3. 10,000 + 300 + 70 + 2; 4. 90,000 + 2,000 + 5; 5. 200,000 + 70,000 + 4,000 + 300 + 20 + 1

Page 42
1. 60,000; 2. 6,000; 3. 700,000; 4. 40; 5. 80,000; 6. 7,000; 7. 200,000; 8. 50; 9. 2,100; 10. 39,000; 11. 46,220; 12. 570; 13. 836,000; 14. 524; 15. 370,000; 16. 142; 17. 400,000; 18. 36; 19. 1,000,000; 20. 90

Page 43
1. 300; 2. 200; 3. 36,000; 4. 100; 5. 600,000; 6. 70; 7. 20,000; 8. 100; 9. 600,000; 10. 10; 11. 2,400; 12. 7,000; 13. 18,000; 14. 5; 15. 540,000; 16. 20; 17. 150,000; 18. 8,000; 19. 280,000; 20. 2,000; 21. 300,000; 22. 40; 23–24. Answers will vary.

Page 47
1. >, Th; 2. >, H; 3. <, Th; 4. <, T; 5. >, Th; 6. >, HT; 7. >, O; 8. 6,580, 5,081; 9. 2,197, 2,745; 10. 34,104, 43,024; 11. 7,500, 7,256; 12. 13,264, 13,604

Page 48
1. 8,581, 8,589, 8,955; 2. 2,527, 3,227, 5,325; 3. 14,734, 15,713, 17,463; 4. 30,412, 34,061, 43,026; 5. 509,235, 590,758, 591,214; 6. 7,610, 71,600, 76,000; 7. 49,324, 483,243, 487,523; 8. <; 9. >; 10. >; 11. <; 12. >, <; 13. <, <; 14. >, >

Page 49
1. >; 2. >; 3. <; 4. =; 5. <; 6. >; 7. >; 8. <; 9. =; 10. <; 11. >; 12. >; 13. =; 14. <; 15. >; 16. <

Page 53
1. 28; 2. 60; 3. 24; 4. 42; 5. 90; 6. 63; 7. 52; 8. 112; 9. 196; 10. 60

Page 54
1. 282; 2. 168; 3. 324; 4. 185; 5. 472; 6. 64; 7. 84; 8. 504; 9. 215; 10. 144; 11. 204; 12. 282; 13. 602; 14. 290; 15. 376; 16. 86; 17. 186; 18. 192; 19. 128; 20. 147

Page 55
1. 642; 2. 568; 3. 2,550; 4. 972; 5. 1,048; 6. 738; 7. 2,056; 8. 1,491; 9. 3,708; 10. 2,526; 11. 1,770; 12. 1,008; 13. 2,448; 14. 711; 15. 2,172; 16. 1,970; 17. 9,369; 18. 8,486; 19. 25,926; 20. 4,912; 21. 11,008; 22. 22,615; 23. 16,926; 24. 25,281

Page 59
1. 306; 2. 228; 3. 544; 4. 451

Page 60
1. 585; 2. 1,302; 3. 1,848; 4. 2,064; 5. 2,700; 6. 2,184

Page 61
1. 490; 2. 3,796; 3. 5,292; 4. 2,132; 5. 2,024; 6. 2,065

Page 65
Check students' work. 1. 1,276; 2. 1,504; 3. 3,648; 4. 663; 5. 462; 6. 418; 7. 1,513; 8. 2,080; 9. 1,876; 10. 3,705; 11. 2,813; 12. 1,232

Page 66
Check students' work. 1. 1,312; 2. 840; 3. 714; 4. 672; 5. 1,092; 6. 1,116; 7. 1,775; 8. 576; 9. 1,408; 10. 1,278; 11. 1,715; 12. 1,015; 13. 4,176; 14. 1,157; 15. 1,960; 16. 1,276

Answer Key

Page 67
Check students' work. 1. 425; 2. 1,260; 3. 432; 4. 1,458; 5. 1,372; 6. 3,612; 7. 2,176; 8. 3,654; 9. Answers will vary.

Page 71
1. 4r2; 2. 6r2; 3. 9r4; 4. 5r2; 5. 3r2; 6. 8r2; 7. 7r5; 8. 9r2; 9. 6r3; 10. 4r3; 11. 4r4; 12. 9r7; 13. 5r6; 14. 3r5; 15. 6r6; 16. 3r3

Page 72
Explanations will vary.
1. 1 bracelet; 2. 13 erasers; 3. 6 miles; 4. 8 packs; 5. 13 students with 1 substitute, or 13 players on one team and 14 players on the other team

Page 73
1. 15 1/2 packs; 2. 13 2/3 miles; 3. 7 1/4 chapters; 4. 12 2/4 yd.; 5. 24 2/3 pieces; 6. 29 1/3 slices

Page 77
1. 13r2; 2. 11r4; 3. 35r1; 4. 11r3; 5. 22r3; 6. 22r1; 7. 46r1; 8. 15r2; 9. 122r6; 10. 132r2; 11. 158r2; 12. 135r6

Page 78
1. 59r1; 2. 56r3; 3. 88r4; 4. 112r1; 5. 74r1; 6. 94r2; 7. 96r7; 8. 41r5; 9. 24r1; 10. 83r3; 11. 173r1; 12. 75r5

Page 79
1. 79r1; 2. 58r3; 3. 42r4; 4. 63r7; 5. 28r4; 6. 39r3; 7. 27r4; 8. 96r2; 9. 72r3; 10. 28r5; 11. 78r6; 12. 97r1

Page 83
1. 5r2; 2. 8r1; 3. 4r1; 4. 3r2; 5. 19r3; 6. 14; 7. 16r3; 8. 11r3; 9. 15r3; 10. 33r5; 11. 22r3; 12. 11r1; 13. 38r2; 14. 56r2; 15. 63

Page 84
1. 105r2; 2. 298r1; 3. 108r1; 4. 108r5; 5. 261r1; 6. 121r2; 7. 150r1; 8. 127r2; 9. 215r2; 10. 714r3; 11. 3,420r1; 12. 1,578r1

Page 85
Check students' work. 1. 180r1; 2. 134r4; 3. 244r4; 4. 1,148r2; 5. 88r8; 6. 117r2; 7. 1,824r1; 8. 77r1; 9. Answers will vary.

Page 89
1. 2/3, 4/6; 2. 1/4, 2/8; 3. 1/2, 3/6; 4. 2/4, 4/8; 5. 2/2, 1; 6. 5/7, 10/14; 7–15. Check students' work. 7. 2/5, 4/10; 8. 2/6, 4/12; 9. 8/8, 1; 10. 2/3, 6/9; 11. 3/4, 12/16; 12. 1/4, 3/12; 13. 2/3, 4/6; 14. 1/3, 2/6; 15. 1/2, 5/10

Page 90
1. 8; 2. 16; 3. 10; 4. 2; 5. 81; 6. 4; 7. 16; 8. 6; 9. 20; 10. 30; 11. 14; 12. 10; 13. 4; 14. 16; 15. 15; 16. 9; 17. 9; 18. 6; 19. 12; 20. 20; 21. 9; 22. 10; 23. 36; 24. 16

Page 91
Numerators; factors: 1. 18, 9, 8, 21, 24; 18, 9, 8, 21, 24; 2. 40, 10, 25, 15, 20; 8, 2, 5, 3, 4; 3. 3, 9, 30, 2, 4; 3, 9, 30, 2, 4; 4. 18, 12, 6, 15, 27; 6, 4, 2, 5, 9; 5. 8, 20, 16, 24, 12; 2, 5, 4, 6, 3; 6. 14, 49, 21, 42, 28; 2, 7, 3, 6, 4; 7. 9, 18, 6, 15, 12; 3, 6, 2, 5, 4; 8. 20, 4, 16, 6, 10; 10, 2, 8, 3, 5

Page 95
1. 1/3 < 2/3; 2. 2/4 = 4/8; 3. 3/8 < 1/2; 4. 1/3 = 2/6; 5. 3/4 > 2/4; 6. 1/2 < 3/4; 7. 2/5, 2/8, 4/6, 1/3; 8. 3/5, 4/5, 9/10, 4/10

Page 96
1. C; 2. <; 3. C; 4. =; 5. <; 6. C; 7. C; 8. <; 9. C; 10. <; 11. <; 12. >; 13. C; 14. =; 15. C; 16. C; 17. <; 18. =

Page 97
1. <; 2. <; 3. <; 4. <; 5. =; 6. <; 7. >; 8. <; 9. >; 10. <; 11. <; 12. =; 13. >; 14. <; 15. >; 16. <; 17. <; 18. >; 19. <; 20. <; 21. >

Page 101
Check students' work. 1. 2/4; 2. 4/6; 3. 7/8; 4. 2/3; 5. 5/8; 6. 3/4; 7. 3/8; 8. 2/6; 9. 3/4; 10. 2/5; 11. 1/10; 12. 3/8

Page 102
1. 3/4; 2. 2/8; 3. 4/5; 4. 9/10; 5. 2/8; 6. 6/10; 7. 8/9; 8. 4/12; 9. 8/20; 10. 80/100; 11. 20/50; 12. 3/15; 13. 6/15; 14. 3/13; 15. 2/8; 16. 4/10

Page 103
1. 4 4/5; 2. 9 8/10; 3. 9 9/14; 4. 6 5/10; 5. 10 11/12; 6. 3 3/8; 7. 9 2/9; 8. 7; 9. 3 3/8; 10. 5 1/5; 11. 1 1/10; 12. 9; 13. 6 1/9; 14. 4 3/4; 15. 4 5/18; 16. 5 2/27

Page 107
1. 1 1/2; 2. 1 2/3; 3. 2/4 or 1/2; 4. 4; 5. 3; 6. 6/8 or 3/4; 7. 1 3/5; 8. 4/8 or 1/2; 9. 2 2/3; 10. 1; 11. 1 1/4; 12. 1 6/8 or 1 3/4

Page 108
1. 10 × 1/3; 2. 8 × 1/5; 3. 1/7 × 8; 4. 2 1/2; 5. 1; 6. 1/2; 7. 3/4; 8. 3 4/7; 9. 1 1/3; 10. 1/2; 11. 2 2/3; 12. 3; 13. 3 3/4; 14. 4; 15. 2

Page 109
1. 8/3 or 2 2/3 cups; 2. 7/4 or 1 3/4 miles; 3. 5/8 of a pot; 4. $34; 5. 28/5 or 5 3/5 cups; 6. 68/8 or 8 1/2 yd.; 7. 18/8, 3 pizzas; Challenge: 1/16 of the cake

Page 110
Start, 1; 3/4 × 6; 4 1/2; 4 × 1/8; 1/2; 3 × 2/10; 3/5; 1/6 × 12; 2; 10 × 2/5; 4; 3/5 × 3; 1 4/5; 1/4 × 12; 3; 5 × 1/2; 2 1/2; 4 × 3/8; 1 1/2; 2/6 × 9; 3; 8 × 2/3; 5 1/3, Finish

Page 113
Check students' work. 1. 5, 5/10; 6, 6/100; 56/100; 2. 7, 7/10; 1, 1/100; 71/100; 3. 6, 6/10; 0, 0/100; 60/100; 4. 9, 9/10; 8, 8/100; 98/100; 5. 5/10; 6. 46/100

Page 114
1. 5/10; 2. 71/100; 3. 70/100; 4. 61/100; 5. 90/100; 6. 95/100; 7. 73/100; 8. 44/100; 9. 84/100; 10. 67/100; 11. 99/100; 12. 82/100; 13. 1 3/100; 14. 1; 15. Answers will vary.

Page 115
1. 86/100; 2. 33/100; 3. 68/100; 4. 11/100; 5. 13/100; 6. 15/100; 7. 87/100; 8. 37/100; 9. 2/100; 10. 1 9/100; 11. X, 72/100; 12. C; 13. X, 64/100; 14. C; 15. C; 16. X, 37/100

Page 119
1. 4/10, 0.4; 2. 5/10, 0.5; 3. 1 9/10, 1.9; 4. 21/100, 0.21; 5. 47/100, 0.47; 6. 1 2/100, 1.02; 7–12. Check students' work. 7. 7/10; 8. 0.70; 9. 57/100; 10. 0.13; 11. 0.8; 12. 62/100

Page 120
1. 0.4; 2. 0.88; 3. 3.25; 4. 6.5; 5. 4.1; 6. 9.30; 7. 6/10; 8. 5/10; 9. 91/100; 10. 7/100; 11. 1 23/100;

Answer Key

12. 4 8/10; 13. 0.65; 14. 6 9/10; 15. 2.12; 16. 21/100; 17. 7.34; 18. 0.99; 19. 16 8/100; 20. 300 24/100; 21. 25 4/100; 22. 25.34; 23. 75.02; 24. 4 3/10

Page 121
1. 1,200, 120, 12, 1.2, 1.2, 0.12; 2. 230, 23, 2.3, 0.23, 0.23, 0.023; 3. 3,070, 307, 30.7, 30.7, 3.07, 0.307; 4. 54,600, 5,460, 546, 546, 54.6, 5.46; 5. 4, 0.40; 6. 9, 0.90; 7. 27, 2.70; 8. 12, 1.20

Page 125
1. 0.5, 1.5, 2.5, 3.5; 2. 4.4, 5.8, 6.6, 7.3; 3. 0.5, 1.0, 1.5, 2.0; 4. 1.5, 2.0, 2.5, 3.0; 5. 0.5, 2.5, 3.0, 3.5; 6. 2.5, 3.5, 4.0, 4.5, 5.5; 7. <; 8. >; 9. =; 10. <

Page 126
1. >; 2. <; 3. >; 4. <; 5. <; 6. <; 7. >; 8. <; 9. <; 10. >; 11. <; 12. >; 13. <; 14. >; 15. <

Page 127
1. N; 2. Y, >; 3. Y, >; 4. N; 5. <; 6. >; 7. <; 8. >; 9. >; 10. <; 11. =; 12. >; 13. >; 14. <; 15. =; 16. >

Page 131
1. 36; 2. 9; 3. 10,000; 4. 6,000; 5. 120; 6. 15; 7. 500; 8. 7,000; 9. 180; 10. 2,000; 11. 600; 12. 4,000; 13. =; 14. >; 15. <; 16. >; 17. =; 18. >; 19. >; 20. <; 21. >; 22. =; 23. <; 24. <

Page 132
1. Answers will vary. 2. 10; 3. 800; 4. <; 5. <; 6. Answers will vary. 7. 144; 8. 16; 9. >; 10. =; 11. Answers will vary. 12. 3,000; 13. 10; 14. >; 15. <; 16. Answers will vary. 17. 300; 18. 6; 19. >; 20. <

Page 133
1. Brooke; 2. 34 in.; 3. no; 4. 32 servings; 5. more; 6. below, 1 oz.; 7. Dion, 95 mm; 8. from first to last: Ansley, Jawan, Nora, Reid

Page 137
1. 18, 22; 2. 16, 16; 3. 12, 14; 4. 21, 20; 5. 10 sq. in., 14 in.; 6. 48 sq. cm, 28 cm; 7. 60 sq. ft., 34 ft.; 8. 24 sq. m, 20 m

Page 138
1. 5 cm; 2. 4 mm; 3. 4 in.; 4. 7 ft., 7 ft.; 5. 10 cm; 6. 5 m; 7. 6 in.; 8. 7 mm; 9. 6 m, 6 m; 10. 9 ft.

Page 139
1. 31 sq. in.; 2. 10 sq. cm; 3. 48 sq. m; 4. 52 sq. cm; 5. 5 sq. ft.; 6. 75 sq. km; 7. 92 sq. mm; 8. 60 sq. ft.

Page 143
Check students' work.

Page 144
Check students' work. 1. 1 3/4 in., 3 in.; 2. 2 1/4 in.; 3. 10 plants; 4. 15 plants; 5. 2 1/2 in.; 6. 1 3/4 in., 3 in.; 7. 16 plants

Page 145
Check students' work. 1. 3 1/4 cups, 2 1/4 cups; 2. 14 players, There are 14 Xs on the line plot. 3. 10 players; 4. 41 3/4 cups; 5. 6 1/4 cups

Page 149
1–10. Check students' work. 5. 4; 6. 3; 7. 4; 8. 3; 9. 4; 10. 6

Page 150
1. acute; 2. obtuse; 3. right; 4. acute; 5. acute; 6. obtuse; 7. right; 8. obtuse; 9. right; 10. obtuse; 11. acute; 12. obtuse

Page 151
1–9. Answers will vary but should be reasonable estimates. 10–12. Check students' work.

Page 155
1. 70°, acute; 2. 170°, obtuse; 3. 30°, acute; 4. 10°, acute; 5. 120°, obtuse; 6. 100°, obtuse

Page 156
1. 45°; 2. 90°; 3. 143°; 4. 29°; 5. 134°; 6. 24°; 7. 139°; 8. 90°; 9. 63°; 10. 137°; 11. 81°; 12. 160°

Page 157
Check students' work.

Page 161
1. 160°; 20, 160; 2. 100°; 80, 100; 3. 130°; 50, 130, 180; 4. 40°; 140, 40, 180; 5. 45°; 45, 45, 90; 6. 60°; 30, 60, 90; 7. 70°; 55, 15, 70; 8. 80°; 80, 40, 120

Page 162
1. 50°; 2. 145°; 3. 75°; 4. 155°; 5. 75°; 6. 60°; 7. 75°; 8. 85°; 9. 25°; 10. 105°

Page 163
1. 70°; 2. 45°; 3. 80°; 4. 65°; 5. 70°; 6. 30°; 7. 125°; 8. 60°; 9. 60°

Page 167
1. ray; 2. line segment; 3. ray; 4. line; 5. line; 6. points; 7. line segment; 8. ray; 9. perpendicular; 10. parallel

Page 168
1. angle; 2. W, X, Y; 3. ray XW, ray XY; 4–7. Answers will vary. 8. parallelogram; 9. Answers will vary. 10. ray AB and line DE; 11. Answers will vary. 12. rays BA, BD, BC, and BE

Page 169
Check students' work.

Page 173
Check students' work. Number given indicates how many shapes should be connected to the center dot. 1. 7; 2. 6; 3. 6; 4. 6

Page 174
1. left: C, D; center: E, F, G; right: H, I, J; 2. top left: G; top center: none; top right: B; left center: E, F; center: C, D; right center: none; bottom: I, J

Page 175
Rows, from left to right: 1. regular pentagon, irregular hexagon, irregular pentagon, octagon; 2. rhombus, square, right trapezoid, rectangle; 3. obtuse triangle, equilateral triangle, right triangle, hexagon

Page 179
1. octagon; 2. hexagon; 3. heart; 4. triangle; 5–7. Check students' work.

Page 180
1–16. Check students' work. 1. yes; 2. yes; 3. yes; 4. no; 5. yes; 6. yes; 7. yes; 8. no; 9. yes; 10. no; 11. yes; 12. yes; 13. yes; 14. yes; 15. no; 16. yes; 17–20. Check students' work.

Page 181
Check students' work.